# Support Partnerships

## Collaboration in action

Penny Lacey

**David Fulton Publishers**
London

David Fulton Publishers Ltd
Ormond House, 26–27 Boswell Street, London WC1N 3JZ

www.fultonpublishers.co.uk

First published in Great Britain by David Fulton Publishers 2001

Note: The right of Penny Lacey to be identified as the author of this work
has been asserted by her in accordance with the Copyright, Designs and
Patents Act 1988.

Copyright © Penny Lacey 2001

*British Library Cataloguing in Publication Data*
A catalogue record for this book is available from the British Library

ISBN 1-85346-568-2

The publishers would like to thank Priscilla Sharland for copy-editing
and Sheila Harding for proofreading this book.

Typeset by Mark Heslington, Scarborough, North Yorkshire
Printed in Great Britain by The Cromwell Press Ltd, Trowbridge, Wilts.

# Contents

# Acknowledgements

I have experienced an enormous amount of help and support from various people who have been part of the research for this book. I would particularly like to thank all the children, staff and parents who have willingly given me information and allowed me to observe their work.

I would also like to acknowledge the following people who variously contributed, commented on my work, typed or corrected parts of it, took on extra work and generally kept me on task:

David Doggett, Valerie Farnworth, Peter Limbrick, Jeanette Lomas, Claire Marvin, Carol Ouvry, Helen Parrott, Jill Porter, Christopher Robertson, Noreen Stacey, Ann Starr, Frank Steel, Christina Tilstone, Philip Tilstone, Graham Upton.

# Introduction

*Support Partnerships* is a book about people working together, in places such as schools, colleges, education or therapy support services, adult or pre-school services and centres. It is based mainly in education and draws on the experiences of people who attempt to work together to meet the needs of children and young people who have difficulties and disabilities. Sometimes there are several people who work with the same individual with disabilities. Sometimes these people manage to coordinate their work and provide 'joined up' services. Sometimes they do not. The book is about the strategies that can help more people to coordinate what they are doing. It is based on several small-scale research studies and years of personal experience either trying to work with other people or listening to and watching colleagues trying to work together. Although research is the bedrock upon which the examples are based, this book is as much a teaching tool as an account of research. It is hoped that the case studies and ideas used will help practitioners to develop what they are doing, however well they are working with other people.

It is also hoped that many people will find this book both interesting and useful, whether they are researchers or practitioners. It is aimed principally at people who work with and care for children who have special needs through disabilities and difficulties in learning, such as teachers, nursery nurses, parents, nurses, therapists, keyworkers, social workers, psychologists, medics and voluntary workers. Although the case studies used to illustrate practice are exclusively about children, it is anticipated that people who work in adult services will also find them helpful. The principles that underpin working together in support partnerships can easily be transferred from education contexts to other parts of the human services, such as community health, adult learning disability teams, hospitals, mental health and social care.

## Part One: The literature

The five chapters devoted to a review of the literature are based mainly on work on multidisciplinary teamwork carried out between the years 1991–7 (Lacey 1997). A variety of perspectives on multidisciplinary teamwork are explored including:

- special education and support services
- mainstream education
- care in the community
- preschool educare
- partnership between families and professionals
- conductive education

- teamwork in business
- teambuilding in business
- shared learning between health and social care
- professional development in education.

There is no claim that this literature survey is exhaustive, although it is hoped that the aspects chosen to be examined provide a broad view of the parameters of the topic. As the research was concerned with *multidisciplinary* teamwork, it was fitting that disciplines other than education (the discipline of the researcher) were consulted.

The five literature chapters do not have to be read all together to make sense of the topic, although they were conceived as a whole. Readers can select the parts that most interest them, building their own pictures of support partnerships, multidisciplinary teamwork and collaboration.

## Part Two: Case studies

The eight chapters that contain the case studies are divided (somewhat unevenly) between examples of support partnerships in practice. The first three (Chapters 6, 7 and 8) are all given over to one case study, that of a special school called 'Pear Tree School' (for the purposes of the book). This school formed the basis of the research mentioned above. The school educates approximately 100 pupils with physical disabilities and learning difficulties and has a strong commitment to multidisciplinary teamwork. Pear Tree became the site for a four year project, during which the researcher collected observational and interview data on how multidisciplinary teamwork worked in practice. After describing the teamwork practice (Chapter 6), systemic aspects of that practice were analysed (Chapter 7) followed by an exploration of various management aspects (Chapter 8).

Chapter 9 contains aspects of a research project set up to analyse the role of learning support assistants (LSAs) who support children with severe or profound learning difficulties when they are being educated with their more able peers. This was carried out during the academic year 1998–9 on behalf of Mencap. The report *On a Wing and a Prayer* (Mencap 1999) is available from Mencap, Golden Lane, London EC1Y 0RT. Observations and interviews were used to gather data regarding the role of the LSAs and how they can work together most effectively with teachers. Alongside the Mencap research is placed evidence from a project carried out in an educational action zone (EAZ) in 'South' LEA where the work of LSAs is being developed alongside a training package.

The material for Chapter 10 has come from two distinct sources. The first is the master's dissertation of Helen Parrott (Parrott 2000) who researched her own practice in setting up, implementing and evaluating a transdisciplinary team in a special school. Parrott's observational and interview data were supplemented by observations and interviews conducted by the author of this book. The second part of the chapter is a snapshot case study conducted specifically for the book in a residential special school for pupils with emotional and behavioural difficulties.

Chapter 11 was inspired by consultancy work in four LEAs, given the pseudonyms North, South, West and East LEAs. All the LEAs were in the throes of change and sought the support of an outside person to help them to move forward and, perhaps, avoid the worst difficulties experienced during major change. The report is based on work carried out from 1998 to 2000 (although it is ongoing in all the LEAs). Three of the LEAs were reorganising their special educational needs provision and the fourth was developing the work and training of LSAs. Evidence for this chapter is drawn from documents and the personal experience of the consultant in the analysis of the partnership between LEAs and outside consultants.

Sources for Chapter 12 were many. The first part is based mainly in the school years on my own experience of family–professional partnership over many years: case studies from the 1980s to the present day. The second part of the chapter is based mainly in the preschool years. Peter Limbrick, who is part of a charity running a keyworker service for families with a child with multiple disabilities, asked two sets of parents to write their stories about partnership between families and professionals. He also provided some of his own stories in addition to documents about his keyworker model.

Chapter 13 describes a multidisciplinary research project on professional development. The project was divided into two parts: practice and training. The researcher developed, implemented and evaluated a teambuilding workshop for members of multidisciplinary teams who desired to improve their practice. Questionnaires and interviews were used to ascertain the impact of the training both immediately following the workshop and again after several months back at work.

The final chapter in the book is made up of three distinct sections designed to answer the question, 'Where are we now and where should we go next?' in support partnerships. The first section contains a summary of the strategies that underpin effective support partnerships and collaboration. The second section is an audit for readers to use to help them to understand the strengths and needs of their own practice. The third section is an attempt to identify current research into partnership and collaboration and to suggest possibilities for future projects. The audit, which forms the centre of this last chapter, is based on that published in the book *Support Services and the Curriculum* (Lacey and Lomas 1993). Despite being written almost ten years ago, the audit is just as relevant today. It is a little disappointing that 'good' collaborative practice has not progressed much in the ten years, although what is encouraging is that there do appear to be more organisations and services that are striving to work collaboratively.

## Partnership

As the topics of this book are partnership and collaboration, it is fitting to acknowledge how much the collection of the case studies has relied upon collaboration. Many people have been involved in the research that underpins the book and individuals have been named in the acknowledgements at the beginning. Schools and services used for the case studies have provided so much more than mere sites for observation or people to interview and some informants have been vital to the research process. (Even though real names have been used in the acknowledgements, fictitious names have been used throughout the case studies.)

It is acknowledged that this book has been written from an educational standpoint, despite the great interest in things multidisciplinary. It is hoped that alternative viewpoints come through the research and that members of other disciplines feel they can learn from what is discussed. Much of what has been written about multidisciplinary teamwork emanates from professionals in either health or social services so it perhaps fitting that there should be an educational perspective in this book.

As was mentioned earlier, this book is designed partly as a teaching tool. It is sincerely hoped that the practice described and analysed within its pages can help to guide other people who wish to develop and/or evaluate their support partnerships. It is not claimed that all aspects of partnership or collaboration are examined but it is hoped that the strategies that lead to effective practice identified in the literature and the case studies can inspire and motivate readers.

## PART ONE

# Collaboration in support partnerships: The literature

## Chapter 1

# Researching support partnerships

This is the first of five chapters that contain a review of the literature surrounding partnership and collaboration in the human services.

In Chapter 1, there is an attempt to set the scene to aid understanding of firstly, how the research for the book was carried out (the research methodology) and secondly, the way in which the different terms and concepts related to partnership and collaboration are conceived.

There are two distinct sections, each with its own set of questions to be addressed within the text:

- case study research
- terminology and concepts.

## Case study research

There were three main questions that underpin this section.

- *What are case studies?*
- *What kind of case studies are used in this book?*
- *How were the case study data collected and analysed?*

Different types of case study research were utilised in the research upon which this book is based, ranging from ethnography, action research to multiple site case studies. All the cases were organisations and structures rather than individuals, although, of course, many individuals were involved.

Robson (1993) refers to case studies as being on a continuum from 'loose' to 'tight'. The 'loose' type of case study is exploratory and intent upon a description whereas the 'tight' type is pre-structured and intent upon confirming what has been discovered elsewhere. The case studies in this book are all on the 'loose' end of the continuum, although semi-structured instruments (observations, interviews and questionnaires) have been used for collecting evidence. They can all be described as qualitative case studies, although some quantitative data were collected.

## Ethnography

Many of the case studies rely on an ethnographical approach. Ethnography is an approach closely related to social anthropology, demanding that the researcher gains an insider view of a particular social context. Participant observation, unstructured interviews and document analysis are seen as the main techniques for gathering data and usually the goal is to produce an analytical description of the culture under study rather than theory creation, although use of 'grounded theorising' (Glaser and Strauss 1967) can be seen as capable of explaining social complexities. Ethnographers are usually either covertly or overtly involved in people's lives for a while, attempting to capture their perceptions of the world and their relationships with other people. It is deemed important that ethnographers take a stranger's view of the society under scrutiny. The usual is treated as unusual and the taken for granted, questioned. Although the course of ethnographic studies cannot be predetermined, plans are needed both at the commencement and at different points during the research. In fact, because of the need to respond to the twists and turns of the revelations of the data, researchers need to create and recreate plans constantly (Hammersley and Atkinson 1995).

Despite some people's doubts about ethnography (Hammersley and Atkinson 1995; Hammersley 1992; Johnson 1990; Woods 1986), it is regarded by many as a legitimate way of attempting to understand phenomena such as multi-disciplinary teams or the effects of an outside consultant on change.

Ethnographical approaches to research were used in almost all of the case studies used in this book, but the most specific example of ethnography is the study that takes up Chapters 6, 7 and 8. This was the study of a single special school and the multidisciplinary teamwork that took place in it. Participant and non-participant observations were carried out during visits (once an month) over four years. Staff and pupils were observed in class, and staff during meetings, in the corridors and in the staffroom. Semi-structured interviews were carried out with the head teacher, the deputy, the senior teacher with responsibility for multidisciplinary teamwork, the speech and language therapist, two occupational therapists, two physiotherapists, a nursery nurse, two parents and four pupils. Many aspects of multidisciplinary teamwork and working collaboratively were pursued during these interviews and observations and analysis of the data provide a wealth of material for discussion in this book.

## Action research

Three of the case studies are based on action research projects, the study of The Meadows Residential School (Chapter 10), the study of the consultant who supports LEAs through change (Chapter 11) and the study of shared learning between partners (Chapter 13).

Action research is not really a definitive methodology but a collection of methods drawn together within the umbrella term 'approach'. One of the most straightforward definitions is given by Elliott (1991, p. 69). Action research is:

'the study of a social situation with a view to improving the quality of action within it'. McNiff (1988, pp. 1–2) suggests it is 'a form of self reflective enquiry', which enables changing a taken-for-granted situation and Lomax (1994, p. 1) gives a 'deceptively simple characterisation' in: 'action research is an intervention in practice to bring about improvement'. What appears to be important to all definitions is the emphasis on development and improvement. It also clearly has a focus on practitioners carrying out their own research into their own practice, intent upon increasing their understanding of, and improving, that practice. Whitehead (1993) claims that teachers can form their own 'living educational theories' through action research and thus not only improve their own practice but also add to the knowledge base through sharing these theories. Lomax (1995) suggests that Whitehead is building on Kemmis' view of truly educational research, as ethical rather than technical enquiry.

McNiff (1988) suggests that neither the empiricist nor the interpretative research traditions help practitioners in problem solving in their own workplaces. She puts forward an enthusiastic case for using action research as it is directly concerned with improving practice through change. Action researchers usually work within cycles of identifying a research question, that is: a problem to solve or a situation they would like to change; information gathering; conceiving of a possible solution; taking action through trying out the solution; more information gathering; evaluating the change; refocusing the original question.

Action research is situational in that it concerns practice in specific situations and it is interventionist in that it concerns taking action to change this situation. It is also essentially value-based as there is reference to improving practice and this implies making judgements. It is participatory and collaborative as practitioners research their own practice 'with' rather than 'on' others. It is also a personal journey for the researcher whose own work stands at the centre of the research. Action research is formative in that it involves cycles of observing, reflecting, changing and acting, each informing the other in a continuous thread (Cohen and Manion 1989).

Critics of action research are not convinced that action research is different from good teaching but McNiff et al. (1996) answer this by explaining the difference between 'practice' and 'praxis'.

> To be action research, there must be praxis rather than practice. Praxis is informed, committed action that gives rise to knowledge rather than just successful action. It is informed because other people's views are taken into account. It is committed and intentional in terms of values that can be examined and can be argued. It leads to knowledge from and about educational practice.
>
> (McNiff et al. 1996, p. 8)

The idea of praxis has been much developed by those who have an interest in encouraging teachers to make explicit their tacit understandings concerning their own practice (Whitehead 1993; McNiff 1993). Through the exploration of these understandings, action research itself can gain credibility as it becomes the source of evidence to support the development of (personal) theory.

McNiff et al. (1996) go on to suggest that action research can be validated as research when it:

- is systematic;
- leads to knowledge;
- provides evidence to support and validate this knowledge;
- makes explicit the process of enquiry through which knowledge emerges;
- links new knowledge to existing knowledge;
- is open to public scrutiny.

(McNiff *et al.* 1996, p. 13)

Although the reports of the action research projects used in this book are not presented specifically to validate them, it is hoped that the accounts are useful to practitioners to aid both their teamwork practice and also their interest in and capacity for conducting their own action research projects.

The study of the residential special school called 'The Meadows' was carried out by Helen Parrott as part of her master's degree (Parrott 2000). She devised, implemented and evaluated a transdisciplinary team (see below for discussion of this term) of teachers, support assistants, occupational therapist, care staff and psychology assistants. Her study was spread over more than a year and involved many cycles of research as she devised structures and systems and then trialled them, altering them for the next trial based on their evaluation. Helen undertook semi-structured interviews with the head teacher and the occupational therapist and administered a questionnaire to staff in the team to supplement the evaluation of her own practice.

The work undertaken for the chapter on consultancy (Chapter 10) is entirely dependent upon the researcher's diary, minutes of meetings and other documentary evidence. The consultancies were conducted in four LEAs (North, South, East and West) each of which enabled the examination of different issues for reflection.

The third case study that utilised action research was that on joint professional development (Chapter 13). A teambuilding workshop for members of multidisciplinary teams was devised, carried out and evaluated. There were many cycles to the research and the workshop was run 19 times. Evaluations took the form of open-ended structured questionnaires and interviews. Much use was made of a reflective diary.

## Data collection and analysis

It has already been indicated that data for the case studies were collected in several different ways. There is much helpful literature concerning ways of collecting data for qualitative case studies (Walker 1985; Cohen and Manion 1989; Merriam 1988; Hamel *et al.* 1991; Hammersley and Atkinson 1995; Maxwell 1996). Maxwell (1996) outlines some of the decisions that researchers need to make as they design their studies. One refers to making a choice between structured and unstructured methods. Although structured methods can help ensure comparability of data across sources, unstructured methods enable the researcher to focus directly on the phenomenon under scrutiny.

The main methods used for collecting data in the case studies undertaken for this book were:

- participant and non-participant observations mainly unstructured or semi-structured;
- interviews ranging from focused to semi-structured and structured;
- open-ended questionnaires;
- reflective diaries;
- documents (mainly meeting minutes or school/LEA documents).

## Observation

Coming from the anthropological tradition, ethnography relies considerably upon participant observation with the intention that the researcher can study the social world, as far as possible, in its natural state and in ways sensitive to the setting (Hammersley and Atkinson 1995). Principles of ethnography suggest that the researcher should adopt a stranger's view of the world and question the 'taken-for-granted' so that the socio-cultural life of the group under study can be exposed and therefore described. This, in its turn, can give rise to theorising or evaluation, although description of what was seen and heard may be the legitimate end-product (Merriam 1988).

Action research makes similar use of participant observation, and often the emphasis is actually on self-observing. The researcher is both the instrument for collecting data and the source of the data itself. Reflecting on one's role using the self-observations can be very powerful in the efforts to change and develop as part of the action research.

Situations that were observed in the case studies included:

- teacher and therapists working together;
- multidisciplinary team meetings;
- parents' and teachers' meetings;
- learning support assistants (LSAs) working with pupils and teachers;
- teachers and care staff working together;
- a consultant working with head teachers, LEA advisers and officers;
- multidisciplinary team members learning together.

## Interviews

Alongside the observations, interviews were utilised in collecting data for the case studies. Some were formal and structured but many were informal and completely open-ended. Ethnographers and action researchers often use interviews because they reach a stage where they need to gather more information or explanations than they can obtain through observations (Merriam 1988).

Several writers suggest there is a continuum of types of interviews from structured to unstructured (Cohen and Manion 1989; Powney and Watts 1987) or variations in the amount of control maintained by the interviewer (Hammersley and Atkinson 1995). It is clear from their typologies that most of the interviews that were carried out in the case studies fall into the least structured, giving the greatest amount of control to interviewees.

In the ethnography of Pear Tree School, the researcher talked to anyone who showed any interest in the research (Delamont 1992), although there was an attempt to get a broad view across the school. Interviewee choice became more 'purposive' as time went on (Johnson, 1990; Maxwell, 1996; Morton-Williams 1985) and lines of enquiry were clearer. Certain people became key informants and were relied upon considerably in repeated interviews as greater and greater detail was sought.

**Questionnaires**

Questionnaires were used in two of the action research studies (The Meadows residential school and the shared learning project). As with observations and interviews, questionnaires can be conceived on a continuum. Depending on the purpose of the instrument, it can contain closed or open-ended questions or a mixture of both (Cohen and Manion 1989). The advantage of using self-completion questionnaires is that a large number of people can be surveyed relatively cheaply. However, often the response rate is low and answers can be very disappointing (Gilbert 1993). In many questionnaires, categories can be decided on and coded in advance which means the analysis will have been begun before the results are received. Categories for open-ended questionnaires cannot be predetermined as these must emerge from the data collected.

Closed questions include all answers possible, although an 'other' category can be offered, which makes them quick to analyse. A major disadvantage of using closed questions is that respondents have little opportunity to give their opinions or record their own particular responses. Open-ended questions, on the other hand, can enable individual responses but are more time-consuming to analyse. Open-ended questions are useful when the issue under research is complex and where the relevant dimensions are either not known or could be multiple (Gilbert 1993).

The questionnaires in the shared learning project were entirely open-ended in character. Participants in the teambuilding workshops were asked to indicate what they learned about working together and what they did following the training. The questionnaire used in The Meadows project contained almost entirely closed questions requiring respondents to tick the aspects of transdisciplinary work that they found worked best for them.

**Data analysis**

The vast majority of the data that were collected through the three major methods outlined above were analysed in an inductive manner, looking for meaning within the data rather than deductively through a predetermined focus (Cohen and Manion 1989). Qualitative analysis methods were employed (Dey 1993; Miles and Huberman 1994) as patterns, causal relationships, explanations, rationalisations were sought across the case(s) under scrutiny. Different approaches were employed as the data were systematically pulled apart and reassembled in the attempts to analyse, interpret and then present effective practice in different kinds of support partnerships.

## Conclusions

Case study research is not unproblematic. One can never be sure that what one sees, hears and reads is what actually happens or whether respondents tell you what they think you want to hear. Case study researchers need to be open-minded but they cannot prevent themselves from forming opinions and making judgements. What is hoped is that these opinions and judgements are based on evidence. Case study research cannot provide large-scale generalisations. By their very nature they are situational and can only provide illustrations of practice.

Despite the limitations, case study research can offer much to practitioners who can read about a situation and glean from it some ideas for their own practice. The ways in which other people deal with challenges and improve what they are doing can be very helpful even if the context is unique. It is hoped that, by bringing together several different kinds of case studies, readers will find many aspects will relate in some way to their own work.

## Terminology and concepts

As well as explaining the case study research used to underpin this book, the aim of this first chapter is to explore the terms and concepts related to working in support partnerships as a basis upon which to approach both the literature analysis and the case studies. This section is driven by the following questions.

- *Who are the partners in support partnerships?*
- *What are the definitions and models of working together?*
- *What are the roles of the partners?*

### The partners

Children and adults who have disabilities and difficulties can have a multitude of different people working with and for them. At times, it can seem like 'pass the parcel' as young children and their families attend endless hospital appointments, repeating their story to yet another specialist who examines a specific aspect of the disability and gives advice, which may be completely conflicting to the advice from the previous specialist. The more complex the disability the more people there are likely to be involved, although the numbers tend to decrease as clients grow older. This is partly because once positioning, medication, resources and support personnel are in place there is less need for constant change. It is also partly because there are fewer adult services than children's and even if a client would benefit from regular physiotherapy throughout his or her life, it may not be available.

There are likely to be several agencies with responsibility for clients with disabilities and difficulties, principally health, social services, education and voluntary bodies, in a rectangle of services (Lacey and Lomas 1993). Each of these are divided into a plethora of specific agencies, such as:

| Health | | |
|---|---|---|
| nursing | physiotherapy | speech therapy |
| medicine | psychology | psychiatry |
| audiology | orthoses | orthoptics |
| dietetics | dentistry | occupational therapy |
| health visiting | complementary therapies | |

| **Social services** | | |
| --- | --- | --- |
| family social work | residential social work | fostering team |
| respite care | support work | job coaching |
| day care centre | workshop | home help |
| housing | benefits | |

| **Education** | | |
| --- | --- | --- |
| local school | special school | local FE college |
| ICT specialists | mobility instruction | educational psychology |
| Portage | home visiting service | hospital school |
| services for sensory impairment | specialist FE college | learning or behaviour support |

| **Voluntary sector** | | |
| --- | --- | --- |
| independent schools | charities | private homes |
| arts therapies | alternative therapies | respite care |

Within each of these agencies are yet another range of people, some professionally educated and others trained 'on the job'. For example in a local authority special school, you are likely to find a mixture of class teachers, specialist teachers, nursery nurses and care and administrative staff, all employed by the school. In an independent special school, you may also find therapists on the payroll.

There are some cross discipline agencies, for example the Community Learning Disability Team, which may consist of learning disability nurses, social workers and therapists or the Preschool Team, which may consist of teachers, nursery nurses and therapists. Child Development Centres are another example of across-discipline teams and they often consist of medics, therapists, teachers and psychologists.

Many services are basically run by one discipline but become the site for other disciplines to meet and work. Special schools may have visiting education services, nursing and therapy services, medical clinics and visiting social workers as well as twice daily contact with bus escorts and drivers who liaise with families. There can be a bewildering number of individuals with whom to communicate and work and a pressing need to identify models and strategies which will enable this work to be effective and efficient. The next section begins this process by examining definitions and models of working together in partnership.

## Definitions and models of working together

One of the intentions of this chapter is to explore the different definitions that people use as they talk and write about the ways in which they work together.

This is partly to attempt to be precise concerning meaning, but also because when talking to people about their partnerships and collaboration, it is clear that people do not always fully understand each other. There have been many occasions on courses where course participants would say something like, 'I thought we were collaborating at school until we started talking about it in the course.' It will be useful, at this early stage, to summarise the findings concerning terminology as this will prepare the reader for understanding the ways in which words and phrases are used in the rest of the book.

Leathard (1994) writes of 'a terminological quagmire' and to illustrate this she lists 52 terms which are used to denote different forms of interprofessional work. Leathard divides the terms into three sections and her headings have been adopted for discussion purposes. These are concept-based, process-based and agency-based.

**Concept-based terms**

Multidisciplinary, interdisciplinary, transdisciplinary are all concepts which are potentially confusing. From experience, multidisciplinary has become shorthand for describing the manner in which two or more professionals from different disciplines, such as occupational therapy and speech therapy, work together or alongside each other. This general term is used throughout this book when writing of the schools, colleges and centres involved as that is the way they describe what they do. There are, however, more precise definitions provided in the literature which appear to be helpful in the analysis of their work.

Although some writers such as Cooper (in Sims and Sims 1993) refer to multidisciplinary work as being concerned with sharing and collaboration, other writers want to differentiate between multi-, inter- and transdisciplinary, seeing only the final term as referring to true collaboration (Orelove and Sobsey 1991; Rainforth et al. 1992; Stainback and Stainback 1990; Lacey and Lomas 1993). For example, Orelove and Sobsey (1991) offer definitions for each of these demonstrating qualitative differences between them. They suggest that the term 'multidisciplinary' refers to professionals from more than one discipline, working alongside but separately from each other. They do not refer to working together but to coexistence. They suggest that those who work in a multidisciplinary manner make no attempt to allocate resources to prevent overlap, but work independently of each other, concentrating on the disability or educational need for which they are responsible.

Moving on to the second term, Orelove and Sobsey (1991) suggest that 'interdisciplinary' work refers to the way in which professionals share information and decide on education and care programmes together. These programmes are, however, implemented separately by members of the individual disciplines. Finally, they go on to describe the term 'transdisciplinary' which they feel represents the most developed model for working with children with special needs. This involves sharing or transferring information and skills across traditional disciplinary boundaries to enable one or two team members to be the primary workers supported by others working as consultants.

Lacey and Lomas (1993) have devised three diagrams to demonstrate the difference between multi-, inter- and transdisciplinary work and these are included here to complete the understanding of these terms used in this book (Figures 1.1, 1.2 and 1.3).

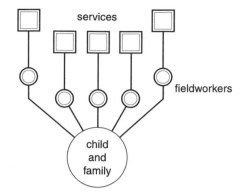

**Figure 1.1** Multidisciplinary teamwork

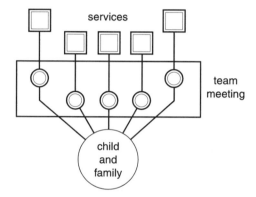

**Figure 1.2** Interdisciplinary teamwork

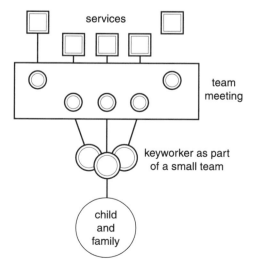

**Figure 1.3** Transdisciplinary (or collaborative) teamwork

As can be seen from Figure 1.1 each service works separately with little or no knowledge of each other. In Figure 1.2 it can be seen that each service still works separately, but they coordinate this work through regular team meetings and report writing. The child and family are serviced by several individuals but they provide different facets of a total package. From Figure 1.3 the importance of a keyworker and a small team in direct contact with children and their families can be appreciated. This helps to prevent a multiplicity of personnel overwhelming families with alternative or even conflicting advice. Most contact with the child and family is through the keyworker and small team, although direct contact with others may be desirable, especially if needs change dramatically and specialist assessment is required.

### Process-based terms

It is helpful in defining concepts to refer to the processes to which they relate and now these will be explored further in the attempt to clarify terms used in this book.

Liaison, cooperation, coordination and collaboration are often, erroneously, used interchangeably. These terms can be conceived of on a continuum, with liaison indicating the least degree of communication between agencies or professionals through to collaboration indicating the most (Lacey 1995). Payne (1993) defines liaison as making contact with other organisations and sustaining that contact. This seems to be the first step towards cooperation which denotes the minimum manner in which two organisations or professionals can work together. They take specific steps to ensure that they do not cut across each other's work or otherwise hinder each other.

The next stage is coordination, where organisations and individuals 'work together when this is necessary' (Payne 1993, p. 4) by streamlining services and timetabling so that children and their families receive a well thought out package of care and education. The final point on the continuum, collaboration, includes processes such as sharing, trusting and handing over skills, joint assessments and mutual training. Professional boundaries are crossed naturally in the effort to meet a complexity of needs. Hornby (1993) uses 'collaboration' as a comprehensive term 'to describe a relationship based on working together to achieve a common purpose'. She also identifies different types of collaboration such as primary (professional and client), secondary (professionals together) and participatory (client and professionals together) and different levels, routine or functional cooperation, simple and complex which refer to the multiplicity of people involved.

Although there are many other terms referring to processes of working together, the most used and misused is 'teamwork'. Most writers on teamwork would agree that a team is made up of a number of individuals who share a common goal and who achieve more, working together, than they could alone (Adair 1986; Hastings et al. 1986; Belbin 1981). Tjosvold (1991) suggests that the most advanced teams work in a collaborative manner and, in the business world, can transform the effectiveness of their performance.

It is often argued that the word 'team' is used when 'work group' would more accurately describe the manner in which people are working together (Payne 1982; Adair 1986; Katzenbach and Smith 1993). They work alongside each other, cooperating and even coordinating their work, but they are not a fully fledged collaborative team. This is a fine distinction, but it is vital to grasp in under-standing the complexities of the way in which staff work together to meet the needs of children or adults who have disabilities and difficulties. The word 'network' can also be associated with work groups. This implies looser connections between individuals or agencies. Networking involves liaison but may also include cooperation and coordination (Payne 1993). It does not imply collaboration, which offers a useful distinction between a network and a team. In terms of children with special needs, it can be explained thus. The team is likely to be composed of teacher, assistant, therapist and parents who work daily with individual children and the network is likely to be composed of a variety of different consultants and representatives of agencies who will provide intermittent or brief services either directly or indirectly to the children and their families (see Figure 1.4).

Another set of process-based terms which will be useful to introduce at this stage is that used in the early attempts at bringing together health and social services to facilitate care in the community. Joint planning, joint funding, joint committees all represent the way in which systems have been set up to encourage agencies to find ways of 'interweaving' what they have to offer in a 'seamless service' for the user (Bayley 1973). 'Joint-ness' in this arena does not necessarily denote a striving towards collaboration, although this may be the desire of some agency staff, particularly in the field of learning disabilities where the complexity of need makes a closeness of working essential. In other care fields, the closeness of collaboration may not be necessary, especially where the user has more control over his or her own care needs. Again, the finer points of the degree of working together are of considerable significance and they will be explored in greater detail in other places in this book.

From this brief discussion, it can be understood that for the purposes of this book, the term 'collaborative teamwork' is the most significant. It could be seen as tautological because the most advanced teamwork is collaborative. However, the two words have been placed together to provide a precision that is so often missing from the vocabulary surrounding the process of working together. This

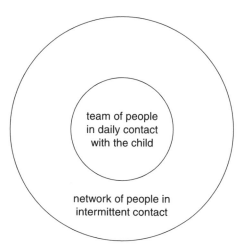

**Figure 1.4** Team and network

is not to suggest that collaborative teamwork is the best and only way to work with children and adults with special needs: liaison, cooperation, coordination, networking may be more appropriate. It is a useful term against which to measure the perceptions and practice of staff involved in the research and practice discussed here.

**Agency-based terms**
In this category there is a similar array of multi-, inter-, trans-agency terms which denotes the degree of closeness of relationship between the different agencies involved in working with people with learning disabilities. Health and social services departments have been struggling for several decades to find ways in which to work together under the auspices of community care. These struggles will be explored in some detail in the next chapter in which there is an analysis of research and literature related to aspects of working together.

Other agency terms include consortium, forum, centre, federation and cluster but none should be confused with the levels of collaborative teamwork. In each case it is possible for agencies to work together somewhere along the continuum of liaison to collaboration within that consortium or federation. It is potentially very confusing that different people mean different things by the same terms and essential that both practitioners and researchers should clarify meanings whenever possible. To help readers of this book a glossary of terms, presented in the way in which they are used, appears at the end.

## Roles of partners

As there are so many different ways in which partners can work together, there are also many different roles that can be adopted by them. Some are very clearly defined by the different professional bodies, for example speech and language therapists have a Code of Practice which defines their role. However, in practice, roles may not be so clear cut and partners will find themselves creeping into jobs and positions which require them to expand their traditional role. For example, some staff who work in schools, colleges and centres could describe themselves as part teacher, part therapist, part social worker, part psychologist, part support worker, part carer. Others, generally those who see clients infrequently, offer a specific specialism such as medical orthoses, eye testing or chiropody and are unlikely to obtain a multiple role.

The multiple role is often adopted or even enforced on support workers who are in first line care with people with learning disabilities in residential homes. This will mean that not only will they support people with learning disabilities to access services in the community, such as education, therapy and leisure, but they will also be expected to run the home as a carer, cooking, cleaning and gardening. It is very hard for this group of workers to get the balance right between housekeeping and supporting clients to access a fulfilling life. The daily grind can dominate.

When partners are working together, it is important that roles are discussed and that each person knows exactly what is expected of him or her. This does not mean that multiple roles are not possible, but everyone must be clear about what this means. At this stage of the book, the advice is that everyone has a main role, such as teacher or therapist, but that the edges of that role may well become 'blurred' in that the teacher may fulfil some therapy tasks, such as positioning a student or practising dressing, and the therapists may fulfil some teaching tasks such as teaching colours or listening to reading. It is also important that partners feel comfortable within their main role or it will be very difficult for them to reach out and take on aspects of someone else's role.

Other aspects of roles and specifically the keyworker system will be explored more in the next chapter and again in Part Two when actual examples will be presented.

## Summary and conclusions

The intention of this initial chapter was to set the scene for the research and practice which follows. Much of the discussion was given over to exploring terminology, while acknowledging its complexity. There is sufficient agreement among writers to support the adoption of definitions of multi-, inter- and transdisciplinary which draw definite distinction between them, although there is no intention to deny subsequent exploration of terms within later chapters.

The title chosen for the book 'Support Partnerships' is deliberately non-specific and is meant to convey that this book relates to anyone who is trying to work with at least one other person in a supportive way in the field of disabilities and difficulties. Those two (or more) people may be from the same or from different disciplines. They may be in the same agency. They may meet often, hardly at all or even never, but they are both concerned with the same client or client group. Partnerships can range from liaison to collaboration and can be about teamwork or about maintaining a network.

# Chapter 2

# Working together in education

The literature for Chapter 2 is based in education, in both special schools and mainstream schools. There are several questions which underpin this chapter. Exploring these can help develop understanding of the 'what', 'why' and 'how' of support partnerships, particularly those that are part of multidisciplinary team-work in special education.

- *What are multidisciplinary teams and why are they needed in education?*
- *Why should members of multidisciplinary teams in education collaborate?*
- *What are the problems and possibilities of multidisciplinary teamwork in education?*
- *What are the strategies that support effective multidisciplinary teamwork?*
- *How do teachers work together when supporting pupils with special educational needs (SEN) in mainstream schools?*

## Multidisciplinary teams in education

Although the term 'multidisciplinary' was defined in the first chapter and placed in an array of similar but different terms, it will be useful now to consider it in the context of working in education. Many children have special needs which derive from roots which are not specifically educational, although some of the solutions to those needs are in the hands of teachers who can adjust the school environment or the curriculum to remove those difficulties (Ainscow 1991). Children with physical or sensory disabilities, speech difficulties, medical problems, social challenges or behavioural difficulties need the support of professionals other than teachers. The more complex the needs, the more professionals are likely to be involved.

There was certainly a phenomenally large number of professionals found in a study undertaken by the Royal National Institute for the Blind (1992) where 27 professionals were in contact with 45 children with multiple disabilities. It is so important to organise them in some way to prevent children and their families from being totally overwhelmed by their ministrations. Although there are a variety of ways to harness the expertise offered by the diverse professionals, the general term used by many is 'multidisciplinary teamwork'.

The most advanced practice, however, can be clearly related to 'transdisciplinary teamwork' (Orelove and Sobsey 1991; McCormick and Goldman 1988; Rainforth *et al.* 1992) or 'collaborative teamwork' (Lacey and Lomas 1993; Gregory 1989; Hart 1991). These two terms seem to be largely synonymous; the first emanating from the United States of America and the second from the United Kingdom. McCormick and Goldman (1988) suggest that in the transdisciplinary model the respective disciplines are directly responsible for initial assessment in their own areas and then are expected to contribute to a comprehensive individual programme for the child. The responsibility for the carrying out of the programme is, however, in the hands of one or two team members utilising the others as consultants. There are examples of parts of the initial assessment being carried out by more than one team member such as the practice at the Wolfson Centre where speech, occupational and physio-therapists collaborate very closely using video and direct observation as the stimulus for combined assessment (Jolleff *et al.* 1994).

Finding agreement concerning definitions of what constitutes multi-disciplinary teamwork does not seem to be an easy task. Different groups of people, even within the same discipline, use it in different ways. For the purposes of this book, 'multidisciplinary teamwork' has been adopted as a general term to denote more than one discipline working together in a support partnership, whether this is minimal contact or full joint working (see Chapter 1 for a fuller discussion of terms). Alongside this has been added the term 'collaboration' to denote the fullest form of working together. By this it is meant that individuals within any team will be working jointly on assessments and children's daily programmes and will be sharing their expertise with each other on a regular basis. They will be working in an atmosphere of trust and support for each other, meeting and talking frequently. By adopting these two distinct terms, it is now possible to combine these into 'collaborative multidisciplinary teamwork', that is, members of different disciplines will be working together in the joint manner described above. There seems to be sufficient literature to support the adoption of these terms and they have been used by the author of this book over a seven year period (Lacey and Lomas 1993; Lacey and Ranson 1994; Lacey 1995; Starr and Lacey 1996; Lacey 1996a, 1996b, 1997, 1998, 2000).

## Why collaborate?

The arguments for why it is desirable for members of different agencies and disciplines to work in a collaborative manner are largely based on common sense rather than on a large body of research (Marshall *et al.* 1979; Davie 1993; Leathard 1994). These arguments will be rehearsed here as they are a vital part of the underpinning of the most advanced practice in this country. It would in fact be very difficult to prove that it is more effective to work collaboratively than in any other way, in a quantifiable manner, as there are so many factors to consider. Is the number of children on a team's caseload significant? Is 'more' better or worse? Does spending more money on bringing professionals together mean that it is less cost effective or does the improved problem solving of the team outweigh this? Which is more efficient, professionals getting on with the work in which they were trained or passing on their skills to others? Common sense suggests that the latter is eventually more efficient, though at first it costs more in terms of time and resources.

A common sense approach offers many examples of the perceptions of professionals concerning the efficacy of collaborative teamwork. One area of interest to many writers is that of counteracting fragmentation (McCormick and Goldman 1988; Orelove and Sobsey 1991). It is very easy for each agency or professional involved with individual children to concentrate only on the small aspect of the child's needs for which they are directly responsible. The physiotherapist is only interested in gross motor movement, the speech therapist in communication, the occupational therapist in hand function and the teacher in intellectual development. With such a fragmentary view it is perfectly possible for individual children to be working in completely different and even conflicting ways with different people. Any advice following assessment can be contradictory and far from the holistic and ecological ideal of educationists such as Bronfenbrenner (1979), Fish (1985) and Linder (1990).

There have long been calls for one agency to be responsible for and respond to the needs of children (Swan and Morgan 1993; Evans *et al.* 1989; Pugh 1992). In the absence of a Ministry for Children, there have been many ideas and attempts to draw together the different agencies under a single council or committee. Some local authorities, such as Strathclyde, integrated their education and social services and allocated management responsibility to education during the childhood years (Pugh 1992) but this new department did not include health authorities, which are not the responsibility of local authorities.

However difficult it is to work together, many people have advocated collaboration over the last 40 years. The arguments have been that not only should this avoid fragmentation, but it should also positively promote an integrated response where individual children have many opportunities for practising the same skills and building up understanding through repeated activities. Working collaboratively means that staff and parents agree to pursue the same goals in a coordinated manner. The physiotherapist advises on sitting position, the speech therapist on the level of language and the teacher on the educational content of work sessions. Parents and classroom assistants can contribute to any or all of these areas. Any one of them can carry out these work sessions as they each know the other's priorities. At a conference on working with children with multiple disabilities, three therapists at the Wolfson Centre discussed what happens when they have competing priorities . They talked of the need to 'jostle' and 'queue', but that they were ultimately influenced by the immediate needs of individual children (Jolleff *et al.* 1994).

Discussions leading to collaborative problem solving is cited on many occasions as being a very clear advantage to professionals working together (Orelove and Sobsey 1991; Losen and Losen 1985; Handy 1985; Payne 1982). The word used is 'synergy' and the implication is that a team of people can achieve more together than each could as individuals. Balanced against this is the very real criticism that many teams find it difficult to use meetings profitably. They waste time that could be spent on solving problems and making decisions through petty power struggles, withholding information or pure ineptitude.

These difficulties in running effective meetings and achieving joint problem solving do not detract from the general agreement among educationists that collaborative teamwork is both desirable and attainable. It is seemingly impossible to find sources where arguments were presented to persuade readers that collaborative teamwork is undesirable when working with children with special needs. There were many which pointed up the problems in achieving it and much advice on how to set on the path to success. These will be the subject of the next section.

## Problems and possibilities

Some of the problems of collaboration have already been mentioned but unfortunately there are several more that beset the best intentions of professionals who genuinely desire to combine their work efforts. One of the intractable problems appears to be that surrounding confidentiality. Despite several well-publicised cases, such as that concerning Maria Colwell, where children have been placed in danger because services did not share information, there is still a great reluctance for professionals from different services to consider modifications to their confidentiality codes. Social services, in particular, have very strict rules governing confidentiality and although it is possible to understand the origins of these rules, it is hard to justify when professionals are trying to work in a collaborative team. The Warnock Report (DES 1978) uses the term 'extended confidentiality' and the Home Office, Department of Health, Department of Education and Science, Welsh Office (1991, p. 13) suggest that 'confidentiality may not be maintained if the withholding of information will prejudice the welfare of the child'. From their research into identifying models of interagency working, Maychell and Bradley (1991, p. 39) report that some of their respondents suspected that information of a non-confidential nature was withheld in the interest of maintaining power and control over others. One of their examples concerned the reluctance of social workers to pass on case history information on a student to his new college in the name of confidentiality. College staff felt that unfortunate incidents that had arisen could have been avoided, had they known the student's background and that withholding the information was unnecessary.

It can be argued that members of collaborative teams should trust each other to the point of feeling that confidences can be shared among them and remain within that group of people. There may be some cases where this is not in the interest of the child and his or her family. When this happens, the agency in question must be very clear about why the confidence is not to be shared. Many writers discuss trust and sharing, suggesting that these are central to effective teamwork (Hornby 1993; Rainforth *et al.* 1992; Rouse 1987). Trust is difficult to build up especially as so many writers mention problems with territorial disputes between agencies and professionals (Clough and Lindsay 1991; Solity and Bickler 1994), power struggles (Fish 1985; Gregory 1989) and feelings of job insecurity (Maychell and Bradley 1991; Thomas 1992). The present climate of dividing the 'purchaser' from the 'provider' within the human services may be adding to these difficulties and encouraging competition rather than collaboration.

Miller's (1996) research points to the importance of professionals from different disciplines sharing a language and understanding each other's point of view. Her study, of the outcomes of training speech and language therapists and teachers on the same course, shows that both sets of professionals felt that they could communicate more effectively; plan and work together more closely; and generally experience a better professional working relationship after being on the course. She does, however, point to some negative results which suggest that some participants felt threatened by sharing knowledge.

The sharing of expertise is implicit in the way in which a collaborative team works. Through natural observation of each other at work, joint problem solving and professional discussion, skills and understanding are exchanged and put into practice (Bailey 1991; Connolly and Anderson 1988; Hanko 1990). Like all teamwork, it is relatively easy to find isolated examples of good practice, but very difficult to find evidence that this trust and sharing is the norm in multidisciplinary teams who work with children with special needs. It is a difficult and demanding thing to achieve and there are so many factors militating against it in schools today, particularly the demands of a crowded curriculum, inspection and league tables.

Research by Wright (1992) has contributed something to the understanding of the problems and possibilities for collaboration across disciplines. Wright looked specifically at pairs of speech and language therapists and teachers working together to try to ascertain what each felt they gained from the partnership. From her interviews, she found several ways in which the pairs felt they had gained from working together. These included benefits to the child, such as less fragmentation; personal benefits such as sharing concerns, support and reducing stress; and professional gains, such as new knowledge in specific areas ('cognitive gain'). Problems included the difficulties in finding time to collaborate, the added strain of working with another person and loss of autonomy. Wright (1992) recommends the use of a facilitator when teachers and therapists first start to work together, as a strategy to help them to identify their own personal and professional benefits from working together, as well as the disadvantages.

## Strategies for enabling collaboration

Wright's suggestion is one strategy that can assist effective collaboration to become more likely. From the literature it is possible to build up a picture of other possibilities. The detail of such strategies is a central theme in the second part of this book and will be dealt with only briefly at this point.

### Legislation

Legislation underpinning multidisciplinary and multi-agency work is largely facilitative and encouraging rather than demanding. *The Code of Practice on the Identification and Assessment of Special Educational Needs* attached to the Education Act 1993 (DES 1993) is a good example of this. One of its principles is: 'There must be close cooperation between all the agencies concerned and a multidisciplinary approach to the resolution of issues' (DfE 1994, p. 3). However, in the detail that follows, it appears that agencies who support schools can choose not to respond to demands for assessments and reports if they feel the request is unreasonable in terms of their own available resources.

Even though the legislation lacks compulsion, there is evidence to suggest that agencies are committed to working together and have devised certain strategies to facilitate this, for example bringing together joint committees, departments and teams financed through joint budgets.

## Contracts and job descriptions

One of the strategies explored by several writers is that of written contracts and service agreements (Bowers 1991a, 1991b; Clough and Lindsay 1991; Swan and Morgan 1993). Clough and Lindsay's (1991) research into the support services in 'City LEA' reveal that contracts can vary in their format, but are basically a tool to aid clarity of purpose in relationships between services and schools. They were in no way legal documents but agreements concerning the way in which schools and services could work together. The results of the research suggest that contracts are useful 'milestones' in an evolutionary process of affecting change in schools but that their usefulness is largely governed by the success with which individuals interact with each other while fulfilling the contract. The researchers suggest that relying on contracts could have the effect of ensuring that special educational needs continues to be seen as the responsibility of outside services rather than of the school itself.

## Meetings

Meetings of all kinds have also been seen as having the potential to support collaborative teamwork. Rainforth *et al.* (1992) suggest that interaction is particularly important when teams are setting up. But throughout their lives teams need time to talk together and to work together. This includes time allocated to carry out joint assessments, plan programmes together and actually work side-by-side (Linder 1990; Losen and Losen 1985). This implies support from management who must facilitate time spent together. Cocker (1995) points to the importance of non-contact time for class teachers and special educational needs coordinators (SENCOs) to work together. She claims that she could not carry out her role as SENCO without being given time to meet with other people.

## Structure

Generally, there is the need for a structure to promote collaboration if teams of professionals are to be effective in their work. Facilitating time for meetings and joint work is one aspect and encouraging the imaginative use of time is another. Traditionally, support from outside services or therapists has been in regular, short bursts. This works quite well while there is generous staffing, but in the age of diminishing resources it leads to frustration as parents and class teachers feel that they are being short-changed. Where once the speech therapist could offer time to work directly with individual children in special schools, now often she has an increased caseload and responsibilities elsewhere in the service and consequently can offer less time to individuals (Wright 1992). Rainforth *et al.* (1992) argue for the blocking of time not just as an expediency, but because it makes sense to use therapists as consultants rather than expect them to give small amounts of time to individual children for direct work. This might result in the therapist making an initial assessment of several children and jointly writing programmes with other team members within one block of time, then leaving the classroom staff to carry out the programmes for a few weeks. Later the therapist returns to monitor the programme and help with adjustments or further assessments. This could be done in several classrooms or schools with the effect that the needs of more children are discussed and those needs can be met daily by classroom staff, instead of twice weekly for ten minutes by the therapist.

## Keyworker systems

One of the structures which requires examination is that pertaining to the keyworker system. Collaborative teamwork implies the use of a keyworker or core member who takes the main responsibility for meeting the needs of individual children (Orelove and Sobsey 1991; Rainforth *et al*. 1992; Linder 1990). This is not quite synonymous with team leader in the sense found in industry, but appears to be more of a coordinator's role combined with an advocate's role. Any member of the team can take the lead or core role in terms of planning and implementation of programmes, using other members in a consultative role. The keyworker role, as developed mainly by health workers for very young children with disabilities, is explored in more detail in the next chapter.

## Special education in mainstream schools

So far, the discussion has mainly ranged round education that can be found in special schools for children with the most severe and complex difficulties and disabilities. The mixture of medical and educational needs means there are often a large number of professionals from different disciplines involved. In mainstream schools there are some occasions when representatives from different disciplines will be working together, but by far the most likely teamwork to be found in this setting is that between teachers who have different specialisms. Either by training or by experience or both, some teachers have become sources of good practice in a variety of special educational needs. The trend recently is for these teachers to support classroom and subject teachers in meeting the needs of children who are displaying difficulties, rather than to use their expertise directly working with the children (Dyson and Gains 1993).

The inclusion, in mainstream schools, of children with SEN has been on both the political and educational agenda for more than 20 years. The Warnock Report (DES 1978) clearly set out how this might be achieved but the two Audit Commission Reports (Audit Commission/HMI 1992a and b) equally clearly demonstrated how little had been achieved in the intervening years. The 1993 Education Act (DES 1993) with its Code of Practice (DfE 1994) has given new impetus and strengthened the role of the SENCO, expecting this role to be formed in every school, not just those with good practice. Much has been written recently on this role and also the role of the peripatetic educational support service provided by the local education authority (Dyson and Gains 1993).

One of the greatest problems identified is that of two teachers working together in the same classroom. Support teaching involves a variety of approaches: from developing techniques with specific children to modifying worksheets and translating for hearing impaired pupils; from diagnosing learning difficulties to advising on resources and training classroom teachers to meet the needs of all pupils in their classes. This is potentially a threatening situation and both supporter and supportee can be overwhelmed by the proximity of working and by the relationship needed when one teacher takes advice from another (Thomas 1992; McLaughlin 1989; Hart 1991; Hanko 1990). Thomas' (1992) research identified one of the difficulties as a possible mismatch between the two teachers in terms of ideologies and styles, which creates stress and the suggestion that the presence of the extra person in the classroom actually detracts from the teaching and learning instead of enhancing it.

Thomas conducted surveys, interviews and observation of teachers, support teachers and assistants working together in a variety of primary and secondary schools from which he made a number of recommendations based on his data. The main thrust of these relates to the need for individuals to have clear task and role definition to ensure that uncertainty is reduced. He suggests the use of joint planning and regular discussion to facilitate this. He also argues that heterogeneous teams, rather than homogeneous, are likely to have fewer difficulties, suggesting that teachers did not like to be observed teaching by other teachers (Thomas 1992).

Dyson (1994) has been developing over several years, the notion of an 'effective learning consultant' rather than a SENCO. He is anxious to promote the idea that retaining the concept of special needs is preventing more imaginative ways of responding to the learning needs of all children. He supports the work of writers such as Ainscow (1991, 1997), Booth et al. (1992) and Stainback and Stainback (1990) who call for effective schools for all children and a recognition of a diversity of needs across the continuum of ability. Achieving this means teams of staff working together, especially as expertise is built up in mainstream classroom teachers. It also means reconstructing schools to change the structures which perpetuate segregation. Research from The University of Newcastle-upon-Tyne (Dyson et al. 1998) has shown that if the general concept of school effectiveness has not been addressed, giving SENCOs a consultancy role in the hope of changing the response to SEN issues has not proved successful. It merely adds another layer of bureaucracy.

Spurred by a natural resistance to the competitive atmosphere encouraged by the present government, some schools have developed relationships with each other which have variously been called clusters (Lunt et al. 1994a and b; Gains and Smith 1994), families (Cade and Caffyn 1994, 1995) and interschool collaboration (Wallace and Hall 1994). What is described appears to relate most directly to cooperation and coordination rather than full collaboration, but there is a real attempt to change structures and accommodate new ways of working, especially in the special needs field. It is helpful to consider Lunt et al.'s (1994b) definition of a cluster.

> A 'cluster' denotes a relatively stable and long term commitment among a group of schools to share some resources and decision-making about an area of school activity. There is a degree of formality, in that there are regular meetings of cluster schools to plan and monitor the activity concerned. There is some commitment of resource (e.g. teacher time) and some loss of autonomy implied, since schools will have to negotiate some decisions about this area of activity.
>
> (Lunt et al. 1994b, p. 74)

Clusters are still in their infancy but they could provide one answer to managing SEN in the harsh world of markets and league tables. The willingness of some schools to enter into partnership with each other is indicative of their commitment to changing their practice to meet needs. From their research, Lunt *et al.* (1994b) suggest that there are several emerging themes which can guide further development: optimum size is between six and eight schools; the focus should be simple; there needs to be a catalyst to get it started; a coordinator is essential; schools need to feel ownership; a particular task is helpful; there needs to be a pay-off for schools to get involved.

## Interpersonal factors

The last aspect of working with pupils with SEN in mainstream schools which will be discussed is that surrounding the interpersonal element of teachers working in partnership. As mentioned earlier, Thomas' (1992) research seemed to demonstrate that the mere presence of someone else in the classroom can cause difficulties. There is very little other research on which to draw to confirm or refute this view, but many writers have drawn attention to the difficulties of two teachers working together (Fish 1985; Rouse 1987; Manford 1991; Jordan 1994; Hart 1991). The shift from working with pupils to working with other adults demands new skills, understanding and knowledge from both parties, but especially from the support teacher who has, in effect, become a consultant. McLaughlin (1989) suggests being guided by the 3Rs: respect (for teachers and their work); reality (start from where the teacher is) and responsibility (which should remain with the teacher).

Teachers are trained to be self-sufficient in the classroom and there is a long tradition of feelings of failure and incompetence if support is sought. This must be coupled with attitudes that children with SEN are someone else's problem and support teaching means removing the problem to another place. In the light of these, it is not surprising that support teaching has taken a long time to become accepted as an in-class activity. Support teachers must be prepared to give away their expertise (Jordan 1994) and be flexible in their response to the needs of the teachers with whom they are working (Hart 1991). Both need to cope with a loss of autonomy and be prepared for teaching to appear more difficult at the outset as new decisions and responsibilities slow the pace (Hart 1991). Hanko (1990) writes of the importance of joint problem solving and how this can be a very effective professional development activity. She advocates the Caplan model which focuses on maximising the teachers' own resources to deal more effectively with problems themselves. This includes a training element where the discussion is broadened from specific cases to principles to be applied to new or other problems.

Some of the difficulties and solutions found in support teaching in mainstream schools can shed light on similar ones found in multidisciplinary teamwork in special schools. The consultant role adopted by many support teachers, both in-school and from peripatetic services, may relate well to that of the way in which some therapists work, particularly speech and language therapists who have deliberately changed their way of working over the past five to ten years from mainly remediating individual children's speech difficulties to mainly supporting teachers in meeting a range of children's speech and language needs (Howard *et al.* 1995).

## Summary and conclusions

This chapter has contained an attempt to bring together what has been written about the ways in which people work together with and for children with disabilities and difficulties in educational settings. There has been an emphasis on the difficulties experienced by partners working together, but there has also been discussion of some of the possible ways in which partnerships can become more effective. Many of these will be taken up in Part Two of this book, where the case studies will be used to explore the practical implications of some of the strategies mentioned at this point.

Education has been a fruitful discipline from which to find literature that sheds light on support partnerships. It is clear, however, that although it is easy to exhort people and services to work together, there is a long history of working alone in education and strong and different discipline cultures that prevent the exhortations from becoming reality. Most individual people are willing to work together in partnership but they spend much of their time battling against the systems and structures that seem to get in the way.

# Chapter 3

# Working together in the human services

After the consideration of support partnerships within multidisciplinary teams in education in Chapter 2, Chapter 3 contains aspects of the literature in other parts of the human services, such as health and social services, families working with professionals and an alternative to multidisciplinary teamwork, conductive education. The questions that underpin this chapter are the following.

- *How are health and social care brought together under community care and what are the implications for services working together?*
- *How do professionals work together with children and families in preschool settings?*
- *What happens if one person takes on the different roles that are usually assigned to different people in a multidisciplinary team, as in conductive education?*

## Community care

In this section, a little of the vast literature charting the progress of developing care in the community is explored to review how health and social services have worked together, including the ways in which multi-agency work has developed in preschool care. Legislation has been more forceful in this sector than in special education with the result that there have been many more attempts to achieve a solution to the difficulties of working together, although the results demonstrate that this has not yet widely been achieved.

Until the 1960s there was little need for agencies to work together as most care services were run under the auspices of health. However by the 1970s, Departments of Health, Social Services, Housing and Education had all become involved in care and had responsibilities for the same body of people. This is particularly so in the area of learning disabilities (or mental handicap as was the term until the late 1980s) where it was no longer deemed appropriate for children or adults to live in long-stay hospitals and their presence in the community demanded the cooperation of several branches of health and social care (Rose 1993; Jones 1989; Pietroni 1994). This has been coupled with a decision that hospitals should be retained for short-term acute care only and that all chronic patients should be cared for in the community, either in their own homes or in small residential nursing homes.

Rose (1993) suggests that in the learning disability field, legislation itself has been less influential in bringing change than the 'secondary' social policy, which includes a whole range of concepts such as 'normalisation' , 'advocacy' and 'ordinary life'. These all represent a move towards recognising that people with learning disabilities have a basic human right to be treated as 'normal' citizens and live as anyone else does, however much support they need to fulfil this role. Their place is rightfully in the community, living in neighbourhood housing and using services which are available for everyone. It could be argued that the work towards the ideal of normalisation, carried out by people with learning disabilities, their carers and professionals who support them, accounts for the success that has been seen in encouraging agencies to work together effectively. Rose (1993) does, however, suggest that there are still many problems to be overcome before agencies and professionals could be said to be working together collaboratively.

## Joint working

From the mid-1970s there has been much encouragement for creating joint mechanisms between social services and health authorities. Joint funding was introduced to pump prime joint planning, but subsequent government enquiries and independent research have revealed a variety of problems and weaknesses with the systems set up (Working Group on Joint Planning 1985; Audit Commission 1986; Hunter and Wistow 1987; Wistow and Hardy 1991). Wistow and Hardy (1991) suggest that these difficulties can be divided into five categories: structural, procedural, financial, professional status and legitimacy. The Working Group on Joint Planning (1985) pointed to particular difficulties with the lack of coterminosity between local authorities and health regions and with the availability of resources, especially bridging finance during the move from hospital to community-based care. To these can be added different management structures, methods of organisation, financial systems, status and pay, basic principles and value systems, priorities and traditions. Append to this the general feeling of threat, which besets any major change, and the failure of joint planning and finance, suggested by the writers mentioned above, can be easily understood.

It has been argued that local authorities are more motivated to make 'joint-ness' work than health authorities, since they stand to gain more in terms of status and control. Westland (1988) suggests that local authorities regarded joint planning as a chance to become more 'respectable' and less politically uncontrollable in the eyes of the government. Certainly, social services have been named the 'lead authority' in the community care legislation and have responsibility for organising case management. In any rise to power, there is always a struggle to resist from those who see their influence diminishing and many of the problems cited above could be said to arise from basic fights for survival. This could be encapsulated in the role of the learning disability nurse. The concept of learning disabilities has been gradually redefined in terms of a social rather than a medical model and people with learning disabilities are less likely to be found in health settings. This has had the effect of threatening the role of the nurses especially trained in this area. What will be their role in the future? They have genuine skills which are not solely medical in character and could be utilised in a care setting. They are, however, professionally trained and thus expensive, which can price them out of the notoriously impoverished social services market.

Creating structures and systems for joint work come up against a variety of difficulties characterised by suspicion and a reluctance to hand over resources and decision-making and by a very real feeling that 'joint-ness' is difficult to achieve and takes an enormous amount of time and effort. Wistow (1988) suggests that systemic change is not sufficient and that attitudinal rather than structural factors are fundamental to the success of community care. He cites research by Etherington *et al.* (being researched at that time) from which they recommend that the starting point should be attacking established attitudes through the development of a shared vision or value base as a foundation for the philosophies and principles on which the new service can be constructed. The All Wales Strategy for the Development of Services for Mentally Handicapped People (McGrath 1991) is referred to as an example of attempts to work in this manner (see below for further discussion).

Knapp *et al.* (1992) summarise some of the key ingredients needed to encourage effective joint working between different agencies. Good interorganisational relationships depend on a shared vision as the foundation for joint action and compatibility in planning and commissioning intentions. They suggest that the preoccupation with paper plans and formal machinery have not been helpful. However, they caution against thinking that getting commissioning right will solve all problems. There are complex procedures coupled with a history of political differences inherent in one service being controlled by central government and the other by local. Their advice is to work at the pace concomitant with local circumstances and begin perhaps with comparability rather than 'joint-ness'.

## All Wales Strategy

The majority of the commissioned reports and research concerned with community care have concentrated on the organisational issues of enabling two fundamentally different sets of professionals to work together. The All Wales Strategy for the Development of Services for Mentally Handicapped People has been examined in a variety of ways giving results in a number of areas in addition to the service organisation level (McGrath 1991). The focus here is on organisational issues.

Following a number of research studies which revealed difficulties of fragmentation and inadequacy faced in services for people with learning disabilities (mental handicap), one attempt at unifying and improving this situation has been in the use of community mental handicap teams (CMHT). These usually consist of a core membership of community nurses and social workers but with support from a variety of different health professionals. The All Wales Strategy was set up in 1983 and represents a unique situation in Britain where policy is based on a rejection of the medical model of learning disabilities in favour of development, integration and wider opportunities. The strong central support for the strategy alongside the extra funding have provided a powerful impetus for development. This has, in turn, been supported by a clearly spelt out philosophy, goals and guidelines and the enthusiasm of most parents and carers.

Collaboration has been at the heart of the programme to the point of refusing to finance plans unless evidence of interagency collaboration and carer participation is provided. Results from the survey conducted by McGrath (1991) indicate that this incentive to work together has been at least partially successful. Success can be seen where there is a broad framework of policies and principles with explicit agreements, representatives of different agencies have delegated authority to make decisions, where there are effective channels of communication between the teams of fieldworkers and county policy-makers and where there are skilled and committed managers.

It would be useful at this point to summarise the recommendations made by McGrath (1991, p. 195) from her study of the development of community mental handicap teams in Wales. She concludes that experience in Wales suggests the need for:

(a) managerial skills;
(b) training and support;
(c) time to establish efficient systems of planning and monitoring;
(d) training in case management, finance management, negotiation and collaboration with other agencies, information systems, monitoring and evaluation procedures;
(e) the establishment of a shared philosophy, clear objectives and feasible targets agreed between stakeholders.

Generally, those who have researched and written about the experience of community care have presented a greater depth of insight and have explored more social issues in their attempts to explain what has happened than the writers concerned with multidisciplinary teamwork in education.

Some of the issues that have been examined are worth mentioning at this point but space does not allow for detailed examination. For example, the encouragement of a quasi-market environment with its competitive elements are contrasted with the call for collaboration by several writers who suggest that developing joint working in such a climate is likely to be problematic (Ovretveit 1994; Hattersley 1995; Ferlie 1994). The difficulties caused through individuals and services engaging in power struggles feature in several different guises and those writing about this topic suggest that these struggles contribute to the problems faced by those wishing to collaborate across agencies (Hudson 1995; Hornby 1993; Engel 1994). The need for shared and joint training to minimise the problems that bedevil teamwork is discussed by several writers (Malin 1994; Brown, J. 1994; Leathard 1994) and this topic will be taken up in detail in Chapter 4 of this book where the subject of training is explored.

## Preschool settings

The literature that has been reviewed relating to community care is chiefly about the relationship between health and social services. Education has little part to play, especially in the world of adults with learning disabilities. In preschool settings, health and social services have very strong roles but education is also involved. At this stage, families of children with disabilities and difficulties are also very prominent, adding yet another dimension to the collaborative picture.

Like special schools for children with complex disabilities, preschool care and education is provided by a variety of different services with their own histories and objectives. There is a variety of services, from child development centres and social services nurseries to nursery classes in schools and home visiting systems. Staff, some of whom are qualified and others who are untrained or voluntary, come from a range of different backgrounds. They are governed by different and sometimes conflicting legislation and policy. Potts *et al.* (1992) call this a 'jigsaw of services' and suggest that its complicated nature makes it very difficult for families to get the provision they need for their children.

Much of the literature devoted to management issues in preschool education relates to the need to reduce the variety of provision and bring together the two elements of care and education into what Sharp (1994) calls 'educare'. Sharp writes about the project in which Sheffield brought together the work of the two departments of education and social services in an attempt to promote unified practice. They wanted coherence, flexibility and quality provision which they tried to achieve through setting up three joint centres. She reports that although setting up the centres was important, changing practice within them needed a 'radical rethink' (p. 176). She suggests that the creation of new posts for under-fives coordinators was useful in moving ideas forward.

Pugh (1992) writes more generally about local structures to support a coordinated approach to under-fives provision, which seem mainly to be in the form of subcommittees in local government with cooptions of health authority personnel or delegation of duties to either education or social services. In whatever way each area decides to structure its agencies, the experience of the Early Childhood Unit of the Children's Bureau enables Pugh (1992) to advise on effectiveness. She suggests that there needs to be clarity in terms of policy, roles, responsibilities, lines of communication and support from elected members and chief officers. She also urges nurturing relationships with health authorities and voluntary groups.

In the same book, Whalley (1992) writes of a specific multidisciplinary centre which was set up by both education and social services with some input from health. Staff came from several different backgrounds and Whalley suggests that this was a strength as they were able to take the best from all the different models of provision. All had the same title, 'family worker', although some posts were more senior than others, and everyone took on a responsibility commensurate with their training and experience. Rigid interagency roles were relaxed as everyone broadly fulfilled similar functions. Whalley writes of some of the managerial difficulties they experienced as they developed their teamworking and of how they settled on a 'side-archy' rather than a hierarchy so they could focus on strengths of staff rather than traditional seniority. She also points to the importance of closing the centre on one afternoon a week for staff meetings and training, believing that fitting in times to talk during breaks is not sufficient for a team to work effectively.

Whalley (1992) is quite clear about the benefits of working in this way, especially for those children and families who have a special need. Instead of having to see several different people from different agencies all asking similar questions and giving sometimes conflicting advice, families can self select one or two people with whom they can work within their own communities, on a long-term basis. The Portage scheme is built on a similar principle that one person will become a keyworker for families and help them to meet their children's needs in their own homes and act as a link between them and a range of agencies (Potts *et al.* 1992). The Wessex Project, reported by Smith (1986), demonstrated how people from different professions (teachers, therapists, specialist teachers of children with sensory impairments) could be trained in the same way to be home teachers, but also use the skills and expertise derived from their original discipline, so that, in a sense, these people became 'multi-professional'. Although many writers claim much success for Portage, it must not be forgotten that the scheme is not without its critics, not least that the training of home visitors is often limited, focusing on teaching behavioural skills to parents rather than on the wider problems they have to address (Sturmey 1987).

However, recent research on Portage by Nunkoosing and Phillips (1999) shows that Portage is more often used by professionals than by untrained workers and that these professionals rely less on the checklist of activities and more on supporting the family in general. The home visitors interviewed as part of this research talked of adapting their role to the perceived needs of the family rather than forcing their own agendas.

## Professionals supporting families

It would be useful, at this point to consider in more detail some of the aspects of professionals supporting families of young children with special needs as this encompasses both a support partnership, that of parents and professionals, and the relevant aspects of multi-agency work.

There are a number of models of partnership between parents and professionals:

- the *expert* model, where professionals make decisions for parents and work directly with the children;
- the *transplant* model, where professionals train parents to work with their own children;
- the *consumer* model, where professionals provide information for parents and let them choose what services they want;
- the *negotiation* model, where professionals and parents work together having negotiated the way forward between them (Dale 1995).

Although it is generally considered that the negotiation model is the most advanced, it can be that parents would want to negotiate working within one of the other models or even within a combination. Certainly, some parents can be relieved to use elements of the expert model, especially if they have many different kinds of stresses in their lives.

Murray (2000), a parent of a child with multiple disabilities, writes that the phrase 'parental partnership' has been used and misused to such an extent that it now carries little meaning. It seems to be a concept which is worthy in principle, but which is so difficult to achieve in practice. Murray (2000) explores some of the reasons for the continuing dominance of professionals over parents, suggesting that the medical model of a disabled child as imperfect or impaired is still prevalent, which gives power to professionals at the expense of parents and of disabled people themselves. Until disability is viewed in terms of rights, families will continue to be at the mercy of professionals and the agencies they represent.

Sinclair and Grimshaw (1997) also discuss aspects of power relationships in their research study on partnership with parents while planning care under the Children Act 1989. They found that the longer children remain in the 'looked after' system, the less their parents were involved in the planning of their future care. They suggest four strategies which can promote and maintain a partnership: the use of supporters for parents in meetings; the provision of interpreters where the family's first language is not English; an informal chairperson able to put families at ease; social workers who really listen to parents' views. They also recommend moving away from the model of a formal set-piece all-encompassing review meeting in favour of smaller meetings, the results of which can be brought together prior to final decisions. All these suggestions seem somewhat obvious, but it is clear from a large amount of the literature that families are not valued and are more likely to be blamed than appreciated.

Carpenter (1997), a parent who is also a professional in special education, writes of the need for families of children with special needs to be accepted as equals in the partnership with professionals. He suggests that professionals should recognise the 'uniqueness' of each family and how much can be learned from them. His view of partnership is of each valuing the contribution of the other. Carpenter (1997) also calls for a coordinated and coherent approach from services, a cry that is supported by many other writers and researchers (for example, Tozer 1999; Beattie 1999; Limbrick-Spencer 2000).

## Service coordination

There have been several reasons given for poor coordination of services for disabled young children and their families. For example:

- the needs of the group are not central to each agency's services (Middleton 1998);
- there may be large numbers of professionals involved especially in meeting the needs of children with multiple disabilities (RNIB 1992);
- this is exacerbated by the trend towards professional specialisation which means even more people are likely to be involved (Department of Health 1998, Circular 1998/201);
- children's needs can fall between agencies or are met sequentially by different agencies rather than simultaneously (Malcolm et al. 1996);
- agencies have different eligibility criteria and families can feel that they are being pushed around from agency to agency in search of the 'right' service (Bridge 1993).

One of the solutions that is often cited by parents is to have one person to whom they could relate and who could coordinate all their services. This person could prevent hospital appointments being made on consecutive days, or two different agencies carrying out the same assessment, or home visiting at the same time. The coordinator might not always be able to prevent conflicting advice being given to families, but he or she could be available to discuss its implications.

Despite government advice to other groups needing coordination of care, there is little guidance about how to coordinate services for disabled children (Challis et al. 1998). Some local areas have made attempts at coordination, but little has been evaluated. Beattie (1999) cites some US studies evaluating coordination, but warns that the context differences may be too great for direct transfer. Of these US studies, following coordination, there was evidence of improvements in:

- access to services
- provision of more services and help
- access to equipment
- family involvement
- service brokering
- parental satisfaction
- comprehensiveness of provision
- job satisfaction for coordinators.

Beattie (1999) points to the fact that parents' views were not included in the studies. However, from the studies she is able to suggest that a coordinator role appears to be very different from that of the usual professional roles. A coordinator would have long-term and proactive involvement that is not aimed at specific problem solving. Thus if it was taken on by a professional from a particular agency, that person would need to set aside agency loyalties and task-orientated solutions in favour of an unbiased and flexible response to family needs. From her own study, Beattie (1999) drastically altered her own view of service coordination, eventually feeling that introducing a local coordinator may not be possible in the current climate. From her interviews of seven professionals, she concluded that the role of the coordinator is important but powerless, unquestioning, irrelevant and threatening:

- *important* because families need a benevolent accepting representative;
- *powerless* because agencies would not be answerable to him/her;
- *unquestioning* because none of the professionals questioned the existing organisational structures;
- *irrelevant* because it carries no status and is not a desirable role;
- *threatening* because it might blur the distinctions between disciplines which might make some professionals redundant.

This is a very small study, but it is a little discouraging for those who would like to promote a coordinator role, not least the families themselves. It makes partnership between professionals and families even more difficult to achieve, if one of the partners is recommending a solution that is basically unacceptable to the other.

## The keyworker role

Despite the results of Beattie's (1999) study, there are examples of the development of care coordination through keyworker systems which do appear to be successful. A survey of 455 parents by Limbrick-Spencer (2000) called the UK SOFTY (Support Over First Two Years) postal survey was carried out to identify the support needs of parents in the first two years following disclosure of diagnosis of their child's complex needs. Limbrick-Spencer works within the One Hundred Hours keyworker model of support and she designed the survey to see if this model could or should be universal.

   In the One Hundred Hours model, the intention is that the keyworker works for the family, is responsive to the changing needs of the child and family, acknowledges and responds to the emotional needs of the family and helps them to join together all the separate strands from the various therapists and teachers working with the child. The intervention from the keyworker is needs-led and concerned with the whole child within the family setting.

The results of the survey indicate that parents feel they need support in six distinct areas:

- emotional support, especially someone to talk to and who had some counselling skills;
- information about their child's condition given at a pace parents can manage and in language they can understand;
- information about services, that can help parents to understand what is available;
- accessing what is needed, rather than having to battle for services;
- coordination of services, to manage an array of appointments and information;
- the whole picture, so that the family needs were being seen as one.

Limbrick-Spencer (2000) is clear that the response to the needs of the parents in the survey is a keyworker approach: one person who could meet the needs identified in the six areas above. She goes on to suggest that to achieve coordination of services, the keyworker would need to be supported by a degree of multi-agency working.

From the literature on coordinating services for young children, it can be concluded that parents face a bewildering array of services that are often badly coordinated. The parents would like one person to help them make sense of what is available and support them during what is a very difficult time, but this role is hard to develop and sustain in the current climate. Schemes such as the One Hundred Hours model suggests that the appointment of keyworkers can successfully meet families' needs and part of that success may be due to the independent nature of that worker. From Beattie's (1999) study, it was concluded that professionals who belong to a particular agency could find it difficult to step outside their professional role to provide the independence necessary for an unbiased view of complex situations. The keyworker model will be explored again in Chapter 12 which is devoted to case studies of partnerships between families and professionals.

## Conductive education

The final aspect of the literature that will be examined in relation to models of multidisciplinary collaboration in the human services, is that pertaining to conductive education. The specific interest is in the role of the 'conductor', which, rather like the 'keyworker' or 'educarer' of the previous section, attempts to combine several aspects of education and care into one person, thus cutting out the need for several people to come together in a multidisciplinary team.

Conductive education is described as 'a system for overcoming motor disorder' (Cottam and Sutton 1986) and emanates from Hungary where it was developed mainly for children with cerebral palsy. It is described as education rather than therapy although it does combine many traditional features of both disciplines. The conductors are the people who carry out the mental-motor development work with the children, although there are other staff to support (technicians, domestic, administrative and medical staff) but no assistants in classes. Sutton (1986) quotes the words of Holt (1975) suggesting that conductors take on a mothering role with sole responsibility for their charges, although there are usually three working alongside each other. Sutton's observations in Hungary show that rarely do the conductors communicate with each other during work time, but what they do is highly planned and coordinated.

Sutton (1986) argues that conductors are not merely combinations of teacher and therapists, but something unique and exciting. He is particularly impressed by their drive, determination and optimism and the way in which they can work with groups of children, while attending to individual needs. His description of their training refers mainly to educational topics, though there are several medical aspects as well. Trainees are school leavers who work at the Institute of Conductive Education in Budapest as they study. Sutton was told that training young people rather than those already experienced in education or therapy, meant that they were not averse to carrying out even the most menial tasks with the children.

The example of conductive education in this country described by Cottam (1986) had experienced teachers, nursery nurses and therapists trained, minimally, as conductors. There is no discussion concerning whether this was as successful as the training of school leavers in Hungary, although Cottam does say that they combined their knowledge and experience to provide an educational approach to the whole child. She goes on to describe their daily meetings, considered essential to provide a consistent approach to the children, and the fact that their specialist knowledge was used to advantage (physiotherapist responsible for seating, teacher for education, speech therapist for communication system). Both Cottam (1986) and Titchener (1986) suggest that prior to using conductive education they had been working in a multidisciplinary environment, where children were treated separately by therapists who withdrew children from the classroom and that there was little carry-over to general classroom teaching. They both saw conductive education as the catalyst for working in a more integrated manner.

The main interest in this brief consideration of conductive education has been in the role of the conductor as, in its purest form, this contrasts with combining teachers and therapists in a multidisciplinary team. There has been little research into the efficacy of conductive education and thus little evidence concerning whether a team of conductors is more effective than a team of professionals from different disciplines. The Birmingham research project came to the conclusion that there was little difference between the progress made by project children in the conductive education group in comparison with a control group (Bairstow *et al.* 1993). This research has, though, been heavily criticised for its small size and for being carried out too early in the project to be fair to its success.

Comparing this brief literature review with that in previous sections, conclusions are that teams of professionals from different disciplines are likely to be more effective than those of conductors, but only if they work together in a collaborative manner. Coming from different disciplines, they have a wealth of expertise and experience on which to call and bringing them together can produce the synergy of 'the result being greater than the sum of the parts'. It also fits in with Thomas' (1992) conclusion that heterogeneous teams work better than homogeneous. This is by no means conclusive, but lends weight to supporting the continuation of separate professionals working collaboratively, rather than the creation of a new worker trained in more than one aspect.

## Summary and conclusions

The literature that has been reviewed so far in this book has been dominated by change and development. Recent legislation in the human services has had the effect of challenging the way in which agencies have worked over many years. Resources are being spread ever more thinly which makes traditional ways of working less viable. Changes in understanding concerning the rights and needs of children and adults with special needs are also challenging traditional practices and the results can be uncomfortable, particularly for some of the older members of staff.

There is much in the literature to guide new thinking, not the least that there are so many individuals from different disciplines and traditions who are agonising over the same issues. The concept of collaborative teamwork appears in many different guises offering researchers a variety of facets for study. From the growth of care in the community, much can be learned from the failure of joint planning and finance as well as from the successes in the All Wales Strategy. The concerns of those working in preschool provision have offered a growing experience in developing structures to support integrated services. The keyworker system of working in partnership with families is deemed by parents as an effective way forward, although many professionals find this a difficult model in the current climate.

Collaborative teamwork is a complex concept. It has several different elements, all of which need to be placed under the microscope if, firstly, understanding of present practice is to be reached and if, secondly, teams are to become more effective in the future.

# Chapter 4

# Working together in business

The content of this chapter is drawn from a different literature from the others. Chapters 1 to 3 are all firmly rooted in the human services and have been presented as perspectives on support partnerships from education, health and social care. Chapter 4, by contrast, has its foundations in the business world, in industry in particular. The questions that drove the literature review for this chapter appear below.

- *What are teams in industry?*
- *What can be learned from the way manufacturing teams are developed and run?*
- *What is known about leadership in teams?*
- *What contribution does teambuilding make to the effectiveness of teamwork?*

## Teams in industry

The research and scholarly writing concerning teams and teamwork in manufacturing brings together two different views of the ways in which individuals are organised in groups. Both psychology and the social sciences contain perspectives which are useful for the researcher anxious to understand how support partnerships and collaborative multidisciplinary teams work. The result has been a rich source of data from which there is remarkable agreement across countries and cultures on the importance of enabling teams of people to work together if manufacturing companies are to be successful in the future.

It would be helpful to begin by examining the notion of a team and teamwork in terms of business so that comparison with work in the human services can be based on a clear understanding. Babington Smith and Farrell (1979) provide a definition of a team which appears to contain most of the elements mentioned by other writers.

> A team is a group in which the individuals have a common aim and in which the jobs and skills of each member fit in with those of others, as ... in a jigsaw puzzle pieces fit together without distortion and together produce an overall pattern.
>
> Babington Smith and Farrell (1979)

The two strands to this definition seem to be important, that of a common aim and that of complementary contributions. It is the bringing together of these two things which writers suggest makes the team effective, but which are its greatest challenge.

Introducing teamwork into manufacturing industry has meant a complete change of the principles and values upon which business is built. Morgan and Murgatroyd (1994) describe it as a paradigm shift, especially if firms embrace the whole concept of Total Quality Management and the belief that quality is the responsibility of the whole workforce. Hierarchical autocracy is no longer seen as the most effective and efficient way to manage. Flatter management structures associated with teamwork, where small groups of workers are responsible for a whole product such as a car, have improved both production and working conditions (Drucker 1974). Results of Liswood's (1990) research suggest that there are also real gains in learning and development when workers are organised into teams because they provide an environment where learning can be articulated, tested, refined and examined against the needs of the organisation.

It is very easy to become carried away with enthusiasm and expect teams and teamwork to be the answer to every situation. Several writers warn against this (Klein 1956; Critchley and Casey 1986). There are many operations and decisions which are better dealt with by one person in their specialist capacity although it is suggested that the more uncertainty there is in a task, the more likelihood there is need for that task to be shared by a team. Even those who are fully committed to the power of teamwork, admit that creating effective teams is highly challenging. Hastings et al.'s (1986) book on 'superteams' begins by admitting that they have not, as yet, seen or worked with a superteam but they use it to present an ideal.

## Team development

Much research has been carried out on the way in which people form themselves into groups and teams and the stages through which they go as they struggle towards effective performance. One of the best known is that of Tuckman (1965) who suggests that groups proceed to harmonious working in four stages: forming, storming, norming and performing. At the forming stage, individuals exchange ideas and gather information about what they have to do and find out about each other's strengths and needs. At the storming stage, they jostle for position and struggle to work out rules and expectations. This can be a stage full of conflict. The third stage is characterised by the working out of ground rules by which the group is going to function so that it can pass into the final stage where attention can be given to the tasks in hand rather than to the group itself. Some evolving teams may reach performance level very quickly, but others may linger at different stages or even return to stages already left behind. Changes in team membership can necessitate beginning the whole process again (Guirdham 1990).

Group dynamics have been extensively researched and although Adair (1986) suggests that its results are culture-bound to the humanist psychologists of the 1950s, there is still much which offers useful explanations and illustrations when attempting to understand the way teams function currently. Studies of the conditions under which groups will tend to become more cohesive have shown that the more important factors are physical proximity, similar work, homogeneity of characteristics, personality tolerance, flow of communication and relatively small size (Adair 1986). Over-cohesiveness can result in 'group-think' (Janis 1972) where members of the group become complacent and oblivious to outside influences or criticisms.

Work on the roles people play in groups and teams has also revealed interesting results. The work of Belbin (1981) is well-known in this area. He found that there are basically eight 'useful people to have in teams'. These he defined in terms of typical features, positive qualities and allowable weaknesses. For example, the *shaper* is highly strung, outgoing and dynamic. She or he has drive and a readiness to challenge inertia, ineffectiveness, complacency or self-deception. However, she or he is prone to provocation, irritation and impatience. The *team worker* is socially orientated, rather mild and sensitive with an ability to respond to people and to situations and to promote team spirit. However, his or her weakness is indecisiveness in moments of crisis.

Although Belbin found eight roles, he suggested that there is no need for every effective team to contain eight people. Individuals can take on more than one role or the characteristics of more than one can be amalgamated. Even if one is a little sceptical of the need for all the characteristics listed, there is certainly recognition that complementary roles are important. Common sense suggests that if every member of a team is an ideas person and no one has the capacity to make these ideas come to fruition, little would be achieved.

## Communication

Communication has been identified as a vital ingredient of effective teamwork and this has attracted considerable interest from researchers and writers. The work of Berne (1964) and Harris (1973) on Transactional Analysis can assist in understanding some of the interactions between people in groups. The theory contains concepts which can be directly useful for improving communication. For example understanding the part played by *games* increases awareness of the power of communication and provides a set of tools for working more effectively with other people. Realising that a power game is about to begin can warn an individual to make use of a 'stroke' or verbal reward to avert unnecessary conflict.

Consensus and conflict have also been much studied with the effect that their places within teamwork are both more fully understood. No longer is it believed that conflict is necessarily a destructive force. It can be a healthy element within teamwork (Dyer 1977; Payne 1982; Adair 1986; Guirdham 1990). Personal conflict is often cited as an excuse for poor communication within teams, but research suggests that the personal element is not as important in reality as is generally thought. Application to the task is considered to be of much greater significance than the personal chemistry of team members (Katzenbach and Smith 1993). Clear performance demands appear to be essential, as is discipline in that performance.

Educational sociologists such as Ball (1987) or Glatter (1982) have a great interest in the struggles for power which are endemic in organisations. These struggles can be manifested in visible conflict or more usually in invisible machinations. Writers in this tradition have a phenomenological or political view of organisations. They are interested in the micro-politics of what happens when people work closely together. A central issue is identified as power and control and there is an exploration of the ways in which individuals exert these over each other. Legitimisation is another issue and much consideration is given to the idea of actions being proper or improper within the terms of the organisation. Any innovations are seen to be mediated through the existing patterns of social interaction within the particular institution (Ball 1987).

Micro-politics usually focuses on group activity rather than on the organisation as a whole, which can be helpful in attempting to understand the way in which small teams of people work together. Writers in this tradition have much to say concerning the way in which people bargain and negotiate with each other and arrive at decisions based on the relative power of the participating groups and individuals (Bush 1986). There is also interest in the significance of external influences on internal decision-making (Sergiovanni 1984), something which is of great importance to multidisciplinary teams of people who originate from different departments or agencies. Sergiovanni (1984) suggests that schools are open systems which are integral parts of a larger environment, receiving, often conflicting, inputs from outside itself.

Within an organisation such as a school, different forms of power can be discerned. A major source is that accruing to the individuals who hold official positions, but there are also those who have a particular expertise which renders them powerful. Individuals can also exert personal power through their charisma or verbal skills. There may be others who have control of rewards or who have the power of coercion (Bush 1986). Exchange theory (Blau 1964; Homans 1974) explores the extent to which dependence and/or interdependence are central to social relationships and the reliance on giving and taking in work situations. Negotiation and bargaining are central to a micro-political view, suggesting that organisational structure is formed as groups jockey for position rather than from a rational picture of what is needed. This implies that the relationships between organisations and their environments are basically unstable and subject to constant change.

As with all theoretical standpoints, although there is much of interest to aid analysis, there are also limitations to the model. The central interest in power and control seems to prevent discussion of the various processes of management nor recognise that most organisations operate according to routine bureaucracy most of the time. Organisations as a whole are largely ignored and conflict dominates at the expense of collaboration. It is, however, a point of view with which many staff in schools and other learning centres can identify.

## Effective teams

To add to the phenomenological models, there are other aspects of organisational theory which enable exploration of collaboration and teamwork. Rational-structural-functional views explored in the majority of the literature on business organisations appeared to offer some interesting insights which can be used to examine what might be found in schools, colleges and centres.

Katzenbach and Smith (1993) suggest that 'potential teams' abound in organisations. They see these developing into 'real teams' when individuals in them take risks involving conflict, trust, interdependence and mutual accountability. This can be achieved through establishing urgency and direction, selecting members based on skills and skill potential rather than on personalities, paying meticulous attention to initial meetings and actions, setting clear rules of behaviour, setting and seizing on a few immediate performance-oriented tasks, challenging the group regularly with fresh information, spending lots of time together (not in formal meetings) and exploiting the power of feedback, recognition and reward.

There are similar suggestions from researchers and writers such as Adair (1986), Hastings *et al.* (1986), Larson and LaFasto (1989), Tjosvold (1991) and Shonk (1992). They are all convinced of the worth of teams and teamwork. Tvjosvold cites the research of Johnson *et al.* (1981) which was a meta-analysis on the results of many research projects on teamwork. Their findings suggest that cooperative groups are significantly more productive than individuals working competitively or independently (three fifths of a standard deviation above). According to Tjosvold (1991, p. 4–5) 'Teams get extraordinary things done ... synergy, synchrony and integration are their (managers) guides to innovate ... groups are becoming the basic building blocks of organisations and are vital to rejuvenating them.' However, even the most ardent supporter realises that teams are only part of the answer to effective performance. Teams and hierarchies are not necessarily mutually exclusive (Katzenbach and Smith 1993) and some tasks are best kept departmental (Morgan and Murgatroyd 1994). What appears to be of great importance is the self-managing capacity for teamwork. The flatter structure which usually accompanies teams means that some form of responsibility for management is given to each individual in the organisation. Everyone is engaged in ensuring the quality of performance. This has implications for leadership and team coordination.

## Leadership

Leadership must be one of the most researched and written about aspects of management in organisations and only a tiny proportion of this literature can be reviewed here. Early theory expounded the importance of born leaders, but much has also been made of leadership style and the importance of developing this when in a leadership role. Trethowan (1985) suggests a continuum of: authoritarian (tell them), persuasive (sell it to them), participative (share it with them) and delegating (trust them to get on with it) with most leaders fitting into one or other of these categories. Other research suggests that there is no one style suitable for all occasions and that the most effective leaders use all of them for different situations (Hersey and Blanchard 1982).

Virtually all writers concerned with teamwork stress the importance of leaders to the success of teams. Shonk (1992) sees team leaders in terms of *coaching* members by helping them to define, analyse and solve problems as opposed to managing them. Katzenbach and Smith's (1993) concern is that managers should concentrate on facilitating team leader performance. Tjosvold (1991) advises that cooperative leaders are more effective than those who are competitive and that when a new team forms, the leader must work closely with members, but can withdraw and enable it to be more self managing as it develops and begins to perform. Hastings *et al.* (1986) single out inspiring team members as important, helping them to respond to the team vision by keeping their performance on track and celebrating success.

From Adair's work (1983, 1984, 1986) it can be suggested that effective team leaders are not dominant but directive in a democratic way. They enthuse about their work, lead by example, are aware of the needs of the team and exhibit trust in team members. They also feel personally responsible for resources (human, financial and material) and are active in setting direction and accepting the risks of leadership. They can articulate direction and objectives clearly, use the most appropriate style of leadership for the situation and maintain high standards of personal performance and demand that of others (Adair 1986). Adair is so committed to the importance of a good leader that he says: 'Team work is no accident, it is the by-product of good leadership' (1986, p. 125). This is particularly pertinent when attempting to understand multidisciplinary teams in the human services. In most cases, multidisciplinary teams consisting of teachers and therapists in classrooms do not have appointed leaders and leaders do not always naturally emerge, although it is often teachers who take on some of the coordinating duties of a leader. If Adair is right, then leaderless teams are ever likely to run into difficulties.

## Teambuilding

One other aspect of leadership which will be helpful to consider at this time, is that of being a teambuilder, as this clearly relates to encouraging teams to form and perform effectively. According to Tjosvold (1991), much teambuilding has been based on the work of McGregor, Lickert, Lewin and Blake and Mouton and emanates from sensitivity training designed to simulate individual awareness and interpersonal skills. Other training has shifted the emphasis to examining and improving processes within ongoing organisational groups (Tjosvold 1991). Shonk (1992) supports this latter approach to team development. He sees the importance of teams exploring together and determining what is most appropriate for them in terms of how they should meet, communicate and make decisions. This fits his view of leaders as coaches. Robinson (1988) also points to the importance of teams training together if there is to be lasting change, but he warns that not all team problems can be solved by team training. Sometimes a change of personnel or training an individual in specific skills can be successful. It is interesting to note that Tjosvold (1991) cites the research of Woodman and Sherwood (1980) which concluded that 19 out of 30 studies of teambuilding showed a positive impact. This is sufficient to feel that teambuilding is generally worthwhile, but there is plenty of scope for improving the quality of the training to be sure of an impact on the remaining 11.

The call for teamwork training appears to transcend areas of human endeavour and can be found in relation to: business (Robinson 1988; Shonk 1992); social work (Poulin *et al.* 1994; Iles and Auluck 1990); nursing (Williams 1992); education (Evans *et al.* 1989; Balshaw 1991) and globally across many work situations (Nash 1994). However, several writers warn that teambuilding is not the answer to all organisational ills (Critchley and Casey 1986; Iles and Auluck 1990; Penson 1996; Robinson 1988).

Adair (1986) suggests that most teambuilding takes one of two forms. Either it is based on substitute team tasks such as outdoor activities and case studies, or on real tasks as when teams have a weekend away together to work on the real problems that they experience at work. Several writers support the use of substitute activities which enable members to isolate their team performance for examination (Lowe 1991; Lawn and Woods 1988; Teire 1986) but Adair (1986) points to possible difficulties with participants failing to see the links between these activities and the reality of the workplace. Bennett (1984) suggests deliberate teaching for transfer is important.

## Effect of teambuilding courses

Several teambuilding courses have been evaluated, and the effects reported demonstrate a general success for training which focuses on ways of working together. First, these can be summarised as:

- more positive attitudes and job satisfaction (Barker 1980; Kersell 1990; David and Smith 1991; Lowe 1991);
- greater understanding of and communication with team members (Barker 1980; David and Smith 1991; Rainbird 1994; Whalley 1992);
- development of new skills (Barker 1980; Adair 1973; Kersell 1990; Lowe 1991);
- higher productivity or new designs (Adair 1973; Crom and France 1996; Lowe 1991).

Some of the studies were studied in detail to try to ascertain the factors which might affect subsequent practice. For example, Lowe (1991) conducted a small-scale study of the teambuilding training of two interdependent automotive departments whose relations were poor. The teambuilding included outdoor training, which Lowe indicated had increased enormously in the manufacturing industry over the recent years. His results fell into three broad categories: individual reactions, changes in job behaviour and changes in the organisation. He claims that the most striking effect of the training back in the workplace was the way in which attitudes had improved on the shopfloor. This was mainly attributed to getting to know each other better and consequently being able to communicate more effectively. Ninety five per cent of participants reacted favourably to the training and 65 per cent reported changes in job behaviour. Despite this, only 10 per cent of participants felt that the training had led to changes in the organisation which enabled improved organisational performance. Lowe suggests that factors explaining this lack of organisational change could be that top management were not involved in the course, that not everyone in individual teams attended and that bonds were forged between individuals who did not normally work together, so there was little scope for improving performance in their day-to-day operations. There was also no follow-up to the training. Thus a general importance can be given to:

(a) management involvement in the training
(b) follow-up to the training
(c) training together, those who work together
(d) everyone being present.

## Methods and techniques

Other writers concern themselves with methods and techniques for improving teamwork on teambuilding courses. Again, the common factors will be enumerated before exploring two studies in more detail.

Several suggest brainstorming, discussion, case studies, problem solving, role play and action learning are all appropriate techniques (Anderson *et al.* 1993; Bennett 1984; Iles and Auluck 1990; Merry and Allerhand 1977; Robinson 1988).

Robinson (1988) provides a list of approaches which he has used over many years of running teambuilding courses. These include simulation, 'action maze' case studies (gradual increasing of information as decisions are made), 'fishbowl' problem solving (one team solves a problem while another observes and evaluates), 'true and false' questionnaires and sensitivity training (to increase awareness of behaviour).

Barker (1980) provides an in-depth example of a five-day teambuilding programme which includes a combination of formal input, exercises and teambuilding activities which have a high emphasis on feedback and goal clarification. His aims within this course are to develop openness, increase awareness of others, examine relationships, resolve interpersonal and authority conflicts, increase personal control and transfer learning to an organisational situation. He makes use of simple questions to bring out important information about the way in which the team is working now and how it might be more effective in the future. For example, 'What can the group do more of or start doing?' and 'What can the group do less of or stop doing?' followed by 'What can the group continue to do the same of in order to maintain and increase its effectiveness?' (Barker 1980, p. 176). Results of the evaluation of this course show that participants reported improved feelings of commitment to the group and its goals, a greater understanding of themselves and others and an increase in choices and skills in interpersonal and group behaviour. Barker does not report on impact on work performance.

Iles and Auluck (1990) have a greater interest in the impact of teambuilding on practice, criticising many techniques as shallow or as encouraging personal development but not organisational. In their study, the East Dorset Community Drug Team (consisting of members from five different professions) were given 'task oriented team development' (p. 160) devised initially by Rubin *et al.* from the United States. This is in contrast with many teambuilding courses which concentrate on relationships and procedures rather than specific tasks, priorities and goals. The course enabled participants to spend time talking with each other to resolve issues of conflict as well as to attend drug training together so that they had a shared knowledge base. Iles and Auluck (1990) conclude that teambuilding is not a one-off event, but something which involves periodic review, re-evaluation and maintenance.

## Summary and conclusions

Generally, there has been much of interest in the literature from the business world to guide the understanding of the workings of multidisciplinary teams in the human services, particularly that pertaining to teamwork and leadership. It is always wise to be cautious when making direct comparisons between manufacturing and the human services as there are fundamental differences between the two. For example, Bush (1986) suggests that there are six major areas in which the management of *educational* institutions differs from the management of other organisations.

1. The objectives of educational institutions are much more difficult to define than those of commercial organisations.
2. It is more difficult to measure whether objectives have been achieved in education than in commerce.
3. It is also difficult to be sure who are the clients of an educational institution. Are they the pupils or the parents, or both?
4. Schools are staffed predominantly with professionals who expect to have autonomy over their own work rather than be closely supervised, as would happen in manufacturing.
5. There is a fragmented organisational and management structure in and around schools, thus making it more difficult to locate responsibility for decision-making than in commercial organisations.
6. Many senior and middle managers in schools have little time for the managerial aspects of their jobs and the majority of time is spent in teaching.

Schools, colleges and centres in the new millennium are being encouraged to consider themselves more in business terms so that the differences pointed out by Bush (1986) appear to be becoming less important. Teamwork, especially in the field of disabilities and difficulties, is expected more and more and the greatest experience can be gleaned from the commercial world.

One of the more important lessons to be learned from business relates to leadership. Team leadership is deemed to be of vital importance, especially in project management. Success, or lack of it, can be decided on the expertise of the leader of a project. The importance of leadership is increasingly being recognised in the human services in the twenty-first century, although the failure of some of the 'superheads' of 'fresh start' schools has dented the belief that effective head teachers alone can turn round failing schools. Generally, though, leadership is seen as important and expected to be evident in most situations. Where this expectation seems to be missing is in the leadership of multidisciplinary teams. It is rare for one member to be appointed as leader and usual for no one to be responsible. It is not surprising in the circumstances that multidisciplinary teams find it hard to flourish.

The chapter concluded with an exploration of teambuilding as, although it can be found in many different workplace settings, it originated from the business world. The need for training for working together is beginning to be recognised by different groups in the human services and although full-scale emulation of commando-type training is not often transferred, the concept of examining roles in teams and ways of working together have been.

# Chapter 5

# Learning together to work together

The last part of the previous chapter provides a good introduction to the topic of this final literature chapter, 'Learning together to work together'. Teambuilding is an important aspect of people learning how to work together, but the whole phenomenon of shared learning across disciplines is explored in detail below.

This chapter is driven by three main questions that relate to the human services and the training of support partners working together with and for people with disabilities and difficulties.

- *What is shared learning and how can it help partners to work together?*
- *What are good professional development courses?*
- *What is the most effective way of teaching professionals?*

## Shared learning

There are several aspects to investigate regarding training people to work together in teams and there are many examples in the literature of both initial and post-experience courses which cross a variety of different boundaries, most of which are expressly designed to promote teamwork. Several have been evaluated but as the majority are relatively new, very few have evidence concerning the long-term effects of training staff together.

Shared learning has provoked much interest over the last 30 years, especially in health and care related contexts (Horder 1995). It is significant, perhaps, that education has had very little involvement in shared learning, with the exception of child protection work following the 1989 Children Act (Department of Health 1989a). Other recent legislation has acted as a spur to those interested in shared learning, particularly the NHS and Community Care Act 1990 (DoH 1990) which gives prominence to health and social welfare professionals working together. The 1989 White Paper *Caring for People: Community care in the next decade and beyond* (DoH 1989b) contained a firm commitment by the government to multidisciplinary training both at pre-qualifying and post-qualifying levels (Brown, J. 1994).

Alongside this government interest, a series of conferences, surveys and reports in the 1980s led to the formation of the Centre for the Advancement of Interprofessional Education in Primary Health and Community Care (CAIPE) in 1987 during which a national survey of interprofessional educational activity was conducted. The main findings revealed that there were many courses in the UK (695 examples) but that the majority (53%) lasted one day or less, with a further 28% lasting between two and four days. Fewer than 1% of the courses led to a degree or diploma. The participants involved included district nurses and/or health visitors (96%), social workers (50%) and GPs (33%) (Pietroni 1994).

More than 80% of the courses reported in the CAIPE study were at post-qualifying level; Barr's (1994) study of 50 professionals, with experience of shared learning, confirms this. His interviewees spoke of a variety of activities, ranging from clinical audits to open learning programmes, in-house programmes and university-based courses. Storrie (1992) suggests that the Master's level courses provide ideal opportunities to consider interprofessional issues because participants have experience to call upon and have an understanding of the problems and possibilities of working together. His study of 12 higher education courses in England and Scotland revealed flexible, modular designs where the development of knowledge and understanding of a particular client group or a system of care was the focus, rather than collaboration. However, most were multidisciplinary in approach, recruited from a range of professionals and were concerned with increasing mutual understanding and interprofessionalism. None claimed to have a balanced intake of health and welfare workers and all but two emanated from single discipline departments. The two exceptions were Southampton (medical and social work) and Hull (nursing and social work). Storrie (1992) found it difficult to tell the extent of the exploration of the dynamics of teamwork and collaboration in the courses he surveyed and as all began in 1990, his report could contain no evidence of the production of inter-professional practitioners through training. In contrast to Storrie, Pietroni (1994) suggests that waiting until Master's level to explore interprofessional issues in shared learning is too late. His study revealed very clear and distinct occupational identities at a relatively early stage of professional development and, more seriously, negative stereotyped perceptions of other professionals.

One response to this problem has been to institute dual qualifications (health and social work) for staff intending to work in community care settings. This practice appears to be most advanced and innovative in the area of learning disabilities (Brown 1995; Robson and Sebba 1991). Brown, J. (1994) argues that a fringe area such as learning disabilities can adapt more quickly to changes in policy directives than the mainstream of a profession. He does point out, though, that early attempts at joint training were not well received by everyone. There is a particular challenge for learning disability nurses to find a place in the new regime of social care for people with learning disabilities and although they are a highly skilled workforce, in a world where learning disabilities is recognised as a social rather than medical condition, they are too closely connected with medicine. There was also a resistance from the nursing profession to the suggestion that the Certificate in Social Work (CSS) should be the replacement qualification for Registered Nurses of the Mentally Handicapped (RNMH) as this was considered a downgrading (Mathias and Thompson 1992; Shaw 1993).

Wood (1994) presents a study of one of, what he cites as, the only two joint schemes of training between nursing and social workers in the UK which provide qualifications in both professions (Hovering College and Bromley College). (There are at least five courses, as of July 1997.) Both schemes are jointly validated by The Central Council for the Education and Training in Social Work

(CCETSW) and The English National Board of Nursing (ENB), and students obtain the CSS and the certificate for RNMH. Wood suggests that getting these two bodies to collaborate was an achievement in itself, as a sense of 'professional preciousness' pervaded them throughout the discussions. Goble (1994), writing of his experience of a European network for the development of multiprofessional education in health sciences, would support this, suggesting that difficulties arise from perceived attacks on the different professions and a fear of the dilution of skills.

Wood (1994) describes many difficulties in designing a joint course, not the least the fact that social workers and nurses feel unable to trust each other with 'sacrosanct elements of their own courses' (p. 76), neither were they prepared to 'promote a separate professional identity' (p. 77) to create a new brand of careworker for the successful candidates. They were simply trained both as social workers and nurses. Workers with young children in education and social welfare have attempted to create a new professional with the title 'educarer' but this is, as yet, undeveloped (Hevey 1992). Objectors feel that, as their training would contain elements from both professions, there would be a dilution of skills and the result would be second-class workers (Sharp 1994).

Long-term effects of joint training cannot yet be seen, but Wood (1994) highlights some aspects of implementing the course in which he was involved. He suggests that students found the absence of a unified approach a difficulty. He attributes the difficulty to tutors being ignorant of each other's training and having entrenched attitudes, a split site arrangement, mixed and confusing messages from both professional groups and a lack of integration in the teaching. Differences in supervision practice were a source of disagreement, as was the perceived inflexibility of the structure of the social work course. However, students from the first intake commented, on completion, that the course had 'come together' by its conclusion and that they could see how the different parts were complementary. Some felt that they had two models of practice which could be used in different settings.

After exploring the current forms of shared learning, the variables attributable to its success will be explored next. This will involve inquiring across pre- and post-qualifying levels, short and long courses and across health, social work and education.

## Variables for success in shared learning

From the previous section, it can be conjectured that shared learning is difficult to achieve and this appears to be attributable to a variety of reasons. Brown, M. (1994) suggests that funding differences in a competitive world force different agencies to remain separate and to charge each other for training across boundaries. Thus, it could be argued that those individuals who are able, and willing, to ignore these difficulties are likely to be more successful in sharing learning than those who cannot. Carpenter and Hewstone (1996) are convinced of the worth of overcoming problems to increase the effectiveness of working together. They cite a study by McMichael and Gilloran (1984, in Carpenter and Hewstone 1996) which concluded that merely placing students in the same classroom is not sufficient to encourage them to improve their teamwork. It can, in fact, actually make matters worse. Carpenter and Hewstone (1996) suggest that direct approaches focusing on acquisition of knowledge about the other profession and exploration of attitudes are more profitable. Barr (1994) echoes this view, citing:

- learning from each other's experiences and perspectives;
- exploring the distinctive part each profession plays;
- appreciating the need for a rounded view of the client;
- actually experiencing working together;

as important ingredients for a successful course.

Based on his experience as a trainer, Casto (1994) argues for six assumptions and nine conditions for education for interprofessional practice. His assumptions are:

- programmes should naturally overlap;
- collaboration will be in the best interest of the client;
- skills and knowledge in interprofessional practice will be enhanced;
- it is an essential lifelong element;
- learning in the course moves from sensitivity to others towards cooperation between them;
- such a course requires a commitment from the institutions involved.

His conditions are:

- a neutral base;
- administrative support;
- a shared interest and commitment;
- shared credit;
- shared resources;
- partnership between the professions in the community;
- an inclusion of training in collaborative skills;
- building horizontal bridges between professions;
- rewards for those who undertake the shared learning.

These assumptions and conditions appear to relate well to the results of the studies of courses included in this section, although Casto (1994) offers no research of his own to support his ideas. One could also argue that even ensuring that all these are present does not guarantee the success of the programme.

Funnell (1995), while discussing his opinions of the value of interprofessional shared learning, urges caution and questions its value, suggesting that for it to succeed, curriculum planners must structure interactions and content in such a way that they offer relevant and stimulating learning opportunities. He also warns that:

- sharing a role can only be undertaken by those who feel secure in that role;
- we should not assume that learning about each other requires shared learning;

- teaching methods are an essential ingredient;
- there is evidence to suggest that enthusiasm for teamwork fades following training.

These are interesting thoughts which alert readers to caution when planning shared learning. Certainly there is a need to consider carefully the teaching methods employed and how to reduce the likelihood of enthusiasm fading.

From their experience of shared management learning at the University of Derby, Forman *et al.* (1994) have a slightly different list of key factors for ensuring success. They include:

- the need to consider logistics carefully;
- team building needs to begin with tutoring staff;
- there have to be positive expectations and a cooperative atmosphere;
- students must have equal status;
- emphasis in tuition must focus neither on differences nor similarities between professions.

The last two points are particularly interesting. Ensuring 'equal status' for participants seems to be a strong contender for inclusion, but *not* focusing on 'differences' or 'similarities' is an unusual suggestion. It could be argued that exploring these differences and similarities would actually increase understanding of each other. Other writers appear to support this view.

Gill and Ling's (1995) study aimed at investigating shared learning as applied to students on the DipHE Professional Studies course (Health Visiting, District Nursing, Occupational Health Nursing) at Suffolk College showed that personal contact is very important for shared learning to be successful in understanding each other's roles. They also demonstrated the importance of having small numbers on courses so that maximum interactions between participants are possible. Leathard (1992), writing about an interprofessional course she set up at South Bank Polytechnic, extols the virtue of basing learning on developing reflective practitioners. The journal in which this paper appears, *The Journal of Interprofessional Care*, contains several articles on the appropriateness of this approach to learning for encouraging interprofessional work (for example: Ash 1992; Goble 1994; Gilbert *et al.* 2000). Ash (1992) for instance, suggests that reflection on practice is particularly useful as it enables the exploration of the different viewpoints present when professionals work together. Reflective practice will be explored in greater detail in a later section in this chapter.

Apart from endorsing the use of reflection, only a few writers have anything to say on the subject of teaching approaches in the area of shared learning. Fox (1994) lists some of the small group work used on the Sheffield Multidisciplinary Health Studies' Master's course:

- writing short papers;
- role play;
- seminar presentation;
- responses to published papers.

Funnell (1995) suggests that there are more likely to be positive effects from shared learning if experiential methods are used. There are other sources for discussion of teaching methods, but these can be found in the education literature and will be explored later in this chapter.

Some writers about shared learning do, however, express opinions on content. Horst *et al.* (1995) for instance, writing of the St Joseph's Community Health Centre model of community-based interdisciplinary health care team education, cite themes from the literature as suitable to be included:

- role issues;
- teambuilding;
- the value of teamwork;
- including the consumer as a team member;
- a team approach to meeting complex needs;
- collaborative learning and sharing.

Macleod and Nash's (1994) list of themes for multidisciplinary education in palliative care include:

- the exploration of similarities and differences in roles;
- skills, knowledge and ideology;
- the recognition of complementary skills and resources.

They also extol the virtue of small numbers to ensure the full involvement of participants. Their list, taken with that of Horst *et al.* (1995) above indicates the importance of recognising that team members have different roles to play and that exploring these in the context of teamwork will be profitable.

At this point, it will be helpful to summarise the main thrust of the literature concerning shared learning before turning to the body of evidence relating to outcomes of professionals from different disciplines studying together.

1. Shared learning is increasing, particularly in the area of health and social care.
2. Proponents appear to be convinced of its worth in terms of encouraging understanding between members of different disciplines.
3. It is difficult to achieve in practice, as can be understood from the few studies which have charted the setting up and implementing of shared courses.
4. From the few studies which exist, it can be suggested that:
   - shared learning should begin early in professionals' careers;
   - course tutors from different disciplines should work together collaboratively;
   - courses should offer opportunities for participants to get know each other's roles;
   - participants should discuss their attitudes to each other;
   - participants should learn to work together in practice;
   - teaching approaches should include an element of reflection.

## Outcomes of shared learning

Several studies contain self-reported effects on participants of learning together. For instance Carpenter and Hewstone (1996) interviewed 85 final year social work and medical students who had participated in shared learning programmes in equal pairs and small groups on shared tasks in a cooperative atmosphere. They particularly reported on increased knowledge of the attitudes, skills, roles and duties of the other profession and how to work together more effectively. However, they found that male medical students were less favourably inclined towards interprofessional learning than female medical students or social work students and that 19 per cent of the cohort (all students) actually appeared to become more negative towards the other profession.

Horst et al.'s (1995) small-scale study of a community-based interdisciplinary health care team's education provides evidence that participants felt it promoted new learning and that it was exciting to share and problem solve together. They felt they had learned about each other and had begun to develop as team members. They enjoyed the variety of opinions, the small group discussions and felt the experience should be available for all. Although there has been no long-term follow up, participants said that they would use what they had learned, especially that pertaining to team conflict styles, management and resolution of conflict, team development and dynamics.

Macleod and Nash (1994) report on their small-scale study of workshops for team training for general practice, including doctors, nurses, health visitors, receptionists and secretaries. Their findings suggest that outcomes included greater understanding of roles and practical skills in listening and communication and they anticipated improved communication as a result. Two difficulties were evident: that doctors tended to dominate discussions and team members without direct care roles (receptionists and secretaries) found it difficult to contribute.

An evaluation of three days of joint training on the abuse of adults with learning disabilities (Stein and Brown 1995), run for social workers and police, revealed particular problems concerning gender and male dominance as the majority of social workers are female and the majority of police male. However, results showed that participants learned much and particularly valued the interchange of information. Other somewhat vague reports of usefulness and enjoyment resulted from studies by Cooley (1994), Forman et al. (1994) and Freeling (1993). Shaw (1994) also reported positive and significant changes in understanding between groups of health and social care staff following shared learning, but he also found regression five months later. He attributed this regression to a lack of support for interprofessional activity in the organisations of the participants. Funnell (1995) agrees with this as an important element of ensuring positive effects from shared learning. Ling et al. (1990) are cautious concerning some of the assumptions made about the advantages of interdisciplinary learning.

In little of the research in the literature studied was there an attempt to demonstrate any long-term effects of shared learning. Renshaw et al. (1990) did look for effects three months after three one-day workshops for staff working in the mental health field and found that:

- issues of communication had been aired;
- a new model of care had been considered;

- trust between agencies had improved;
- the sector teams were stronger and did not always look to the consultant for leadership;
- links between professionals had been formed;
- there was a joint policy of care.

In summary, although there is firm evidence to suggest that participants perceive shared learning to be helpful in improving their understanding of other professionals, there is almost no evidence from which to judge the long-term effects of this. This lack of evidence is partly due to the comparitive newness of such courses, but it does appear to be a missing layer in the research. Like the general call for collaboration in the workplace, there is a common-sense argument for providing opportunities to train together. Whittier and Hewitt (1993) provide an analogy with football training, suggesting that it is necessary to train the team together for it to perform effectively. Exhortations such as that, are no substitute for research data.

# Professional development courses

In order to understand how to develop courses to help support partnerships to flourish and be effective, it will be helpful to examine the literature concerning the training and education of professionals. It is necessary to turn to the education field to examine in-service education and training for experienced teachers mainly because educationalists have written a significant amount concerning professional development and in-service training (INSET). The few studies carried out by health and social work educators appear to contain very similar concerns to those expressed by teacher educators and they will be included, where appropriate, in the discussions which follow.

## Professional development and INSET

The professional development of teachers and other professionals contains a great variety of activities of which training and education is only one aspect. Writers cite mentor schemes, working parties, committees, job rotation and curriculum review groups among other examples (Lyons and Stenning 1986; Jones *et al.* 1989), but the aspect which is the concern of this chapter relates specifically to INSET. Particular interest lies in the impact of courses on subsequent practice in schools, colleges and other learning centres.

INSET has been of great concern over the past 20 years, partly because it has changed enormously in that time and partly because, in general, it has been very disappointing in its ability to bring about improvements in schools (Bradley *et al.* 1994). Fullan (1991) describes it as 'frustratingly wasteful' (p. 315). He is particularly critical of college courses, which tend to produce 'hero innovators' who 'are eaten up for breakfast by organisations such as schools and hospitals' (Georgiades and Phillimore 1975). Conner (1994), while attempting to demonstrate a justifiable place for teachers studying at Master's degree level, agrees with

Fullan's view, pointing out that prior to the 1980s, most professional development consisted of long courses at universities which were individualistic experiences which rarely gave benefit to the school or college.

Many changes have been made since this time, yet there remains considerable criticism of the lack of impact on practice of INSET courses whether they are run in universities, LEAs or in schools themselves. Halpin *et al.* (1990) cite Henderson's 1976 study from which he found little research into, although much interest in, the effectiveness of INSET. They go on to point out that most of these are case studies of particular forms of INSET carried out by course leaders. They also criticise the research community for failing to build on previous studies and thus provide an accumulative dimension to the research.

In recent years, INSET has become far more school-based in response to the criticism that long courses in colleges do little to improve practice. Day (1989) points out that although there are benefits from the move towards school-based INSET, variety and quality are difficult to maintain and Conner (1994) suggests that there is a danger of becoming parochial and failing to debate and assimilate new ideas. Day (1989) also argues that government initiatives and 'categorically funded' topics have prevented in-school INSET from fulfilling the needs of individual teachers. Lally *et al.* (1992) add that school managers may lack appropriate training either to develop or lead training in their schools. They also point out that Teacher Education Days or 'Baker Days' have been imposed and that sometimes teachers can have negative attitudes to the sessions arranged for them. They accuse Teacher Education Days of being a 'quick-fit' solution to training and education needs.

According to Newton and Newton (1994), there can be problems with an arbitrary use of Teacher Education Days. Schools have been allocated five days per year for INSET purposes which can be used in whatever way they think fit. Newton and Newton's (1994) study of approximately 100 primary and secondary schools, revealed that the majority of time was spent on planning and preparation and not specifically on professional development. More time was given to professional development in secondary schools, but that was mostly aimed at National Curriculum subjects. From these results, Newton and Newton (1994) recommend that schools could benefit from guidance on how to use their training days to greatest effect.

Fullan (1991) calls for more evaluations of the effects of INSET on teaching and learning in the classroom. As was pointed out earlier, such studies are still not many in number. One useful study was carried out by English (1995) who wanted to find out the role of INSET in bringing about change in classrooms, with reference to mathematics. He located examples of change and then asked teachers to trace back and see what influenced it. He did not mention INSET as a possibility, wanting teachers to keep an open mind. He had 369 responses to his questionnaire, through which he identified 73 changes. The most important factor in these changes, attributed by teachers, related to the National Curriculum (47%). In only 15% of cases was INSET mentioned. English (1995) concludes that if such a small percentage of change is attributable to INSET then it could represent an enormous waste of money. He does, however, continue by suggesting that INSET is about creating individual and organisational habits rather than implementing specific innovations. He cites Henderson's (1976) argument that INSET is not useful for initiating change, but is essential for supporting a predilection for it.

## Impact of INSET

The impact of INSET on school and classroom practice, such as that by English (1995), has been studied by several researchers. Kinder *et al.* (1991) provide examples of the impact on specific teachers from their in-depth study of six primary and six secondary teachers. Most of them were able to identify aspects of their practice which had been affected by certain INSET experiences during the year. They suggest that the degree of impact seems to relate to a combination of the length of the courses and the participants' commitments to the messages conveyed. Halpin *et al.*'s (1990) study of almost 200 primary and secondary teachers attending courses provided by four LEAs in Avon during 1987–8, also set out to assess impact. Teachers identified the highest impact on knowledge (84%) and attitudes (87%). Least affected were school organisation (38%) and classroom organisation (39%). There were several mentions of an increase in self-confidence, a rise in status and opportunities to meet others. Halpin *et al.* (1990) conclude that individual professional development is a weak way of changing institutions, but there are valuable gains in teachers' knowledge, teaching approaches and pupil attainment.

Conner (1994) and Rouse (1994) both conducted studies to gauge the effect of university-based courses, leading to advanced level work. Rouse (1994) quotes Balshaw's M.Ed. dissertation to suggest that, following the course, there had been changes for individual teachers in areas such as:

- confidence
- classroom skills
- collaborative skills
- understanding.

There were also changes for schools in terms of:

- classroom practice
- new policies
- ethos
- better use of staff

and for pupils in terms of:

- classroom groupings
- curriculum provision
- support for SEN (the focus of the course).

Conner (1994) writes of the York Outstation MA, as an example of linking higher education and schools. He conducted a small-scale study of 24 students most of whom were teachers in schools, but a few of whom were teachers of health professionals. There were many reports of the effects of the course on practice and, in contrast with Halpin *et al.*'s (1990) study, most of these were in the organisation. Other outcomes reported were that participants felt their practice was now based on evidence rather than on gut-feelings and that both knowledge and confidence had improved. Conner (1994) attributes much of the success at organisational level to the fact that participants were able to base their assignments on school needs.

## Conditions for successful INSET

Following the somewhat meagre and rather mixed evidence regarding the impact of INSET, it will be useful now to consider what writers have to say concerning the conditions necessary for the success of INSET which has an impact on practice. Dempster (1991) suggests certain conditions for success:

- any agency concerned with INSET must hold the belief that it provides long-term learning for teachers;
- any programme should be negotiated between providers and receivers;
- it should have high task specificity;
- it should be co-managed with teachers.

Several writers discuss the role of INSET providers who become facilitators for schools, enabling teachers to reflect on their practice and, over the long term, experience changes in attitudes, conceptions and beliefs (Lally *et al.* 1992). Newton and Newton (1994) also see INSET's providers as supporters of personal and professional development, which cannot be achieved in one-off sessions. The case study presented by Webb (1989) of a team of language advisers using consultancy to improve the classroom impact of INSET, provides a good example of how long-term support of teachers can be effective. The teachers in the study felt that success was due to:

- the role models provided by the advisers;
- the information they could provide;
- their facilitation of collaboration;
- their confidant role;
- the exchange of ideas generated by the relationship.

Webb (1989) suggested that the climate and relationships within the schools were also important factors.

Several other writers discuss the importance of conditions within a school for the success of INSET. Ainscow *et al.* (1994) suggest that the school is the context for professional development and their book contains many examples of activities to promote such development. Bradley *et al.* (1994) agree with the need to place professional development in school, saying that positive conditions in the workplace are vital if teachers and schools are to progress. They extol the importance of active leadership and support for, alongside teacher involvement in planning of, INSET. They see little place for short 'how to do it' activities, as these do not bring about sustained development.

Although INSET has become much more school, than individual, orientated over recent years, many writers agree that without individual professional development, school development is impossible. Butt (1989) argues that individual training days can only raise awareness and both Conner (1994) and Law and Glover (1995) suggest that government support of skill and knowledge acquisition, in place of sustained professional education, does not ensure long-term impact in practice. Day (1989) adds his opinion, that sustained professional development takes time and reflection. However, it does appear that both types of INSET have a place. The creation of learning environments in schools involves the commitment of several leading members of staff, supported in sustained education by higher education institutions alongside opportunities to up-grade skills and knowledge through short, school-based workshops. Most of the arguments that have been rehearsed in this analysis of the literature concerning INSET have set school-based training days against long-term college-based courses, suggesting that the latter are superior to the former. The two are not incompatible: they are complementary.

## Teaching and learning approaches

The conditions for the success of INSET identified above, are only part of what makes it effective. What happens within the sessions is also of vital importance. There appears to be strong agreement among writers and researchers concerning the attitude to teaching and learning most likely to be successful when educating professionals. There are variations on the common theme, but half of the 74 articles, chapters and books consulted for this part of this literature review refer to the importance of enabling professionals to become reflective practitioners or to engage specifically in action research. The other half either do not refer to teaching and learning at all, or recommend the use of action learning, problem solving, discussion groups, coaching, case studies or observation; all of which are compatible with the generic idea of a reflective practitioner. No writers suggested that it was appropriate to train professionals in skills and knowledge alone.

### Reflective practice

When analysing the many references to reflection or action research, a number of themes emerged. The first relates to reflection itself and what it offers to teachers and other professionals. Brookfield (1986) suggests that adult, self-directed learning involves critical reflection which can lead to changes in action. He expands on this by referring to the need for learners to use reflection on matters previously unquestioned to enable them to examine their values, beliefs and behaviours. Schon (1992) distinguishes between reflection-on-action and reflection-in-action which adds another dimension to its power. He suggests that practitioners need to stop and think and then apply the ideas in a problem-solving manner (reflection-in-action) and that reflection 'on' enables their implicit or tacit understanding to become explicit.

There is remarkable consensus throughout the literature reviewed concerning the importance of reflection on experience as an ingredient for ensuring that INSET has an impact on practice. From a common-sense point of view, it appears sensible to suggest that the recalling of past experiences and an analysis of their positive and negative points can become the basis for future developments. It can also be suggested that there is much support for encouraging practitioners to articulate not merely their experiences but also their own theories concerning why they work in the ways they do. Several of these writers have developed both the theory and the practice of action research, using it to help make explicit their own ideas. Although this is still a relatively new approach to research, it is beginning to gather credence, especially because it does encourage impact of learning on practice (Elliott 1991).

## Learning facilitators

To encourage change in the workplace, adult learners need tutors who can facilitate both the active learning and their reflection upon it. Brookfield (1986), Gould and Harris (1996) and O'Hanlon (1991) all explore the facilitator role. O'Hanlon (1991) suggests that facilitators can work through exposing professionals to a range of concepts, theories and models of knowledge to help them solve their problems, as well as enabling them to evaluate and respond constructively to issues that they encounter in their practice. She suggests that there are two sides to the role: practical and inspirational.

Joyce and Showers (1982), Sebba (1994) and Wideen (1992) suggest that coaching from tutors or from colleagues is another important activity in encouraging professionals to relate their learning to practice. Other writers demonstrate the use of case studies to ensure the perception of relevance (Coulshed 1993; Eraut 1988). Problem solving in practice is also seen as a specific way of making use of adult learners' need to see their learning as relevant to them (Borger and Tillema 1993; Coulshed 1993; Schon 1992; West-Burnham 1987). Discussion groups are specifically supported by Coulshed (1993) and Eraut (1988), although many other writers imply that discussion among peers and with tutors underpins their work, for example, Bailey's (1991) interest in using classroom observations as the basis for discussion for teacher education.

Conclusions can be drawn from considering the recommendations of the writers on the tutor's role in INSET which is aimed at encouraging impact on practice. They all see an active role for the tutor, but not one where the activity entirely concerns the traditional function of giving information. It is an enabling role where participants are encouraged to discuss and carry out activities aimed at improving their day-to-day work. This is not without its difficulties for tutors who may be more used to lecturing than providing opportunities for active learning. They do not necessarily possess skills in leading discussions, supplying pertinent case studies, engaging in dialogue, analysing video tapes, provoking discourse and generally providing opportunities for participants to relate actively to new ideas, try them out and report back.

## Summary and conclusions

It is encouraging to find examples of the importance of the same kind of attitude to professionals' learning from writers and researchers in all three disciplines of education, health and social welfare. This suggests that there are no basic differences in position that need to be overcome when attempting to teach representatives from the different disciplines together.

From the example of education, it can be suggested that the pendulum swing from long courses for individuals towards workplace-based short courses to try to improve the impact on organisations has not solved all the problems faced by those who are concerned with impact on practice. Although many more individuals can be involved in workplace training, it is often short-termist and shallow in nature. What is needed is a combination of the best of long-term personal education with the relevance of institution-based projects, with particular help for participants in transferring learning to practice.

In terms of the conditions needed for in-service education which provides impact on practice, writers suggest that professionals should be involved in negotiating their own courses, which should contain opportunities to conduct projects which are likely to be of specific benefit to their daily work. They appear to work best when presentations are interactive and when there is a mixture of reflection, experiential learning, case study work, problem solving and discussion. Active support during, and following, learning appears to be very important, especially from the management of participants' organisations. Evaluations should be built in to ensure accurate feedback to providers.

## PART TWO
## Collaboration in support partnerships: Case studies

## Chapter 6

## Teachers and therapists working together

This chapter is mainly based on research data collected at an all-age special school for pupils with physical disabilities and learning difficulties, known as Pear Tree School. There are approximately 100 pupils in the school, 10 teachers, 17 classroom assistants, one speech and language therapist, a speech and language therapy assistant, one full-time plus four part-time physiotherapists and four part-time occupational therapists. The multidisciplinary teamwork in the school is relatively advanced in that therapists work mainly in the classroom alongside teachers and classroom assistants, especially with the younger children; there is a senior member of teaching staff responsible for multidisciplinary teamwork and active management support for non-contact time for meetings.

These are the questions that are explored in this chapter.

- *How do members of multidisciplinary teams work together?*
- *Why do motor groups promote effective collaboration?*
- *How important is it for team members to have a shared culture?*
- *What part do multidisciplinary meetings play in supporting effective collaboration?*
- *What is a collaborative curriculum?*
- *What does effective collaboration look like?*

## Working together

Teachers and therapists at Pear Tree School work together in a support partnership which enables them to meet both the education and therapy needs of the children.

**Example**

Pam's class consisted of eight pupils of junior age all with multiple problems caused mainly by cerebral palsy. All had physical disabilities but many also had sensory impairments, communication difficulties and medical problems. There was a great need for input from several professionals. Those who were on site formed a classroom team of a teacher, nursery nurse, classroom assistant, physiotherapist, occupational therapist and speech and language therapist (supported by a speech and language therapy assistant).

Therapy was as important in the classroom as education. Even if an individual lesson was driven by the National Curriculum, physical positioning was a major consideration as was the method of communication. Individual programmes were a mixture of education and therapy needs and were either written jointly or at least were influenced by each other. Children were assessed jointly. One multiply disabled child was observed being assessed for access to the computer which would become her means of communication in the future. Present at the assessment was the speech and language therapist and the occupational therapist. They worked together using a suitable computer program provided for them by Pam. Although Pam was not able to be at the assessment she was part of both the briefing and the de-briefing meetings. The two therapists worked together for about an hour, trying out different switches and positions, combining each other's knowledge and expertise to solve the problem.

**Example**

A group of nursery and infant pupils were brought into the physio room by a variety of teachers and classroom assistants. On this particular day there were five children and three adults, two classroom assistants and Lesley, the physiotherapist. Other observations of similar sessions included a different combination of adults, depending on who was available. For example the speech and language therapist, her assistant, teachers, classroom assistants and an occupational therapist were all involved at different times.

During the session the physiotherapist, Lesley, took the lead and employed a combination of educational and physiotherapy techniques. She had a variety of aims and objectives ranging from encouraging rolling, sitting, reaching, straight lying and pushing an object to teaching colours, size, laterality, counting to five, body part vocabulary and recognition of personal clothing.

From the discussion following this session, Lesley indicated that she has her own priorities for the motor session, but that she weaves in educational objectives where she can. These are group rather than individual objectives, although the level of engagement was varied according to the ability of each child. The children appear to be viewed in an holistic manner and therapy and education can be seen to be running side-by-side in an integrated manner.

Members of the multidisciplinary team are clearly physically working together where this is possible, using the synergy created by more than one mind coming together to solve practical problems. They also work very closely in what the school calls 'a motor group', that is a small group of children working with a number of staff on functional movement such as unaided sitting or reaching for objects.

In both those examples, teachers and therapists are working alongside each other in the classroom and are clearly allowing their specialist work to overlap. This is relatively easy to achieve at the nursery level where the curriculum is more general but becomes more difficult as pupils move into more discrete subject work and perhaps easier again in further and adult education where individual curricula are more common.

## Motor groups

It would be useful to examine what happens in motor groups in more depth to attempt to develop the framework for understanding why they promote teamwork so successfully. It might be possible, from this, to suggest other aspects of special education where this degree of collaboration would be appropriate.

Motor groups at Pear Tree School involve all therapists and classroom staff, although they do not all have the same amount of input (see Figure 6.1).

The lead specialism in motor groups is physiotherapy, as the prime focus is on enabling children to gain control over their own bodies. It is seen as a precursor to full involvement in the school curriculum. Motor education can be said to be an English derivative from conductive education, a system of educating children with motor disorders in Hungary (Cottam and Sutton 1986). It was first developed in residential schools run by Scope (formerly the Spastic Society) by Ester Coton who was a physiotherapist (Cottam 1986). It is based on the idea of motor function and on enabling children to become functional in everyday living. Many English state day schools for children with physical and/or learning difficulties took up some of the ideology and practice in the 1980s (Steel 1991) and staff at Pear Tree School have developed their own brand.

Motor education is different from conductive education in several ways. The most important for understanding multidisciplinary teamwork is the way in which staff are trained and work together. In conductive education, each member of staff is trained in several different disciplines. Individuals learn about motor

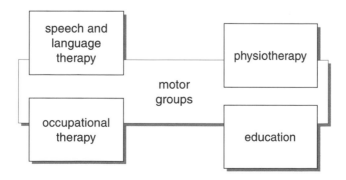

**Figure 6.1** Staff involvement in motor groups at Pear Tree School

disorders from the angles of physiotherapy, speech and language therapy, occupational therapy and teaching. They are, in fact, multiprofessional. The term 'conductor' is used to describe their job which is likened to a conductor of an orchestra who wants each individual to work together for the whole group. Staff teamwork in conductive education is thus about like-disciplines working together rather than different disciplines.

Although it appears that developing the role of the conductor could be a powerful example of bypassing the difficulties encountered with multi-disciplinary teamwork, this may not be the case. One of the strengths of multidisciplinary teamwork is that, when collaboration works, it feeds off the differences between people as well as the sameness. There is little doubt that individuals from different disciplines have different mind sets upon which to call. They view problems presented by children's difficulties in diverse ways which can greatly improve the quality of the solutions offered. If every member of the team has been similarly trained, their problem solving may not be as imaginative as those whose training was diverse. This has by no means been proven in this or any other research and is offered as a tentative suggestion.

Motor education at Pear Tree School (and others in this country) relies mainly on bringing together individuals from different disciplines, who work together in a collaborative manner to cross the divide between teaching and therapy. All the staff involved are included in devising and carrying out of programmes and the common goals set by the team seem to act as a binding force for them. In some versions of motor sessions, every move and every word are scripted so that the children experience both exact repetition of exercises and continuity across personnel. At Pear Tree School, some of the exercises are treated in this manner, but there is greater flexibility for responding to immediate needs than can be seen in the strictest of regimes. It appears that individuals are trusted to keep within the bounds of a brief and also exercise their imaginations where appropriate.

There are many occasions when more than one discipline is represented in a session and there are opportunities for discussion alongside the work with the children. In observations, the sessions were not interrupted by these discussions, but they are part of the way in which teaching and therapy are constantly adjusted to meet changing needs. The opportunity to work alongside each other provides a forum for immediate and constant problem solving.

In summary, motor education seems to be effective in bringing different disciplines together in a collaborative relationship because it contains the following elements:

- common goals which integrate teaching and therapy;
- concentration on a defined aspect of the child's life (motor function);
- teachers and therapists working physically side-by-side;
- teachers and therapists problem solving together on-the-spot;
- whole-team involvement in planning and carrying out programmes.

It has already been pointed out that it is more difficult to create these conditions as pupils get older, but there are other difficulties faced by therapists and teachers attempting to work together in partnership, for example differences in the ways they work, have been trained, are paid and are managed. The two groups come from very different backgrounds. Health and education start from very different premises and view disability and difficulties in very different ways, using different vocabularies and different expectations. It can be very taxing for partnerships to combat these differences.

## Shared culture

Although these differences in the culture of health and education undeniably exist, there are also many things that they have in common. It would be helpful to explore these in more detail as it appears that those people who work together well perceive more things in common than those who do not.

Although teaching and therapy come from different disciplines, they are both concerned with progress and development, use assessment to diagnose problems and devise programmes to meet individual needs. Special education has been influenced strongly by a medical view of children's needs, although the trend is to move away from a perception of 'within child' factors towards an ecological view of disability and difficulty. Both teachers and therapists are moving in this direction and many share the current social perspective which encourages them to concentrate on adjusting the environment to meet needs. They are also developing an holistic view of the child which enables them to see therapy and teaching as complementary rather than competing.

Teachers and therapists operate from different frameworks but in reality their areas of knowledge overlap: with speech and language therapists in the area of language and communication; with physiotherapists in the area of gross motor development and with occupational therapists in the area of fine motor development, daily living skills and aspects of reading. Some individuals perceive this as positive overlap where knowledge and expertise can be pooled, but others either do not recognise how much they share or find it threatening and so resist.

At Pear Tree School, staff who work most closely together appear to believe that they share much in common. The motor groups are an obvious example but there are other ways in which teachers and therapists cross over, blur the edges of their roles and hand over skills to each other in order to ensure pupils' needs are met in an holistic way. For example the speech and language therapist, Lena, spends time with each teacher jointly writing programmes with them which can then be carried out by any member of staff. She also works alongside classroom staff, jointly solving problems and passing on her expertise. She knows that children's speech and language needs will be addressed routinely and that when she is called away from the school to attend to management matters elsewhere in the service, pupils' needs will continue to be met. She said, 'I would feel I had failed in my job if everything came to a halt just because I had a bad term and wasn't in a lot.'

Lena also talked of blurring the edges of her role with others in the classroom and how some professionals find this threatening, thinking that if they give away their skills they will no longer be in demand. On the contrary, she said, 'the more you get to know about physios, occupational therapy and nursing, the more you realise you need their skills.' So giving away skills does not result in redundancy, but in renewed interest in what individuals have to offer. Of course, this does not always work smoothly. Lena, at another time, bemoaned the fact that Pear Tree staff had rewritten their spelling policy without inviting her to contribute, although she had much to offer on the topic.

## Multidisciplinary meetings

Finding things in common and working on children's learning programmes together take time to organise and facilitate and teachers and therapists need to work out how to achieve this. Again differences in working practices and culture make finding common time difficult (see Chapter 7 for a more detailed discussion). Pear Tree School organises formal annual multidisciplinary meetings for each class and enables other informal meetings to be arranged when necessary.

The annual meetings are organised for each summer term. Teachers are released from their classes to be able to attend and therapists arrange that their time will be dedicated to the meetings. Although a senior teacher responsible for multidisciplinary teamwork activates the process, each teacher is responsible for arranging the details. Although there is only one meeting per teacher, there will be several for the therapists, especially for the speech and language therapist who works on her own (with an assistant) in the school. Recently the occupational therapy service has re-organised itself and only one therapist (Jane) is working in the school (instead of four); the rest work in the community so Jane will have to attend the multidisciplinary meetings for each class. There are usually five or six physiotherapists involved in the school so they divide themselves between meetings depending upon their client group. At the meetings every child in the class is discussed in turn. Individual targets are discussed for the next 12 months and general approaches are agreed.

The informal meetings that occur throughout the school year are called when the need arises. These often happen after school hours or in the lunchtime. The therapists have sufficient flexibility to be able to arrange meetings to suit school hours. They are also largely placed on the school site so that it is relatively easy for them to meet with school staff at short notice in an *ad hoc* manner. For therapy staff who work under different circumstances it is likely to be more difficult to meet informally and thus more formal meetings will be necessary. If meetings can only be arranged during school hours, then arrangements for non-contact time for classroom staff will be necessary. Some schools devote some of their budget to this to ensure that multidisciplinary teamwork is properly supported (see Chapter 8 for more discussion of management issues).

Multidisciplinary meetings can be excellent fora for joint problem solving, especially if everyone has a chance to present their own point of view and there is an efficient chairperson to draw it all together and facilitate decision-making. The synergy released when professionals from different disciplines problem solve together demonstrates that 'the whole is greater than the sum of the parts'. However, not all multidisciplinary meetings manage to reach these heights as there are so many aspects that can conspire against efficiency and effectiveness:

people are unable to attend at the last minute; those who can attend have not had time to study preparation papers; service representatives cannot or will not commit resources; jargon is misunderstood or deliberately used to obfuscate; professionals jealously guard their own service interests; and the chairperson does not keep members to the agenda. These are just a few of the ways in which multidisciplinary meetings can be sabotaged.

Avoiding such chaos can be very time-consuming, but time extremely well spent. Before any multidisciplinary partnership can flourish and give rise to synergy, there needs to be investment of time. Individual team members need time to get to know each other, what each service can offer, the resources available and the constraints under which each operates. Jargon needs to be explained, along with the basics of each other's training and service principles. Common aims need to be discussed and agreed. One multi-therapy service describes a process of 'jostling and queuing' between members of the team as they offer their own priorities for the multiply disabled children they are working with. They explain that this is a positive process and leads towards a more unified approach once priorities have been decided by the team.

This particular team, working in the Wolfson Centre in London, is made up of three therapists rather than therapists and teachers, but the principles by which they work can be applied to other teams. When a multiply disabled child is referred to the Centre, one of the therapists takes the lead, usually based on the child's most major difficulty, and conducts the initial assessments. Prior to this, the three therapists have shared their assessments and trained each other to undertake the basics. They trust each other to carry out assessments from a different discipline, but call upon each other if they run into difficulties. The assessment sessions are recorded on video tape and can be shared between the therapists when they meet. Alternatively children can be assessed in a room with a one-way mirror so that observers can be placed in an adjoining room.

In this way, not only does the child work with just one adult instead of three but families only have to tell their story once, to one professional. This reduces family frustration and the likelihood of confusion from alternative advice and enables children to receive a much more unified approach to meeting their needs. It can be the case, for families of children with multiple disabilities, that they can be passed from professional to professional getting more and more confused. For some, hardly a week passes without an appointment with someone who can offer some of the help they need. In fact, what they really need is a consistent keyworker figure who can represent as many other professionals and services as possible (see further discussion in Chapter 12).

Children themselves, especially young children, need to build up a close relationship with one person who can bring together all the strands of what can be offered by a multidisciplinary team, or at least a very small group who all work in a similar manner. In schools this is likely to be the classroom staff and any therapists who work daily or weekly with the child, in addition to the parents. It is helpful if most other professionals work through this small team, although it is recognised that sometimes new ideas from recognised 'experts' can help to re-energise the team, and developing these ideas may involve hands-on work with the child (see further discussion in Chapter 7).

## A collaborative curriculum

Effective multidisciplinary teamwork appears to contribute towards what could be called a collaborative curriculum. This is a curriculum that employs the best of the practice in motor groups, builds on a shared culture and multidisciplinary problem solving and utilises a small classroom team approach. It is a curriculum that binds together the many different aspects of children's lives during the school years and is based, as far as possible, on a bottom-up view of curriculum planning rather than a top-down.

A bottom-up view of curriculum planning enables the multidisciplinary team members to start from the children's needs and not solely from the demands of the curriculum. Of course, in the current climate, team members cannot ignore the pressures of the National Curriculum, the Literacy and Numeracy Strategies and target setting, but the driving force can be the children's needs *within* the context of a prescribed curriculum. Children with complex needs warranting input from a multidisciplinary team rarely learn conveniently in tune with a curriculum written for non-disabled children and require the kinds of modifications sanctioned by the Qualifications and Curriculum Authority (QCA) and Department for Education and Employment (DfEE) in *Curriculum Guidelines for Pupils with Learning Difficulties* (QCA 2001).

For teachers and therapists working together collaboratively, the most important aspects of the curriculum are those that are shared between them. It will be useful to consider the work of the physiotherapist in a collaborative curriculum to illustrate this point. Physiotherapists aim to help children to improve and/or make the best use of their motor abilities. They have expertise in optimum positioning for ease of motor function and can advice on and/or make orthoses to aid children's positioning and movement. This relates well to the physical education (PE) curriculum. Traditionally, physiotherapists have withdrawn children from lessons to concentrate for a set period of time on physical exercises and alternative positioning. Children have been observed lying in a piece of equipment such as a side-lying board in the physio room doing nothing, having been taken away from lessons which have carried on without them. There seems to be nothing gained by divorcing the positioning from the lesson: the two could be occurring concurrently.

Not only can positions be changed within the classroom context, but many of the exercises used by physiotherapists could be incorporated into the curriculum if teachers and physiotherapists plan together. What appears to be most difficult to achieve is fitting into the day separate programmes that have been written by teachers and therapists in isolation. Either there is the unsatisfactory separation of activities, as above, or teachers become stressed as they try to find time to supervise or carry out exercises written by someone else.

In a collaborative curriculum, teachers and therapists have spent time writing programmes together and training each other in the aspects of their work where their expertise overlaps. Physiotherapists and teachers can gain much from planning classroom organisation together. Natural opportunities for stretching, grasping, balancing and strengthening muscles can be found in many different areas of the curriculum which will obviate some of the need for allocating special time for exercising. If the PE curriculum is jointly written, lessons can be led sometimes by the teacher and sometimes by the physiotherapist so that the children can benefit from the expertise of both.

Not only do pupils experience a less fragmented curriculum when teachers and therapists work together on a collaborative curriculum, but also they are given many more opportunities to have their needs met than if the therapist only worked with them during their appointment time. It is tempting for therapists to work in the same way they would in a hospital or clinic when attached to a school, but this rarely works well for anyone, least of all the children (see Chapter 8 for a fuller discussion of this point). If everyone in the school setting is aware of the therapy needs of the children, they can ensure good positioning and encourage exercises at all times of the day. In this way, the children are not seen as a combination of legs, hands, speech or intellect, but holistically in terms of their education and care.

## Effective collaboration

For the last section of this chapter, it will be helpful to use the evidence from Pear Tree School and others to draw together the best of collaborative practice between teachers and therapists working in partnership in an attempt to describe what effective collaboration looks like. This will lead into the next chapter where the management implications of multidisciplinary teamwork will be explored.

### Overlapping of roles

Teachers and therapists work together specifically in the areas where their knowledge, skills and expertise overlap, so that the edges of their roles become blurred and children experience similar input from both people. Working together in areas of overlap enables partners to begin at a comfortable level and then to branch out a little and introduce aspects of their work to each other that are more specialised. Passing over of skills from one partner to the other can thus begin with the familiar and progress to the less familiar.

Overlapping roles and blurred role edges do not mean that specialist skills are not needed. Each member of the multidisciplinary team has a different and distinct role, complementing each other in experience and expertise.

### Joint planning of children's targets

If children are to be seen as whole people and not collections of disabilities, therapists and teachers should write targets and programmes jointly. They should discuss the needs of the children together and decide between them on priorities. Thus the programme will be balanced and everyone will feel ownership of it. It will be an integrated programme based on ways of bringing together the different parts of the children's curricula.

## Working together

It is important for teachers and therapists actually to work together: to watch each other at work and learn from each other. Leadership can shift from one to the other as the emphasis changes, although in the case of a system such as motor groups, the emphasis remains the same and any team member can lead at any time.

Sometimes it is helpful to have direct training sessions, but the informal training while working side-by-side can be very valuable. It is very important to have discussed what it might be possible to learn from each other and to reflect on what changes can be made to the environment or teaching to ensure children are learning and developing.

## Mutual and common training

The formal training should be two-way. On the whole schools are good at asking for training *from* therapists on health and therapy techniques, but are less good at giving them training on aspects of the curriculum or teaching and learning. Each group needs to understand the other and training sessions are opportunities for conducting directed discussions as well as for listening to information.

Common training is also helpful. If therapists and teachers attend the same course together, they are likely to have a common understanding of the topic. They are also likely to work together on the same topic after the course has finished. (See Chapter 13 for more discussion of this.)

## Working intensively with individual children

There are times when teachers and therapists need to work together and directly with individual children. More often than not, good multidisciplinary teamwork results in one professional taking on some of the role of another, but occasionally the two people are more effective if they concentrate on one child together. Problem solving can be particularly effective when more than one perspective can be brought to bear at the same time.

## Close physical locality

It is undeniably more difficult for teachers and therapists to work in a collaborative partnership if they do not share a physical locality for a significant amount of their working time. Therapists who travel about and serve many different schools will always find it hard to develop relationships with everyone with whom they work. It can be helpful to arrange their timetable to work with different people for longer periods and then have longer gaps between their contact. If therapists visit one school for a whole day once every three weeks rather than three different schools for two hours once a week then there is a possibility for professionals to get to know each other sufficiently to be able to take advantage of the best of multidisciplinary teamwork. (See Chapter 7 for further discussion.)

## Working mainly in the classroom

If members of the multidisciplinary team all work mainly in the classroom, as opposed to withdrawing children to a special space for therapy, then the conditions advocated in the last few subsections can be achieved. Sometimes specialist equipment is required for the particular therapy that is only available in another room, which makes it necessary for children to be withdrawn. If this is so, then extra effort needs to be put into sharing what has occurred. This can take place in a formal meeting, through informal contact or through relevant paperwork. It does not matter which is the most suitable, what is most important is that team members discuss a) how to communicate and b) what occurs in the withdrawal time.

There are other conditions when it may be best to withdraw children to other spaces, for example if physiotherapy involves undressing or if a distraction-free environment is essential. Team members should fully discuss the reasons for working in one place rather than another and agree between them the most effective environment for learning and development.

## Multidisciplinary team meetings

Discussions such as those advocated above should take place in regular multidisciplinary team meetings. The actual amount of time given to and pattern of meetings should be agreed between the members. There should be sufficient numbers of meetings for members to feel they can:

(a) get to understand each other's role, skills, principles, aims, constraints
(b) problem solve together
(c) plan their work together
(d) review and improve the work of the team.

Some of the meetings should be formal and include all the professionals working with a group of children and others informal when pairs of professionals can get together briefly to exchange ideas and information. (See Chapter 7 for further discussion.)

## A senior member of staff responsible for multidisciplinary teamwork

If multidisciplinary teamwork is to receive the support it requires, it is advisable to appoint a senior member of staff responsible for its smooth working. This could be the SENCO, though not necessarily. This responsible person should be in a position to organise cover for classroom staff to attend meetings that can only be held during school hours. They should also be able to provide liaison with services and have time to negotiate the therapy input with health trusts.

This senior member of staff should have a strong commitment to multidisciplinary teamwork and be able to motivate team members to review their work and set themselves new goals for working together.

## A multidisciplinary team commitment

There needs to be commitment not only from the senior member of staff responsible for multidisciplinary teamwork, but from everyone in the school and therapy services. Attitude is vital where people are being asked and expected to work together in partnership. If individuals are not willing to share with each other, teamwork will be impossible. However, a willingness to share is not sufficient without systems in place to support the partnership. Systems for meetings, written communications, service agreements, review and training are all important too and are the subject of the next chapter.

## Summary and conclusions

In this chapter, the work of one school for pupils with physical and learning difficulties has been introduced. Examples of ways of working together have been given and analysed in terms of the systems and strategies that support effective collaboration. Understanding and utilising the expertise each member brings to the team appears to be very important. If everyone works in isolation, it is very hard for all the child's needs to be met. If one of the team members writes a programme for the others to carry out (as so often happens) it can be very difficult to integrate that programme with the rest of the child's curriculum. If the partners write and run the programmes together then they can adjust and combine in the most efficient way.

Working together collaboratively can be facilitated by certain conditions and factors. Those highlighted in this chapter were:

- promotion and support of collaboration by a senior member of staff;
- opportunities to meet to talk, to work and learn together;
- the integration of the different aspects of the child's curriculum.

Effective partnership or teamwork does not automatically occur when people work in the same organisation, or even the same room. It requires nurture and support as well as commitment from individuals.

# Chapter 7

# Systemic aspects of multidisciplinary teamwork

As in the previous chapter, this chapter draws mainly on the research carried out at Pear Tree School. The analysis is primarily concerned with a systemic view of multidisciplinary teamwork, and is particularly focused on why systems are often either poor or non-existent and on how to improve the situation. In many cases, people from different disciplines are willing to work together, but what they lack are effective systems to support that work. Lines of communication are underdeveloped or non-existent, time for planning is snatched or non-existent, joint bodies are few or non-existent and shared training is rare or non-existent.

These are the questions addressed in this chapter.

- *Why is it difficult for the special school management system to support collaboration between teachers and therapists?*
- *How do differences in flexibility affect collaboration?*
- *Does it help to differentiate between teams and networks?*
- *How can working in a 'consultancy' manner support collaboration?*
- *How can time be managed to enable team members to work together?*
- *What does 'opening the can of worms' reveal about the difficulties team members have when trying to work together?*

## A special school management system

In many special schools there are two management systems running side-by-side. Figure 7.1 shows how teachers and therapists have completely separate lines of management, although, as in Pear Tree School's case, they are all working under the same roof with the same set of children.

The headteacher and senior management team have relatively simple management responsibilities and lines of communication, although there is always scope for ambiguity with teaching assistants. Do they work to the head or to the class teacher? Where an assistant works in several classrooms, who is their boss? In collaborative teams this question should be irrelevant as everyone should support each other without undue evidence of hierarchy. In reality though, most assistants look to class teachers for direction and some are resistant to becoming full members of teams if this means taking responsibility. However, in many special schools, the small number of staff means that hierarchical lines of communication do not usually dominate.

On the therapy side, most therapists work at a distance from their lines of management. In the case of Pear Tree School, there are physiotherapy and speech and language therapy managers on site. The physio has several full- and part-

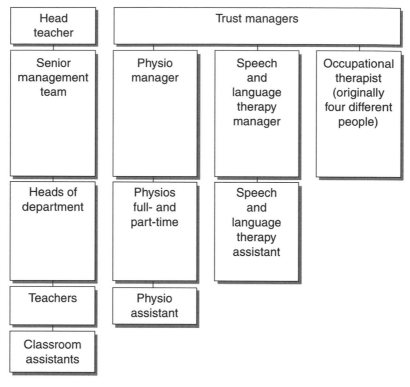

**Figure 7.1** Pear Tree School's management system

time therapists working to her who are also on site, but the speech and language therapist manages other therapists who work within other organisations. The occupational therapist's line-manager does not work on-site. She does have several colleagues who share accommodation with her who work in the community, which means she has a strong discipline support within easy reach. This is the same situation for the physios, several of whom work together at the school. The speech and language therapist is isolated from her colleagues and has the added complication of managing others who operate on other sites unconnected with the school.

The head teacher is responsible for all that goes on in his school, including the therapy, although this is not total responsibility. For instance, he has no direct lines of management with the therapists. All the communication between them is dependent upon goodwill. Therapists operate completely independently from the school management system, although at Pear Tree School there are very strong links that have been developed to ensure that, for instance, therapy is timetabled in sympathy with individual children's curricula.

The head teacher is not consulted at service level concerning the numbers of therapists, their hours nor how they will work in his school. He, and ultimately the children, are entirely in the hands of the trust managers. The following extract is taken from an interview with the head teacher of Pear Tree School.

| Bill | ... currently we're moving into a difficult time because there have been lots of absences of health personnel and a lot of jobs haven't automatically been replaced, allied to the fact that Lesley is the professional adviser for physios and Lena is the professional adviser for speech and language therapy. |
| Penny | So they have a wider brief? |
| Bill | So they have a wider role than just here. Both are having to coordinate resources within the community which takes them out more in terms of admin. time and meetings. Time is being eroded from here. So it's likely to become more problematic in the future. |
| Penny | Is that a change because of trust status? |
| Bill | Yes, trust status is obviously a factor in it, but also the funding that the health authority have got. In order to cover absentees, posts that haven't been filled, then they're having to draw more upon staff here, which is obviously problematic because it compromises what we're trying to do. It's tolerable at the moment, but ... |
| Penny | Do you have specific contracts, say with the physiotherapy service? |
| Bill | No we don't. This is what makes it difficult ... The health authority provided input here, according to the resources (I was going to say according to need) available. Therefore, being a PH (physically handicapped) school, we get a significant degree of physiotherapy. Speech and language therapy on the other hand, we get rather a lesser amount because there are a number of other assumptions which require it also and there is never enough to go round. It's often a case of robbing Peter to pay Paul. So we've been in this situation before where we've tried to put pressure on the health authorities, but when it comes down to it, they will put in what resources there are available, but will withdraw them if they feel they have to. |

This passage has been quoted at length, as it seems to encapsulate so many of the difficulties encountered when trying to match up two entirely different services on one site. The head teacher appears to feel helpless as all the decisions concerning the therapy service are in the hands of others who have little idea of the demands of the school, yet he holds overall responsibility for meeting the children's needs.

His allusion to the underlying assumptions which drive the allocation of resources to a school such as Pear Tree, is interesting. He appears to be suggesting that the health authority have decided that levels of physiotherapy should be higher than speech and language therapy because physical disability is primarily about motor difficulties. The extent of language and communication problems is not recognised, despite the growing number of pupils with complex disabilities entering the school. This is not an unusual misconception, and it reflects the difficulties absentee managers have in trying to allocate resources to situations of which they understand little.

In systemic terms, there are so many factors stacked against teachers and therapists working smoothly together. These have some interesting consequences which are worth pursuing.

## Differences in flexibility

From both experience and from the literature, evidence suggests that teachers who complain most vociferously about the therapists who work in their schools, talk of the way in which they interrupt lessons whenever they feel like it. They walk into the classroom and either extract children or work with them in a corner on what seems like a whim. If a timetable was ever agreed, it is not often kept to. Therapists argue that they work to an appointments system, which everyone knows is very difficult to keep to time. Sometimes the need of individuals takes more time than was allocated and the rest of the queue gets pushed further and further back. Appearing in a classroom at an allotted moment is a problem.

On the other side, therapists complain that it is very difficult to talk with teachers as the latter are regulated by a strict timetable. Classroom teachers are expected to be engaged with pupils between the hours of 9 a.m. and 3.30 p.m. and have little time to talk with other adults.

The occupational therapist at Pear Tree School summed up the problem seen from her point of view:

> It's often difficult to see a teacher because of his or her timetable and I've had situations where I've been talking about a child in a classroom with that child present and been unable to get that teacher any further away from that child.

Therapists come from a culture where their time is flexible and they can arrange time to consult with others and where necessary actually work together with other people. This flexibility enables them to move around more freely than teachers, even though they have pressures of getting through large numbers of patients in this market-driven world.

'Wandering about' in schools is not much encouraged for teachers and teaching assistants, although there are some exceptions. Thus in special schools, it is allowed for heads and deputies (and any other non-teaching senior staff), therapists, medical staff and peripatetic staff. But it is not allowed for teachers, support staff and pupils. In the culture of teaching, people who are able to 'wander about' during school hours are generally those who occupy senior positions. Head teachers and senior staff usually have facets to their jobs which require them to move about the school. They have a certain flexibility which, for some of the time, enables them to choose what to do and when to do it. On the whole, 'wandering about' equates with seniority which can be seen to bring with it status, power and control. If this is related to teachers and therapists, it could be argued that teachers perceive therapists as having more freedom to 'wander about' and thus attribute them with greater power and control than they feel they have themselves. They also feel that there is the potential for therapists to misuse their licence to wander about by entering and leaving the classroom at will.

The head teacher indicates a little of the feeling that can be generated in the following short extract of an interview.

> Therapists are not tied down quite so specifically to certain activities. They've got a little more flexibility in terms of being able to absent themselves, as they do when they've got team meetings at X House, the Health Authority place.

The difference in culture between education and health can be perceived in those few words. There is no doubt that Bill is dissatisfied with the fact that therapists can absent themselves from school without redress. A meeting during working hours is legitimate 'wandering about' and indicates quite clearly that control of the situation is in the hands of the therapists rather than the head teacher. Whatever the actual status of the therapist, this licence to wander about is seen to give that person more power and control than those who hold responsibility within the organisation.

## Teams and networks

It is clear from the argument so far that the two different systems employed by health and education staff make it difficult for them to work together. This is, of course, similar for all the other services and agencies who are trying to collaborate with each other in schools: specialist education services; social services; the police; educational psychology service; careers service. Each one is run in a different manner making joint efforts very hard to achieve. It can be helpful to consider the level of joint working necessary with certain agencies as it can be unrealistic to expect to be able to achieve full collaboration with everyone all of the time. In Chapter 1 of this book, different ways of working together were explored. These ranged from intermittent and brief contact (liaison) to full joint working (collaboration). The significance of developing different ways of working together can be illustrated by exploring two of the terms introduced in that first chapter: teams and networks.

From Figure 7.2 it can be suggested that there is a definite difference between a team and a network. Many people do not understand this and have unreal expectations of what can be achieved within the network. It is indicated in the figure that the team surrounding the child will typically contain the classroom teacher, teaching assistant (in this case a nursery nurse) and any therapists (or other support service staff) in direct contact with that child. It will also contain the child's family as well, but this theme will not be taken up at this point (please see Chapter 12). Everyone else will be part of a wider network and members of the team will have varying kinds of relationships with individuals in this network.

For many, liaison mode will be sufficient for most of their work, but with the possibility to be activated into a closer relationship. This could be illustrated by referring to the disability officer who is associated with Pear Tree School. Until it is time to draw up a transition plan for leaving school, it is not necessary for the disability officer to have any contact with individual children's teams. During

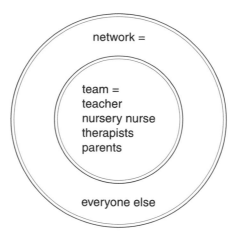

**Figure 7.2** Teams and networks

the time of the first transition review contact moves into coordination mode as meetings are arranged and parallel assessments are carried out under the Disabled Person's Act (DoH 1986) and the Children Act (DoH 1989a). There may even be a time when the young person is leaving school that the disability officer will work even more closely with the class team, although full collaboration will be unlikely to take place for long.

It is suggested, then, that individuals can move in and out of the different modes of working together, becoming members of the class team for short periods and then fading back into the wider network. There are probably several layers to this depending upon the size and make-up of individual schools. At Pear Tree School there appear to be five layers (see Figure 7.3).

In the diagram, the class team has been separated from the multidisciplinary team because although most children will have at least one therapist within their classroom team, there are other therapists upon whom the classroom team can call and who will move in and out of that team. The department team falls somewhere between a group of people who need to work collaboratively and a wider network who can call upon each other as need dictates. Each department has a leader but most departmental meetings consist only of teachers and assistants, with no input from therapists.

The school network embraces everyone else who is part of the school and, of course, there are cross-groupings which place individuals in cooperative, coordinated and collaborative relationships for different tasks. For instance, at Pear Tree School, the nursery teacher and the speech and language therapist talk of language groups that were used to place together children of like needs for teaching purposes. Coordination was necessary across the school and collaboration was needed between the leaders of language groups and the class teachers so that both were working towards the same goals in an integrated manner. Also, individuals can move in and out of the class team, depending on the needs of individual pupils. The information technology coordinator becomes a collaborative partner during the time it takes to assess or reassess a child for

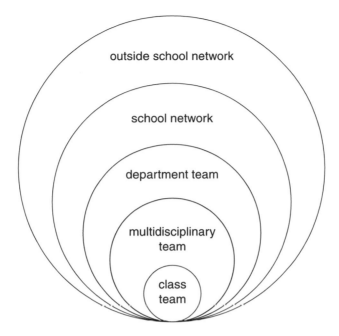

**Figure 7.3** Layers of teams and networks at Pear Tree School

access to a microcomputer, working closely with the class teacher, occupational therapist and possibly the speech and language therapist.

It can be appreciated from the discussion in this section that working together can be very complex for individuals. They may be members of several different teams/networks each of which may have conflicting demands. Consider a physiotherapist who treats children in three different classes (see Figure 7.4).

It appears that the physiotherapist is a member of at least five different teams and is a member of a wider network for other staff in the school and in the wider community where she or he has an advisory role.

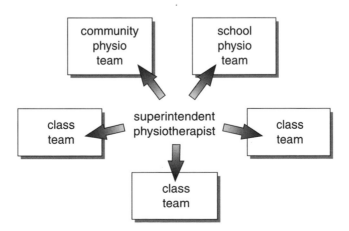

**Figure 7.4** The physiotherapist's teams

Not only is this demanding physically, attending five different team meetings, building relationships with all those involved in each team, writing reports, problem solving with five different groups of people, but there can be potential conflicts between the demands of these five teams, especially in terms of time.

This section has been dominated by the importance of understanding terms and thus the variety of modes possible for multidisciplinary teamwork. Much of the literature indicates that collaboration is the best mode and everyone should aspire to work in this manner with children in special education. It appears that not only is this unrealistic, but it is also unnecessary. Full collaboration between teachers, assistants and therapists in direct contact with the children appears to be possible, if time-consuming, but other people will move in and out of the team on a needs-basis only. This difference might be clearer if, for instance, it was acknowledged that doctors are part of an outer network rather than the team surrounding the child. Expectations may change as a result of that acknowledgement.

## Consultancy

When exploring roles within the continuum of working together, the one that seems to have developed recently is that of consultant. As was seen from the literature review, there is a growing tendency at all levels of special education, for fewer people to have direct contact with children so that teachers and teaching assistants take greater responsibility for the needs of the children in their care. Cynics may suggest that this development is the direct result of cuts in support staff and increases in caseloads for specialist teachers and therapists. This may be true, but it has laid the way open for the emergence of consultancy between professionals that can be enriching for everyone concerned.

At Pear Tree School, there appears to be a mix of direct work with children and consultancy, dependent upon the mode of working together. In the nursery, where collaboration is at its strongest, exchange of expertise is also strong. Although there is much direct work with the children, there is also much consultancy. The class teacher appears to have a leadership and coordinating role and is the focus for integrating education and therapy. She consults often with the three therapists who have frequent contact with her and in turn they consult with her. The result is that each professional is trained as a para-professional in each other's discipline. The teacher is a para-therapist and each therapist is a para-teacher. They all understand enough of each other's expertise to be able to carry out certain aspects independently. For example, the nursery teacher can place children in standing frames and carry out passive exercises as a result of using the physiotherapist as a training consultant.

There is no suggestion that when teachers are trained as para-therapists they no longer need therapists. One of the difficulties in teachers and therapists working together is often attributed to the threat therapists feel that if they train teachers to perform their roles, they will no longer be needed. The speech and language therapist at Pear Tree School said that just had not happened to her: 'The more people know what I can do, the more they want me.' There was certainly no hint in the nursery that Lena was not needed. She was involved in assessments, programme planning and direct therapy, although the teacher and assistants carried out the majority of the day-to-day work with individuals and groups of children.

It could be said that the teacher has taken on a keyworker role, using other professionals to support her. However, it is advisable to use this term cautiously as it has different meanings in different contexts. In residential settings, the keyworker is often an untrained person who is responsible for the daily living skills of the children, but is rarely responsible for integrating these with other aspects of the child's life in the way a teacher is, especially in a collaborative team. The use of the term, 'educational keyworker' may give a clearer meaning to the teacher's role at Pear Tree School. At nursery level this is most strongly a mix of education and therapy, waning largely to educational in the secondary department.

The educational keyworker role falls comfortably within the consultancy model and gives legitimacy to what teachers actually do in terms of leading and coordinating the multidisciplinary team in the classroom. It could be that discussing and using this role would go some way towards minimising problems such as therapists entering and leaving classrooms at will and the lack of flow of information. There is responsibility on both sides to develop and respect the role. The nursery teacher at Pear Tree School holds a large proportion of the information on each child, bringing together what is necessary to know for daily living and learning. She is usually the first point of contact for parents and members of the wider network of professionals. The school has not embraced the idea of having one record for each child to which all teachers and therapists contribute, as the therapists still keep their own records, but the classroom record does contain most of the information available in the school.

Having responsibility as first point of contact is not always in the hands of the educational keyworker. This appears to depend upon the focus of the contact. For instance, if the network member is the orthoses technician, it is likely that the physio will be contacted initially. She will then inform the educational keyworker who plans the visit into lessons. As this system is dependent upon the goodwill of individuals, there are many possibilities for communications to break down. It is possible that discussion can encourage individuals to find ways of facilitating effective communicating systems.

The development of the consultancy model of working in special education is a fundamental change to the thinking of both teachers and therapists. Individuals at Pear Tree School seem to have embraced this to differing degrees. Several informants suggest that the younger teachers, especially those who have been trained in special education, and experienced teachers with advanced special education training, find the consultancy role easiest to embrace. The younger occupational therapists claim that collaborative teamwork is a strong feature in their training. Others who have converted relatively easily include the speech and language therapist (who is in her 40s) which might be explained because the whole of her profession has been transforming itself from 'speech therapy' into 'speech and language therapy' over the last few years, recognising the importance of developing children's language as well as their speech. There is also a perception of a considerable overlap with education.

Resisters to the change appear to be, predictably, the older members of staff and those who work with the older pupils and who have had many years' experience with children who are physically disabled but intellectually able. Major change, such as moving from direct therapy to a consultancy model, is an extremely long-term venture and may be never fully embraced by some of the older members of staff (both therapists and teachers).

From the results of the research at Pear Tree School, it can be argued that the consultancy model explored in this section demands a whole new system to support it. If therapists work as consultants rather than just in direct therapy, time has to be allocated differently. This appears to be extremely difficult to change and the next section is devoted to an exploration of the whole concept of time as expressed by informants at Pear Tree School.

## Time

Almost everyone interviewed at Pear Tree School mentioned problems with finding time to work in teams. Figure 7.5 contains some of the words and phrases used by these informants, demonstrating the strength of feeling roused by the subject.

| | |
|---|---|
| time eroded | swings and roundabouts |
| compromises | robbing Peter to pay Paul |
| at a premium | snatched |
| pressure | trading |
| time-scale intruding | on the hoof |
| crisis management | forage around |
| ration | nightmare |
| governed by time | threatens the very existence of teams |
| this magic day | she lost it |
| depressing | lucky |
| chances | time commitment |
| pressures | a kind of dream |
| time-consuming | it drives me mad |
| utilise | horrendous |
| frustration | things have been put on ice |
| a no-go area | use available non-contact time |

**Figure 7.5** Time words and phrases

Some people talk of time as if it were something with physical presence, for instance: snatched, robbing, lost, consuming, eroded and intruding. Others connect it with moods using words such as depressing, chances, pressures, frustration, lucky, horrendous. At other times it is given business and power structure properties. Crisis management, governed by, trading, at a premium, ration, utilise are all examples of terms taken from the business world. The criminal world also features in words such as robbing, snatched and threatens. There are also a few gambling words such as lucky, lost it, magic day, chances.

The majority of words and phrases are connected with negative feelings and certainly the data indicate that almost everyone faced with re-organising time following the move to a consultancy model is overwhelmed by the enormity of the task. Interviewees smiled when asked to expand on their difficulties connected with time, but they rarely said anything positive. There was almost a feeling of helplessness as if they felt they had no personal control over their own time. Even the head teacher gave this impression.

One possible explanation for the difficulties in finding time for therapists and teachers to work and talk together is the different way they structure their time. Teachers work in blocks of time with groups of children whereas traditional therapists work down a list of patients rather as in a hospital.

As can be seen from Figure 7.6, the two time structures are conceived in different dimensions and both will need to alter if the two groups of people are going to be able to work together. Teachers will need more time outside the blocks of time with classes to fit in more with the therapy way of working and therapists will need to find longer blocks of time to fit in more with the school way of working. If both shift a little, compromises can be made.

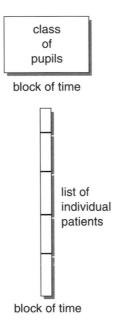

block of time

**Figure 7.6** Time structures for teachers and therapists

From the earlier discussion, it can be seen that time is regarded as something with a life of its own. Several people interviewed at Pear Tree School said they felt powerless in the face of diminishing time in the current climate. There are, however, some aspects of time which can be controlled and which are in some organisations. For example, therapists can 'cluster their time' so that they spend significant amounts of time with a smaller number of staff and children on a rotation basis. If they visit a school or classroom once a week for half a day, then staying for three days every six weeks could have the same effect in total time over that period, but utilises the time differently within the six weeks. The positive argument for working in this way is that during the three days in the school or classroom, it should be possible to engage in all the aspects that have been identified as necessary for working collaboratively, that is meeting together, working side-by-side, training each other, writing programmes together, joint assessment and evaluation.

Earlier in the chapter, the importance of being able to 'wander about' in facilitating teamwork was identified and it should be possible for this to be organised for the teacher involved within the three days, but failing this, the therapist is likely be available for lunchtime meetings and even after school. Clustering of time can pose difficulties during the six weeks between visits, especially if a child presents a problem which needs solving during that time. Children do not tidily keep their special needs until the therapy time comes round again. The argument, at this point, is that if the teacher has been sufficiently well trained during the three day stints, she or he should have, at least, some knowledge concerning where to begin intervention. This could be supplemented with advice over the phone if necessary, a point supported by Lena when referring to her enforced absence from Pear Tree School for half a term (see Chapter 6).

Time clustering appears to fit in well with the consultancy model and enables therapists to move in and out of the classroom team, alternating between collaboration and liaison as modes for operation. It is undoubtedly a different way to work and involves new thinking by both individuals and their agencies. Although therapists have a certain amount of control over their time, they are bound by certain demands such as numbers of patients treated per week. Clustering their time will involve changing the expectations over a short time-scale in recognition that over, say 12 weeks, the case records will be broadly the same. It could be argued that there is a likelihood of increase in caseload because if therapists work in a single setting for several days, it is likely that there will be more time for assessments and programme writing as less time is spent in travelling and readjusting to new situations. It might also be argued that because the therapy is shared collaboratively with classroom staff, more children are likely to benefit.

## 'Opening the can of worms'

Changing systems and ways of working can be stressful for the people involved. All the people involved in the research at Pear Tree School talked about the difficulties they were experiencing with all the massive changes taking place in schools. Some changes relate to the curriculum and all the bureaucracy created by recent government directives, but others relate directly to the demands of multidisciplinary teamwork, a rise in caseloads and the development of different ways of working. Unsurprisingly, many interviewees expressed their feelings quite strongly as they talked about working in teams.

The title of this subsection is a quotation from a teacher who was referring to transition from school and the difficulties she has experienced attempting to work with the social services department. Other people used equally colourful language and that is reflected in the words and phrases gathered together in Figure 7.7.

The two most frequently used categories of metaphors seem to be connected with war (minefield, battle, conflict, fighting, double-edged sword, stick, entrenched) and with anxiety (nightmare, no bed of roses, can of worms, blindness, pulling teeth, back door stuff, treading on toes) and even the emotions expressed have an anxious feeling (traumatic, jealousy, fraught, handled delicately, difficult, hard, etc.). This seems to raise two questions which it would be fruitful to explore briefly: 'What are they fighting?' and 'Why are they anxious?' These two questions have been used to direct the analysis. There appear to be two main categories in this fighting theme: systems and people and each of these can be allocated certain sub-categories. Table 7.1 is an attempt to draw these together.

It can be seen, from the table, that in terms of service structure, not only are

| | |
|---|---|
| entrenched | treading on toes |
| handled delicately | nightmare |
| minefield | difficult, hard, never easy, problem |
| beyond a joke | weren't consulted |
| compromise | hurdle |
| it needs a stick | divisive environment |
| it was like pulling teeth | fraught with potential difficulties |
| quite traumatic | stumbling blocks |
| battle we're still fighting | back door stuff |
| a kind of blindness | conflict |
| jealousy | social services shifted the goal posts |
| opened a can of worms | fighting their own corner |
| no one was pulling it together | double-edged sword |
| no bed of roses | teamwork is a philosophy |
| thou shalt not touch | ne'er the twain shall meet |

**Figure 7.7** Teamwork words and phrases

**Table 7.1** Anxieties of team members

| Systems | What are they fighting? | Why are they anxious? |
|---|---|---|
| service structure | • differences in funding, management, status, pay, hours, culture, training<br>• therapists are members of many different teams<br>• part-time staff | • reconciling differences in practice<br>• torn in different directions<br>• feelings of inequality<br>• don't know each other well enough<br>• difficult to get hold of each other |
| resources | • not enough, rationed<br>• come from different sources<br>• no one wants to pay<br>• lack of investment | • have to prioritise<br>• disappoint some<br>• who pays for what?<br>• how can we pay at all? |
| climate | • marketisation<br>• accountability<br>• competitiveness<br>• constant change<br>• retrenchment | • have to show value for money – difficult for services<br>• have to do more with less<br>• multidisciplinary teamwork is expensive (at first) |
| team structure | • no choice of members<br>• leaderless<br>• *ad hoc* structure | • come together through goodwill rather than planning<br>• who does what?<br>• when do we get together?<br>• how do we get on? |
| demands of the job | • large caseloads<br>• lack of continuity (therapists)<br>• community role of therapists<br>• differences between education and therapy<br>• timetabling<br>• full curriculum<br>• secondary curriculum<br>• the job is never finished | • not enough time to see all children<br>• nor for meetings<br>• difficult to see whole child<br>• how can therapy be integral?<br>• therapists have little say in curriculum<br>• constant interruptions |
| **People** | | |
| roles | • differences between teaching and therapy<br>• keeping roles separate (them and us syndrome)<br>• teachers (especially) are used to autonomy | • don't really know what each other can do<br>• effort to get to know<br>• if give away too many skills, might not be needed<br>• loss of autonomy<br>• can feel like a guest in each other's territory<br>• want to defend own priorities |
| personal | • differences in personalities and in amount prepared to change<br>• personal power struggles<br>• differing amount of commitment<br>• different views of teamwork<br>• having to work with whoever you are given | • don't always 'get on'<br>• feelings of not being in control<br>• lots of emotional energy needed to negotiate with each other<br>• people have their own agendas<br>• difficult to see things from another's perspective |
| demands of teamwork | • based on goodwill not on anything planned<br>• lack of training for teamwork (some are and some aren't)<br>• teachers and therapists aren't available at the same time<br>• monitoring each other's transferred skills | • individuals might not cooperate with each other<br>• communication doesn't always work<br>• don't know how to negotiate<br>• meetings are often snatched<br>• feel threatened by each other |

there differences between the way services function, but many of the therapists are part-time so that they are members of many different teams in different places. Working together under these circumstances can lead to conflicting priorities and potential misunderstandings. The serious under-resourcing of health and education contributes further difficulties and forces individuals to have to decide on priorities and argue over who pays for what. It is hard to be convinced that children's needs are sufficiently central. The general climate of markets and accountability makes collaboration difficult to achieve and while both sets of professionals are experiencing so much change it is easy to understand the automatic reaction to withdraw and regroup within separate services, rather than move forward with new ways to work together.

The demands of people's jobs create a considerable challenge for those who wish to collaborate. There is more than enough to do in terms of curriculum or therapy without trying to integrate the two, especially when, as in the secondary curriculum, integration is difficult to achieve. People get anxious when their roles are threatened in any way and it seems that most education and health professionals feel under threat at the moment and end up defending their territory and thus their own priorities for individual children.

Although the business literature (see Chapter 4) indicated that personalities are relatively unimportant in effective teamwork, evidence from Pear Tree School suggests that the personal dimension does affect what happens in practice. The construction of classroom teams in terms of balance is only partially in the hands of school managers. There is very little choice of members, especially in terms of therapist. There are several physiotherapists, but there is only one speech and language therapist and, since reorganisation, only one occupational therapist. Luckily both of these are keen to work collaboratively and already possess many skills to enable this to happen. Not all the teachers or physios are as eager or able.

From the table and the discussion, it can be concluded that individuals at Pear Tree School feel that they have many battles to fight and it is understandable why they feel anxious. There are, however, several strategies which exist at the school which prevent this anxiety from escalating to the point where collaborative teamwork is abandoned. One of the most important strategies appears to be active management support within the school and this is the first topic in the next chapter which concentrates on aspects of management.

## Summary and conclusions

This chapter began with an exploration of the management systems to attempt to find explanations regarding the difficulties faced by teachers and therapists trying to work together in collaborative multidisciplinary teams. Other aspects of collaboration were explored in a similar way and suggestions were made to try to provide ways of countering some of the 'brick walls' set up by frustrated team members. Team members are frequently heard to say that they desire to work together, but they quickly become overwhelmed by the systems that exist in special education; systems designed to support a way of working that is now changing. The 'brick walls' they set up are usually related to having no time to meet with team members or to therapists having such large caseloads that they race round the countryside ensuring they see their quota of patients. ('I can't wait until the teacher is free at 3.30 as I've got to get to another school before the end of the day.' 'I can't talk to the therapist when I'm trying to teach my class.')

Ways of working have changed (from only direct contact with children to adding consultancy with other adults) but many of the systems that support those ways of working have not. Few people would disagree with the claim that professionals working together in teams and partnerships is an effective way to meet the often complex needs of children with disabilities and difficulties. What they might disagree with is much of current practice. Everything seems to be set up to frustrate the ideal of collaboration. It is timely, therefore, for these systems to be reconsidered. Schools and services might like to ask themselves the following questions.

- Should therapists be employed by schools (colleges and centres)?
- Should there be one line of management for members of multidisciplinary teams?
- Should jobs be re-aligned to prevent individuals being members of a large number of teams?
- Should team members change their practices to enable more time to be spent together (and thus less directly with children)?

These are some of the initial questions that require to be asked if the changes in working practices are to be supported and flourish. At the moment, people are changing faster than the systems.

# Chapter 8

# Management aspects of multidisciplinary teamwork

In this, the last of the three chapters devoted to reporting the research into teachers and therapists working together that was carried out at Pear Tree School, aspects of management will be considered. The areas that will feature relate to what managers can do to support and promote the work of multidisciplinary teams and to the place of leaders in those teams. The questions that drove this part of the case study were the following.

- *What kinds of management support are important for effective collaborative multidisciplinary teamwork?*
- *Is it helpful to have a senior manager designated to support multidisciplinary teamwork?*
- *Should a therapist be included in the senior management team of the school?*
- *Are written contracts helpful in supporting collaboration?*
- *How important is it to have leaders of multidisciplinary teams?*
- *What might be a framework for collaborative multidisciplinary teamwork?*
- *What might be a model for collaborative multidisciplinary teamwork?*

## Active management support

It is very difficult for multidisciplinary teamwork to be collaborative unless there is specific support from management in the school. Data collected from a variety of informants and from observations at Pear Tree School suggest two main dimensions to this support: systems and facilitation. Table 8.1 is an attempt to draw together all this evidence into three categories: things that management do at Pear Tree; things they could do better and things which are outside the control of the school.

Looking across the first category, there appears to be a general recognition of the importance of collaborative teamwork and an appreciation of what that is likely to mean in practice. According to Bill, the head teacher, this has evolved over time and is constantly changing. He was responsible for instituting both the annual multidisciplinary meeting and the post of multidisciplinary coordinator early in his time as head teacher. The post of coordinator for multidisciplinary teamwork has had obvious positive features in raising the profile of the collaborative work between teachers and therapists, but it is difficult to judge whether the post has made any difference. When interviewed after a term at the school, Steve, a teacher in the senior department, did not know that a senior member of staff, Pam, was responsible for multidisciplinary work, although he

**Table 8.1** Management support

| Pear Tree School | Systems | Facilitation |
|---|---|---|
| do | • non-contact time<br>• coordinator for MDT<br>• contract for nurse<br>• written guidelines on MDT work<br>• annual MDT meeting<br>• twilight planning meetings<br>• consultation over class teams<br>• formal liaison with outside agencies<br>• communication channels<br>• motor groups | • delegation of responsibility for MDT to all teachers<br>• therapists explain roles at meetings<br>• therapists train classroom staff<br>• prioritising meetings<br>• open discussions<br>• therapists welcomed in school<br>• use of keen people to develop collaboration<br>• expectations that teachers and therapists will work together<br>• encouragement of exchange of skills |
| could do or could do better | • contracts with therapy services<br>• evaluation of teamwork<br>• have therapist on SMT<br>• induction<br>• joint record-keeping across education and therapy<br>• seating clinics<br>• clustering time | • therapists invited to education training sessions<br>• training for meetings/teamwork<br>• more time for meetings<br>• therapist involvement in class lists<br>• focused training for collaboration in secondary department |
| out of control of school | • therapy time<br>• therapy team members<br>• trust support<br>• resources etc. | • training in lifting (has been taken out of school therapists' hands)<br>• expectations of collaboration at service level |

MDT = multidisciplinary team
SMT = senior management team

did acknowledge that he had received a note reminding him to arrange his annual meeting with the therapists who work in his class. The head of the primary department was asked if Pam's role had made teamwork any easier and she replied: 'I don't think the present level of teamwork has come about because someone has been appointed to a specific role. I think it was there before but it just wasn't designated.' The head of the PMLD (profound and multiple learning difficulties) Department was not sure that having someone responsible for multidisciplinary teamwork meant that it worked any better for her. Others felt that it did contribute towards raising the profile of multidisciplinary teamwork in the school.

From the observations and discussions with both Pam and Bill, the head teacher, it appears that despite the reservations, the role has been instrumental in supporting the teamwork in the school. The therapists express appreciation of the formal channels for liaison and the way in which their work has become more integral to the life of the school and although the speech and language therapist complains about lack of time for meeting together, she says: 'There's a willingness on the part of the team and there's consultation in that we're having multidisciplinary meetings at least once a year. From that point of view it has improved.'

Responsibility for multidisciplinary teamwork is only part of Pam's job but she has been able to inject a sense of need to develop in this area, although of one initiative she says: 'We did try (formal evaluation) the first year the motor groups started. We did try to evaluate it. Oh God! it was like pulling teeth.' The head teacher appears to appreciate that creating the role 'got things going' but he is concerned that it has produced a situation where, because Pam is keen to work with therapists, she commands more of their time than is really equitable.

> I wonder now whether one person having that role is not such a good idea as it was three years back ... It becomes more than one person having the designated role. Human nature being what it is, if you can attract therapy to support what you are doing, then you're going to do it.
>
> (Head teacher)

Other systems supportive of teamwork apparent at Pear Tree School (see Table 8.1) include time given for meetings, through provision of non-contact time and twilight planning time. For the latter, there was agreement across the staff to translate one teacher education day into six twilight sessions, specifically for ongoing classroom planning for teachers and assistants. Generally meetings are viewed as important, although informants in this research were far from satisfied with the reality of what happens in practice. Either there is not enough time to meet,

> but the problem for any multidisciplinary team is the time factor, that you don't have time to share ideas and sit down and talk together then it doesn't ever work, not even if you are in the same building as Pam and I are, when we hardly ever see each other 'cos I'm flitting in and out.
>
> (Speech and language therapist)

or there are too many meetings and people feel overburdened.

> Any meeting that isn't going to be productive is knocked on the head ... By providing more time for evening slots for curriculum development and planning meetings, hopefully that takes some of the pressure off these frantic meetings that have to be held at lunchtimes.
>
> (Head teacher)

Striking the balance is hard and it appears that this has been partially achieved at Pear Tree School. There are not many timetabled meetings for therapists and classroom staff, although many happen in an *ad hoc* manner. At the beginning of the project, Pam suggested that there was room for a fortnightly or monthly meeting to bridge the gap between the annual multidisciplinary meeting and snatched conversations.

## Therapy representation in the senior management team

Although several ways in which there is active management support of teamwork at Pear Tree School have been highlighted, the second row of Table 8.1 contains aspects which were discussed with informants and which they agreed could be helpful, either by being improved or, in the case of suggesting that a therapist should be part of the senior management team, by being introduced. The introduction of this last idea provoked an interesting response from the head teacher.

Penny   What about having a therapist on the senior management team?

Bill   That's a difficult one, Penny, because a lot of the issues that are discussed are not relevant to the therapists.

Penny   How about having a meeting, say every three months?

Bill   We're already looking at changing the onus of the SMT and how that operates. One of the other problems is that there are three therapy teams and they've each got slightly different agendas in that – the fact that the physios are based here, technically to work with the children while they're on site; the OTs are community-based and tend to fit in as and when; the speech and language therapist is part-time.

Penny   But to a certain extent you could say that's so with teachers as well so you could appoint one of your therapists as the senior member to represent the others' views.

Bill   I certainly wouldn't discount that view – I could see how that could fit in quite well, assuming that they've got the time to be able to provide that commitment but that could perhaps be worked on.

It seemed at the time that Bill dismissed this idea as unworkable and there has been no move towards considering this since the conversation, despite his final comments. Is his reluctance to consider sharing management of the school with therapists a sign that he feels that 'togetherness' is good for class teachers but not for managers? Would he feel threatened by their presence on the senior management team? Does he feel they would be an anomaly because they belong to a different management system? Alternatively it may just simply be that he fears wasting therapists' time on irrelevancies or merely that it takes time to set up. Whatever the reasons, there seems to be an argument for having a formal forum for discussion at this level. Constraints on both sides could be better understood and it would indicate to education and health departments that teaching and therapy can be fully integrated at all levels in schools. It is only likely to work in a school where there is such a high presence of therapists. It would be less appropriate where therapists visit infrequently.

## Contracts

The other aspect of providing systems that was discussed with the head teacher and also with the speech and language therapist and the multidisciplinary teamwork coordinator is that pertaining to written contracts. It was suggested that writing down what was expected of both education and therapy would be beneficial, not only in terms of clarity of service provision, because it would provide a forum for exchange of ideas, so important to building understanding between disciplines. All three informants are generally in favour of contracts but could not really see them working in reality. This is Pam and Lena's discussion concerning classroom level contracts:

Pam     We've said that at an individual level, if we go and do an assessment and work that isn't followed up, there should have been a contract set up saying 'I will do that', 'what I did' and 'I've given to you' and 'you will now do'.

Lena     We do have these report forms which say 'our expectations of you basically are ...'

Pam     There's the downside of that (in) that if we have a contract saying 'I'll come into your classroom once a week ...'

Lena     We'd always be breaking it!

Pam     We all know the reality don't we? And the other side too, classes will say 'well, we're going out today.'

Lena     I think you have to keep away from too much paperwork. To be honest, I think if you had an written agreement with some of the teachers, I don't think it would be worth the paper it was written on.

Bill was a little evasive when asked about service level contracts, suggesting that they would be worth little as the health authority allocates input according to resources rather than need. He seemed to suggest that discussions would be useless as decisions had already been made concerning how much therapy Pear Tree School will get. When pushed a little, he was evasive.

Penny     Would a contract help? Is it something that has been considered?

Bill     It hasn't been considered because you step into a situation where *status quo* is maintained to a greater degree. You move into a situation where you're used to having physios around and used to having some sort of therapy input and because it has been provided by health, you don't tend to challenge it.

This is difficult to interpret. It sounds either as if Bill has never really considered contracts for therapy services, so his answer is just unprepared, or that he feels helpless in the face of the health authority machinery. He does go on to talk about a contract they have for the new school nurse, but his expansion of this point is more concerned with her post and her appointment than with the contract itself.

Conclusions at this point are that contracts have not really impinged on staff at Pear Tree, but this fact does not mean they have no use, as long as they are flexible and in fact evidence from elsewhere supports their importance. The actual process of discussing who can do what and what resources are needed and who will provide them can only aid in the attempt to work together.

## Leadership

Another aspect of active management support that would be useful to analyse is that pertaining to leadership and the part it appears to play in the way teamwork functions at Pear Tree. There are several different levels to this, school, multidisciplinary, classroom and a variety of different complications, especially the implications of running basically leaderless teams as is the case with multidisciplinary teams across the school.

Bill has a traditional leadership role in the school as head teacher, although he has little jurisdiction over the therapists who work in the building. Figure 8.2 is an attempt to sum up Bill's approach to leadership and the effect that it has on what happens in the school. The categories chosen relate to the literature on leadership and those which are thought to have an effect on teamwork in organisations. The remarks in the right hand column are based on interpretation of observations and interviews with Bill and others.

**Table 8.2** School level leadership at Pear Tree School

| Category | Remarks |
| --- | --- |
| team make-up | • the head teacher<br>• has no choice of therapists<br>• has no say in which therapist works in which class<br>• can create classroom teams<br>• considers personalities when putting teachers and assistants together<br>• doesn't look for complementary skills in teams<br>• must wait for natural wastage before choosing new team members |
| teamwork training | • training through demonstration concerning conducting meetings<br>• some time given to training of classroom staff by therapists, but none the other way<br>• minimal time spent in twilight sessions specifically on teambuilding<br>• encouragement of team members working side-by-side for mutual training on-the-job |
| school climate and structure | • climate which encourages open discussions<br>• staff are involved in decision-making<br>• democratic structure of committees and working parties<br>• therapists are marginally involved in drawing up class lists and timetabling<br>• curriculum groups can include relevant therapists, but involvement is not usual<br>• no therapists on SMT |
| communication | • direct lines of communication between head and all others<br>• coordinator for MDTwork<br>• therapists and teachers directly communicate<br>• annual MDT meeting<br>• 'corridor' meetings<br>• liaison points with outside agencies<br>• shared planning but no shared records |

| vision/direction | • mission statement contains reference to collaboration across disciplines<br>• specific MDT direction to school<br>• little evidence of planned development of MDTwork<br>• no formal evaluation |
|---|---|
| anticipation | • with little control over therapists and enormous structural changes in both health and education, it is very difficult to anticipate what is going to happen<br>• most management appears to be reactive rather than proactive |
| trust | • structures are provided and staff use them to enable MDTwork to function<br>• senior department does not fully understand importance of integrating education and therapy<br>• some staff need encouragement to work in MDT |
| managing growth | • at the moment, this is really managing change and diminishing resources rather than growth |
| sharing leadership with team members | • as classroom MDTs are basically leaderless, there is a natural sharing of leadership between members in some teams and little evidence of sharing at all in others<br>• curriculum groups enable co-leadership by teachers (therapists not usually included)<br>• classroom assistants have some share, especially some of the nursery nurses<br>• ideas appear to flow up and down the hierarchy |

It appears from this Table 8.2 that Bill is expected to lead a team under some difficult circumstances. Based on the opinions of informants, it seems that, on the whole, he is succeeding, although there are specific criticisms such as that expressed by Lena, the speech and language therapist concerning class lists.

> So, it happens every year, and I will go and say, 'Look, I'm not quite happy about that.' This year, I changed a few round and they listened to some of the changes and went with some of them and not others, which is reasonable. But it wasn't done in the initial consultation stage which is when it should have been done. So I still haven't won that battle. It still isn't an automatic thing, 'Right, we're looking at class lists, let's get the class teachers and the therapists together and try and sort out viable groups. The same goes for the timetable. The timetable will be set by the teachers for the teachers. In September, the physios will probably have the first bite of the cherry, then the OTs and then, because there is only me, I will come last. So when I've seen where they all are, I have to try and fit my timetable around what exists.
>
> (Speech and language therapist)

There is obviously still some way to go before the speech and language therapist feels fully part of the school team. She expresses other frustrations concerning her lack of involvement in, for instance, a policy and curriculum for spelling. Other therapists did not mention that they wanted to become more involved in either curriculum or management matters, so it is not possible to generalise on what Lena says. However, it appears that she feels her expertise is being under-used despite the limitations on her time in the school. There seems to be a delicate balance between consulting therapists and overloading them with matters which are not strictly therapy. Perhaps the answer is to invite them but allow them to make a decision about whether to attend. It maybe that integration of education and therapy will only come about if teachers and therapists are all involved in every aspect of school life.

## Leaderless teams

It can be said that, at classroom level, multidisciplinary teams are leaderless. It may be sensible for the class teacher to coordinate education and therapy as they have continuous contact with the children, but there is no formal recognition of this as a leadership role. There is in the case of teachers and assistants working together, but this does not extend to the team which includes therapists. No one person has responsibility for enabling the team to work, creating an atmosphere of openness, providing structures for communication, taking the rap when things go wrong and reviewing progress. These appear to be expected to happen naturally. All the business literature points to the importance of leaders to the success of high-performing teams. Adair (1986) even suggests that success is 50 per cent due to leadership and 50 per cent to the team's performance. So how can teams which cut across disciplines be effective without a leader? Are we being naive to expect this?

The answer is not as simple as the affirmative, partly because the therapists are members of several teams and are constantly moving in and out of different classrooms. It would also be difficult for anyone other than the teacher to be the teamleader because she or he remains more constant than the therapists. Although this may not pose problems, there may be occasions when a therapist in the team is more suited to leadership than the teacher. Despite the lack of one obvious answer, it would be fruitful to explore briefly what might happen if teachers were given the formal role of leadership of classroom-based multidisciplinary teams.

Team leadership is not synonymous with line management responsibility and infers no status hierarchy in a conventional sense. There is, however, a management role in coordinating the efforts of the team, keeping it on track, oiling communication channels and organising evaluations. But leading the team is more than this. If teachers were to take on this role, it would involve less tangible jobs such as creating a climate for success, motivating high performance, helping others to perform, holding the team together when they are apart as well as when they are together, connecting with the world outside the team, setting an example of excellence and celebrating success (Hastings et al. 1986).

Although it is not a formal role, Pam, the nursery teacher at Pear Tree School, does fulfil some of the duties of a team leader. As she is a member of the senior management team and is the coordinator for multidisciplinary teamwork, she has a seniority which makes leading the classroom team easier than for other more junior teachers. It is possible to argue, though, that what Pam does could formally be expected of others. In Table 8.3, the same headings have been used as for considering the whole-school leadership to enable an analysis of the multidisciplinary teamwork in Pam's class.

**Table 8.3** Leadership in the nursery at Pear Tree School

| Category | Remarks |
| --- | --- |
| team make-up | • little choice in team members, although long-standing, good partnership between Pam and Sue (nursery nurse) has been built on<br>• therapists interested in motor work followed Pam when she changed age groups, so self-selecting<br>• keen team created, although unplanned |
| teamwork training | • mostly informal functional training by therapists when need arises<br>• working alongside each other, thus informal mutual training on the job<br>• some formal sessions e.g. lifting/feeding<br>• no training in teamwork skills |
| climate and structure | • team members can move in and out of the classroom freely<br>• climate of openness, opinions expressed freely<br>• everyone in team appears to have an equal voice<br>• Pam describes her style as 'up front'<br>• little conflict<br>• therapists express enjoyment of working in the nursery<br>• only formal structures are annual meeting for whole team and weekly planning with assistants (no therapists) |
| communication | • members are available to talk most of the time<br>• mostly informal through working side-by-side<br>• snatched meetings at break times<br>• some joint planning with therapists<br>• few regular written reports from therapists<br>• education and therapy have separate records |
| vision/direction | • believes 'teamwork is a philosophy'<br>• keen to develop teamwork and integrated experiences for children<br>• gives example of sharing to other members<br>• class has a mission statement |
| anticipation | • senior member of staff has whole organisation view which helps anticipation<br>• no evidence of deliberate anticipation to encourage continuing high performance |
| trust | • team members work without constant supervision<br>• specialist roles are encouraged e.g. Sue's responsibility for positioning children in physio equipment |
| managing change/growth | • Pam appears to offer support for changes at classroom level e.g. involving team members and giving time for discussion<br>• the growth of team ability is managed in a somewhat *ad hoc* manner<br>• little formal evaluation of team's work |
| sharing leadership | • opinions of team members welcomed<br>• individual abilities recognised and utilised<br>• different people take the lead where their specialisms are needed<br>• Sue often left in charge (even when another teacher is present)<br>• no evidence of discussion of sharing leadership |

From Table 8.3, it could be argued that it would not be difficult for Pam to move into the formal role of leader of the multidisciplinary classroom team. She would need to become more conscious of some of the facilitation aspects of the leadership role, develop further structures to enable full collaboration and most importantly set an evaluation system in action. She does, however, create a climate within which teamwork can flourish, she communicates regularly with all members, shares her expertise, uses that of others, trusts team members to get on with their jobs and supports change.

So how possible would it be to transfer this to other teachers in the school? All teachers in special schools are used to working with assistants. It could not be argued that they are all skilled at leading that team of two, but it is certainly a position from which more developed leadership skills can be added. There appears to be some leadership training available in education for those in traditional management positions such as heads and deputies, but it would be very difficult for class teachers to fulfil this role without some form of training or, at least, the opportunity to discuss how to lead effective teams.

## A framework for multidisciplinary teamwork

Over Chapters 6, 7 and 8 it has been suggested that there are two basic aspects to teamwork: systems and people. Systems appear to be unlikely to create effective teamwork entirely on their own. The commitment of individuals to sharing is important to make the systems work. Committed individuals can, however, be effective in their teamwork, at child level, even if they have little in the way of systems to back them up. Pear Tree School appears to have quite well developed internal systems as well as many individuals who are convinced of the worth of teamwork, prepared to work to enable it to flourish. They are much frustrated by external systems and a climate which can be characterised by marketisation and competitiveness rather than cooperation and collaboration, yet they are able to work together effectively, at least in the primary department.

There seem to be several aspects of the systems and people where things can go right or wrong which can affect the outcome in terms of how effectively the team performs. Figure 8.1 is an attempt to represent the main parts.

Relating Figure 8.1 directly to Pear Tree School provides the following summary. The external climate is one of fundamental change which has caused members of individual services to feel threatened. It is market driven where competition is expected although collaboration is the rhetoric. Health and

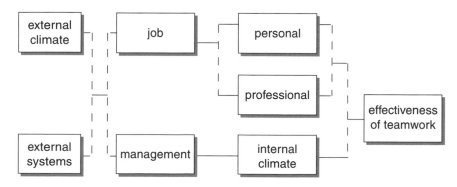

**Figure 8.1** The constituent parts of teamwork

education work separately from each other, though as was heard from informants, there are some attempts to form groups across the disciplines. Cooperation between services is generally quite good, though there is frustration at transition points (especially out of the school). The job expected to be carried out by teachers, therapists and teaching assistants at school level is rendered considerably more difficult through bureaucratic demands, large caseloads and dwindling resources. Management at school level at Pear Tree is generally supportive of teamwork, enabling non-contact time for classroom staff and providing systems for teachers and therapists to work together. The internal climate is generally one of openness and there is involvement of individuals in school development. Therapists are not as involved in this development as some would like. Many individuals are committed to teamwork, both professionally and personally, although it is more pronounced in the primary department than anywhere else in the school. Some individuals have good teamwork skills, though there is evidence of others who could usefully develop these. The result of all this is broadly effective teamwork, especially where staff use motor education as the base of their work (see Chapter 6). The main area of criticism that has been presented has been in the general lack of an evaluation process, so that practice can develop in the future.

In Chapters 6 to 8 of this book, various aspects of the multidisciplinary teamwork at Pear Tree School have been explored in an attempt to provide a conceptual framework within which to understand some of the problems and possibilities for teams of teacher and therapists to work together. It will be helpful in the final section of this chapter to draw all these together alongside ideas from other sources to provide a possible model of effective multidisciplinary teamwork practice.

# A model of effective multidisciplinary teamwork

## Joint strategy

Starting from a strategic level, effective multidisciplinary teamwork requires joint work between directors of services or their representatives. There are examples of joint strategic planning groups around the country. Some are successful in bringing together two or three agencies, but few manage to provide a forum for representatives of all services involved in schools to plan how to work together. Some nominally include services, but attendance at joint meetings is sporadic and thus relationships do not develop as deeply as is necessary for collaboration. Joint work is rarely a priority for individual services so commitment to joint meetings is often low.

## Senior managers

At all levels of joint work (including strategic levels), senior people are needed to make sure that multidisciplinary teamwork is fully supported. If it is part of the job description of a senior manager to facilitate others working together then the systems needed for this are more likely to be in place. Having a forum for senior managers to come together to discuss and work out strategies for supporting front-line collaboration would also be helpful.

## Contracts

Service level agreements and workplace level contracts can be useful, especially if they are drawn up jointly and are flexible. Rigid contracts are difficult to honour on occasions and that can lead to bad feeling. Flexible jointly written contracts and agreements can be very supportive, partly through the process of drawing them up, when information about services and individuals' expertise can be exchanged, and partly through the clarity of the content.

## Systems

There are a variety of systems that are likely to support effective multidisciplinary teamwork. One of the most important is a communication system. Paperwork communication requires joint planning of format and content by the team members. The process of agreeing how the system is to work can be very supportive of future work together. Joint record-keeping, for example, is only likely to become a reality if all agencies discuss its process and content and how duplication can be avoided or deliberately planned in.

## Meetings

Face-to-face communication, usually in some form of meeting, also requires careful joint planning as well as commitment to put aside time for attendance. Multidisciplinary meetings should be in evidence at all levels from strategic level to service level and fieldworker level. It is impossible to run a multidisciplinary team unless time is set aside for members to talk together. Even those people who only liaise with each other occasionally need time to talk about their liaison.

## Joint working

Those team members who work directly with the child, even if only for some of the time, need to work together. This could take the form of joint problem solving over identifying or meeting the needs of children (clients), or it could be one team member observing another in order to learn how to identify or meet the needs of children (clients). What is important is that team members know how each other works and can train each other in aspects of their own work.

## Joint training

Apart from coaching each other in the classroom (workplace), there should be opportunities for team members to attend training together. This can enable members to hear the same message at the same time and also encourage them to discuss what they have heard and how it applies to their joint situation. It also avoids the situation where one team member is struggling to 'cascade' the training to others or persuade them of the need to develop practice.

## Management of time

Although many members of multidisciplinary teams understand the need to work together and talk together, they are often frustrated by the lack of time given to those activities. Across the board there is a need to reallocate time to maximise its use. Caseloads will need to be viewed differently if the greatest number of children (clients) are to have their needs met. Clustering time was suggested in Chapter 7 and this is one way in which time can be managed in a different way to facilitate joint work and meetings. Traditional ways of working will need to be re-examined and changed so that collaboration is possible.

## Consultancy

One of the ways in which tradition is changing is for therapists (and members of other agencies) to work more as consultants instead of entirely as front-line workers. Thus they reduce the time spent with individual children (clients) and increase the time spent advising teachers and assistants (careworkers). This enables them to influence more people and indirectly meet the needs of more children (clients).

## Conclusions

Multidisciplinary teamwork has been gradually changing over the last 30 to 40 years. It is a very slow process partly because no one person or body is responsible for all its facets. Certain individuals and certain teams have been very successful in working together effectively, but there are still too many frustrated people who either do not know how to work with others or who know only too well but are thwarted by circumstances. Certain practical suggestions have been made in this book which have arisen from the examination of practice in schools, colleges and centres such as Pear Tree School, but the single most difficult factor to change is *attitude*. Individuals at all levels need to be committed to the importance of collaborative multidisciplinary teamwork if it is to work. If people do not believe that needs are more likely to be met if agencies work together then joint working will never become a reality. There will always be excuses (particularly that there is no time). Change people's attitude and changing practice will be relatively easy.

# Chapter 9

# Teacher and assistant partnerships

Over the past few years, the partnerships of teachers and teaching assistants have grown enormously from a few examples of people working together in nurseries and special schools to complex networks of SENCOs, class teachers, subjects teachers and teaching assistants in almost every school in the country. The inclusion of pupils with special educational needs (SEN) is reliant upon a whole army of assistants and now added to these are the many people who are supporting teachers and pupils for the Literacy and Numeracy Strategies. This growth has been largely unplanned with the consequence that there is wide variation in the quality of the partnerships between teachers and assistants.

The case studies upon which this chapter is based are numerous. Most come from the Mencap research which was reported in *On a Wing and a Prayer* (Mencap 1999) but some come from the project which is featured later in this book on consultants supporting LEAs through Change (Chapter 10), and concerns assistants working within the Literacy and Numeracy Strategies in a rural educational action zone (EAZ) in 'South' LEA. Other examples come from many years of personal experience or have been gleaned from colleagues.

These are the questions that are addressed in this chapter.

- *What are the complementary roles of teachers and teaching assistants?*
- *How can working hours be managed to enable teachers and assistants to be given time to talk and plan together?*
- *How can communication between teachers and assistants be most effective in terms of helping pupils to learn?*
- *How can teachers and assistants work together effectively?*
- *What kinds of support do assistants require in order to carry out their work effectively?*

Vocabulary is difficult in this rapidly changing world. The latest DfEE documents refer to 'teaching assistants' but at the time of the research reported in this chapter, the term 'learning support assistants (LSAs)' was popular. For the purposes of this chapter, these two terms should be regarded as synonymous.

Before attempting to answer the questions set out above, it is necessary to give a brief outline of the two sources of data for this chapter.

## The Mencap project

Mencap commissioned the Learning Difficulties Team at the University of Birmingham to undertake research to ascertain the role of LSAs in the inclusive learning of pupils with severe and profound and multiple learning difficulties

(SLD and PMLD). A telephone survey of 60 schools was used to establish the models of inclusion for pupils with SLD and PMLD. From the 60 schools, making sure they represented the 9 models identified, 24 schools were chosen to be the subjects of case studies. All these schools were visited for interviews and observations to be carried out over the course of a day. Four schools deemed of particular interest were revisited for a further two days each. During the research, 43 LSAs and 25 teachers were interviewed and most of them were also observed at work.

## South EAZ

South EAZ was the subject of a case study conducted during a consultancy set up to develop the role and training of assistants funded by the EAZ to work in schools for the Literacy and Numeracy Strategies (see Chapter 11). Initial meetings with head teachers and assistants were held to develop an induction pack for assistants. A further set of three meetings of class teachers and assistants who normally work together was used to write a follow-up pack for teachers and assistants to work on jointly to help develop their partnerships.

## Relationships and roles

In the previous chapter, the relationship between teachers and therapist was seen to be more-or-less equal. Each is a trained professional and has been educated using a body of knowledge specific to their discipline. As was seen, there were difficulties that arise from two different disciplines trying to work together. The difficulties faced by teachers and assistants working together are both similar and very different. There are still the challenges of finding time to talk and defining roles, but as assistants do not, on the whole, have prior training before they take on their first jobs, the challenge here relates to inequality of status rather than equality. Teachers have studied for four years in higher education and many assistants have studies little beyond their schooling, although some have had nursery nurse training and some take up training courses during their careers.

Of course equality of professional status is not vital to an effective partnership but it does take time and effort to get right the fundamentals of relationships and roles. How much responsibility can be given to assistants who are not only largely untrained, but also paid considerably less than teachers? What sort of roles can they be given that will be supportive to the teaching and learning that goes on in classrooms? These are not easy questions to answer, but get these two right and all other aspects of the partnership will be much easier to achieve.

Clarity of role is crucial for everyone working in organisations such as schools. Status actually becomes of little importance if everyone feels that they have a role that is particular to them and they are appreciated when they carry it out. Examples of the comments from LSAs in the Mencap research illustrate the frustration some feel when they are not sure of their role.

---

**CASE STUDY**

A new head teacher in an urban special school inherited a group of somewhat 'militant' assistants who kept very strictly to the hours they were paid for, refused to undertake duties they considered outside their brief and generally stirred up discontent around the school. The head teacher grasped the situation as soon as she could by negotiating new contracts with the assistants. Roles were set out clearly and everyone agreed to undertake much more than they had before. Hours were also clearly stated although this prompted many to stretch these further than they ever did previously. When the changes had been completed, there was now a workforce who felt appreciated and valued. They had roles that gave them special responsibilities for jobs that would not have been done or would have fallen on teachers, for example keeping the staff room notice boards tidy and up-to-date, or making sure the video equipment was in working order and in the right place at the right time. The head teacher reported that, on occasions, she had to insist assistants went home when they were still in school an hour and a half after the children had left. This was a complete turn-around from the situation she had inherited.

---

- 'I'd like to know my place in the classroom, for example, how much to give other children or can I make decisions?'
- 'The role is not defined.'
- 'Who's my boss?'
- 'Some staff see us as threats.'

The last comment indicates the difficulties teachers have when they are not sure of the role of the LSA. Generally teachers are not used to having other adults in the room with them and may feel uncomfortable, especially if they have not had a chance to learn how to make the best use of the extra help. Often LSAs accompany a child with SEN and having a child in the class whose needs are different from other pupils may be stressful in itself without the presence of another adult to employ gainfully. Some teachers see an LSA as a legitimate way of passing on to someone else the responsibility for meeting the needs of the child with SEN. Some more comments from the Mencap project help to illustrate this.

- 'Some teachers find it difficult to relate to a child with SEN.'
- 'Sometimes there are no concessions to the pupil with SLD.'
- 'Teachers aren't trained in SEN or working in teams.'
- 'Sometimes the LSA does everything including planning.'
- 'Some teachers just let the LSA get on with it – they don't know how to break things down for Lisa.'

So who has what role in the partnership between teachers and assistants? Of course, there is no one answer. It depends completely on the situation, but what is important is that the partners are given time to discuss what is right for them.

Balance is also important. For both partners to feel good about the relationship, it is helpful for the teacher to be seen to be ultimately responsible for the learning of all pupils in the class, but to share the day-to-day responsibility with the assistant. For example, assistants deserve to be included in planning what goes on in the classroom, though they should not be left to plan for and teach certain pupils completely on their own. Nor should they enter a classroom completely unprepared for what is going to happen. One LSA said 'I may go into a lesson on a wing and a prayer', rather than following careful planning with the teacher: a situation which is totally unsatisfactory.

It has been stressed that teachers and assistants need time to talk together to sort out their complementary roles in the classroom and the following audit which was developed with teachers and assistants in South EAZ may be helpful for partners wishing to do this.

- Estimate how much time you spend together planning, reporting back, in meetings and in children's reviews in an average week.
- Make a note of the sort of topics covered.
- Gather together any planning and record sheets you use.
- Describe your roles in specific lessons.
- Estimate how long you spent on different parts of your roles (just the bits that are to do with working together, e.g. how long the teacher spends on writing plans for LSAs, or how long LSAs spend on filling in record sheets).
- Estimate how much time is spent on unplanned activities (e.g. a sick child).
- Estimate how much time LSAs spend not actually supporting anyone (e.g. teacher-led activity when LSAs are listening, but are not actually supporting an individual or a group.)
- Estimate how much time LSAs feel that they are 'teaching' (e.g. rephrasing something in the lesson; asking questions to make children think; explaining why they have got something wrong).
- Estimate how much time LSAs are supporting individuals or groups (e.g. keeping a child on task; pointing out the different steps of a task).
- Estimate how much time LSAs are supporting the teacher (e.g. 'controlling' disruptive pupils; conveying to the teacher when pupils don't understand or need a different approach).

Estimating how much time is spent on different aspects of the work of LSAs can help in the joint reflection of how to develop the effectiveness of that work.

## Aspects of time

Finding time to conduct an audit such as that can be very difficult, especially if assistants are working part-time. In South LEA assistants, paid for by EAZ funds, can be employed for only a few hours a week and might arrive and depart part way through the morning. They may work with several teachers and have no paid for time other than the hours when they are to work with pupils. They also might have other jobs within the school such as midday supervising or bus escorting. This is a very unsatisfactory situation for everyone. The pupils are unlikely to get a coordinated response if there is no time for teachers and assistants to talk together. Teachers are unlikely to get the best out of the assistants and the assistants are unlikely to know what they are supposed to be doing. There are, of course, exceptions to this and some assistants are working very effectively with little time for talking with teachers, especially those who are following a prescribed programme such as those attached to the Literacy Strategy.

The situation where everyone seems to benefit is that when assistants are permanent members of staff, working full-time with preferably only one teacher or one department (in a secondary school). This situation means that they can be full members of the school staff, arrive a little before the pupils arrive and leave a little after they depart. In this way time can be found for briefing meetings and feedback as part of the working day. Training days which are attended by all full-time members of staff can contain time set aside for planning and for teachers and assistants to review and plan to improve their working together. It may seem attractive to employ several people to help with the Literacy or Numeracy Strategies, but it may not work in practice. One LSA in South EAZ said that she worked with 13 different teachers. It is no wonder she could not find time to plan with them all!

One of the primary schools that was part of the Mencap project had one way of approaching time for planning.

---

**CASE STUDY**

The special school for pupils with SLD and PMLD had been closed and classes of pupils with SLD and PMLD had been established in three 'resourced' primary schools in the locality. 'Meadow Bank' Primary School had a class of six pupils with SLD and PMLD, one teacher relocated from the special school and five LSAs. Pupils were allocated to mainstream classes and spent at least 50 per cent of their time with their more able peers, mostly supported by an LSA. The remaining time was spent in the resource class with the specialist teacher.

In order for there to be sufficient planning between the different staff involved with the pupils with SLD and PMLD, the resource class teacher was responsible for liaising with class teachers after school which she then passed on to the LSAs first thing every morning. The pupils with SLD and PMLD were met from the buses by their non-disabled peers who escorted them into the mainstream class. They remained there unsupported for the first half hour of the day while the LSAs were planning with the resource class teacher. In the planning session, all six children's needs were discussed and each LSA knew what was her role for the rest of the day. Long-term planning was carried out every half term at a time agreed by all involved, but out of school hours.

---

Meadow Bank School had achieved involvement for LSAs both in long-term planning and in short-term daily planning. In this way they:

- are valued for their knowledge and skills;
- are sharing responsibility for children's learning with teachers;
- understand the purpose of the activities;
- have 'ownership' of the plans;
- feel part of the team who meet the needs of the pupils;
- are achieving far more than 'minding' pupils who have special needs.

Other examples of ways of creating time for teachers and teaching assistants to plan and feedback are:

- devoting one of the training days to planning by not using the day itself, but dividing it into half hours that can be added to the end or the beginning of the school day throughout the year;
- negotiating with teaching assistants to finish 10 minutes earlier on four days a week in exchange for 40 minutes planning before or after school on the fifth day;
- employing assistants to work, for example, 15 hours a week but only 14 are to be spent directly with the pupils.

If these ideas are put together with earlier suggestions regarding employing fewer assistants for longer in the week or attaching them to departments rather than pupils, it should be possible to create a situation where teachers and assistants can spend at least the equivalent of an hour a week talking together.

## Communicating

Once time for talking has been established, even minimally, consideration can be given to the content of the talk. What are teachers and assistants communicating about and how can the communication be most effective in terms of helping pupils to learn?

There seem to be several purposes to communication between teachers and assistants:

- to exchange professional information about each other;
- to establish common aims and goals;
- to decide upon each other's roles;
- to agree how best to work together;
- to discuss the strengths and needs of individual pupils;
- to plan what to help pupils to learn next;
- to explore possible teaching approaches and plan which to use;
- to feedback to each other on the success of their plans;
- to evaluate how well they are working together.

The first two bullet points will perhaps only be necessary when setting up a new partnership, whereas the rest should form a cycle that will be used time and time again. From the case studies it can be said that the most effective partnerships make good use of this cycle, although some of them may not spend sufficient time on evaluating how well they have worked together and how they should alter what they are doing to maximise effectiveness. Some partners never give time for general evaluation although they may be extremely good at evaluating pupil progress.

Once the purposes of communicating are established, there seem to be two main ways achieving them:

- in face-to-face meetings
- through paperwork.

The dominance in a partnership of communicating via either meetings or paperwork depends largely upon the amount of time given to communicating. If there is little time for face-to-face talking then it is vital to achieve the most effective paper communications possible. This does not necessarily mean the creation of huge files of notes and records as these may even impede communication. Evidence from the case study partnerships suggest that effective written communications have a format that has been devised between the partners and contains elements that directly affect teaching and learning. Each of the partners may want to keep their individual notebooks to which they can refer back if necessary, but the shared paperwork is best kept very succinct and focused.

The following questions may be helpful when evaluating current paperwork such as planning and recording sheets. Any evaluation should be carried out by teachers and assistants together.

- What paperwork do we have at present?
- Who contributes to it?
- Who works from it?
- What does it cover?
- Where is it kept?
- How often is it used?
- Can we easily understand what to do from planning sheets?
- Can we easily see pupil achievements and progress from recording sheets?
- Are information sheets clear and unequivocal?
- Is it effective in contributing to the quality of teaching and learning?
- What might we want to change?

Although some communication will quite rightly be through the written word, it is vital to have face-to-face meetings where partners talk to each other. Being handed a piece of paper containing today's lesson plans is not sufficient for an effective partnership between teachers and assistants. The planning sheet can serve as a reminder of plans that have already been discussed, or provide the detail of the broad ideas discussed previously but they should never have content that is a surprise to the assistant. Many assistants have said that they could have gathered resources or had ideas for differentiation if only they had known the topic of the lesson prior to its start. Not giving assistants a chance to do that is not only wasting their talents, but also likely to give the pupil an experience that is less than satisfactory.

Face-to-face communication between teachers and assistants is usually through formal or semi-formal meetings, although much can be discussed informally over a cup of coffee, snatched between lessons, in the corridor or even with the child in class time. Both planning and recording can be very effectively conducted within lessons, especially if pupils are also directly involved. Consulting pupils over their learning in a three-way conversation can lead to both good teaching and effective learning. Sometimes this can be cursory such as in verbal feedback in a plenary session or planning an individual's learning goals. The sequence of Plan-Do-Review can be supportive of fully shared face-to-face communication between teachers, assistants and learners. For example:

---

**CASE STUDY**

Sam, supported by a teaching assistant, was planning what he was going to learn during the extended writing lesson with his teacher. As he was helped to plan not only the content of his writing, but also the strategy for learning spellings he was going to practice, much information was passed between the two adults. At the end of the lesson, Sam reported back briefly on what he had written and how well he managed with the learning strategy he was using. Together they all planned what he would do next time. The assistant checked with Sam what she wrote on his record sheet before the episode was complete.

---

Exchanges such as these are only fully effective when topics such as learning strategies have been more fully discussed between the partners, either as part of a training day or in a meeting set aside for exploring such issues. The time spent in discussion can be very profitable, not only to tease out the different aspects of the topic under discussion, but also for getting to know the views, experience and expertise of the participants.

Although exchange of views can be part of the agenda, usually formal meetings are used for the following purposes:

- giving information
- making decisions
- solving problems.

On the whole participants in meetings feel satisfied if at least one of the above is achieved. Other things people like about effective meetings are:

- clear definitions of members' roles and aims of the meeting;
- starting and ending on time;
- being listened to and having their opinions respected;
- an informal relaxed atmosphere;
- good preparation with relevant materials provided before the meeting;
- commitment of all members to the aims of the meeting;
- a record of the meeting (which may be formal minutes);
- occasionally reviewing the way meetings are run;
- someone who takes responsibility for getting through the agenda;

- feeling that meeting with your partner(s) has achieved something that couldn't have been achieved without meeting.

Participants in the development of the training package for teacher and assistant partners in South EAZ were sceptical about being able to find enough time even for informal meetings about immediate and practical things, let alone more formal meetings where views are expressed and decisions made over teaching and learning. However, by the end of the project, they were recognising the importance of enabling them to happen and celebrating the difference that meetings and developing paperwork together had made to their work.

## Working together

Creating good lines of communication, vital though it is, is only one aspect of the way in which teachers and assistants work together. Sometimes they are physically working side-by-side doing the same things, sometimes doing different things. Sometimes they are working apart trusting each other to keep to the plans they have agreed or sometimes they are fulfilling complementary roles based on a general plan conceived of together.

From the Mencap research it is possible to present a list of what effective LSAs do to encourage the inclusive learning of pupils with SLD and PMLD. Although the list refers to a specific group of pupils it corresponds well with other research carried out at a similar time but with a more diverse group of children (Farrell *et al.* 1999).

An effective LSA:

- works with groups of pupils to encourage interaction between them (even when primarily acting as a mediator for one child);
- enables pupils to participate in lessons through a variety of means (such as repeating parts of the lesson using simpler vocabulary or using different resources);
- is sensitive to (and constantly adjusts) the amount of support that is needed to enable the child or children to learn;
- shares responsibility with teachers for planning and working with individual pupils;
- has a clearly defined role in the classroom;
- is given time for planning and reporting back;
- is adequately resourced to meet pupils' needs;
- has access to good communication systems;
- is part of a team approach to meeting special needs;
- has opportunities for relevant training on meeting pupils' needs;
- has a career structure within which training and experience are recognised.

One of the most important aspects of this list, in terms of the partnership between teachers and assistants, is the way in which LSAs and teachers share responsibility for the children's learning. Not only do they plan together and generally have time to talk, but they both work with the pupils with SEN, giving them the benefit of two focused adults. Good LSAs do not become a barrier between the child or children they are supporting and the rest of the class, including the teacher. They encourage interactions of all kinds and facilitate communication.

Effective LSAs usually work with several pupils, even if they are nominally assigned to one. By doing this, they reduce the stigma for those children who are singled out as needing help; they can be available for any child who needs support however minor; and they can encourage pupils to work together. By working with groups of pupils, they can also reduce the amount of dependence the pupils with SEN have on adult support, encouraging them to develop strategies for learning that are self-reliant. There are some children with very complex needs, particularly those who are deafblind, who may need a constant 'intervenor' through which they can access the world, but even these people will be working towards withdrawing support gradually to encourage greater independence.

One of the difficulties voiced by several assistants throughout the case studies have been that sometimes teachers can give too much responsibility to assistants, especially with those pupils with more severe difficulties.

---

**CASE STUDY**

One infant school teacher said that she was having a child with Down's Syndrome in her class but she didn't think she would be having much to do with him as he had his own assistant. It was gently suggested to her that she would ultimately be responsible for him and that she could not leave his learning to the assistant. After a few weeks, she reported back that she was finding William very interesting, but very time-consuming. It transpired that she was hardly using the assistant at all with William, but taking responsibility for him completely. It was suggested that she should plan jointly with the assistant and together they could attempt to meet his needs. After a few more weeks, the teacher reported a much better balance in her work and the assistant's work with William and some progress in his learning. She expressed how difficult it was to manage someone else in the classroom while trying to teach the whole class.

---

Managing assistants is, of course, exactly what teachers are being asked to do with little or no training. Tim Brighouse in the *Times Educational Supplement* (2000) forecasts that in 2050, the teacher will be an expert highly paid person 'orchestrating a cast of teaching assistants, teaching associates, resident and visiting artists and scientists and business people, not to mention personal fitness mentors' (p. 15). He suggests that primary teachers today would rather have a trained assistant than a slightly smaller class. There may be a very strong case for both, especially when the class includes children with complex needs.

There are some potential difficulties with this vision of teachers managing assistants, not because this is not what teachers are trained to do at the moment, but because the principle of one person managing another is hard to reconcile with a partnership between two people working together. This can be a delicate relationship, especially when the quotations from the beginning of this chapter are recalled, for example, 'I want to know, who's my boss?' The situation is more complex than it appears to be. True partnership, as has been seen from this book, it about sharing, joint-ness, trust and communication. One person should not need to or be required to dominate the other, or even tell the other what to do. Equality cannot necessarily be achieved, but equity can. Each voice is important and should be heard on equal terms, whether or not the partners have similar status. This point, is, of course, relevant for parent partnership which is explored in Chapter 12.

So the dilemma for teachers is, 'How can I manage this situation while enabling equity between partners in the classroom?' Many teachers feel that it is their job to plan for all the learning in the classroom and then inform the assistants what they are going to do within that plan. Some tell assistants in advance, but some, as we have seen, tell them seconds before they are expected to respond. Effective partners do not work in this way. Not only do they plan together in advance, but they agree jointly on roles in the learning process. It is an agreement between two people who have complementary roles to play and does not depend on dominance of one over the other.

The previous chapter contained discussion of team structure and leadership and the same arguments are important here, especially because one partner seems to be expected to lead and manage the other. Leadership is still important, but that leadership does not necessarily have to be confined to teachers all the time. There may be important times when it is natural for the assistant to take the lead. For example, assistants who have very detailed knowledge of individual pupils may be the best person to take the lead in annual reviews or in meetings where those pupils are the subject of in-depth discussion. It can be frustrating for assistants if they are either not involved at all (which is not unusual) or not fully consulted in such situations.

It maybe that assistants are performing at least some of the duties of a keyworker in that they have regular long-term contact with the child and family; are the source of information to the family about what school provides for the child; identify the child's strengths and needs (in collaboration with teachers); advise and support the child; coordinate the services the child receives, especially if these stem from different agencies; and act as an advocate for or with the child. These are potentially vital and responsible activities and deserve recognition, support and training.

## Support and training

Support and training were seen as important to the LSAs in the Mencap research. Table 9.1 contains the results of an analysis of the responses of the 25 LSAs in the first round of the case studies to the question 'What kind of support do you need (or have you had) to help you to be an effective LSA?' There was more than one response from each LSA, that is 125 in all.

Formal training was seen as important by the LSAs. They cited examples of induction and INSET days while in their jobs, as well as previous training such as nursery nurse training. Several said that there was not enough training, or not

**Table 9.1** Support valued by LSAs

| Nature of support | Responses (out of 125) |
|---|---|
| opportunities to learn from others | 39 |
| opportunities to train | 21 |
| good communications | 16 |
| previous experience and confidence | 15 |
| support from others | 14 |
| whole-school positive approach and consistency | 10 |
| career possibilities and recognition | 6 |
| adequate staff and resources | 4 |

enough that was relevant to them, but they still cited it as being important to the development of their role. It is not surprising, however, that they felt that learning through watching and talking to other people was even more important as this was part of their everyday job. Some were very enthusiastic about how invaluable it can be to watch others at work and talk to parents about their children.

Interestingly, previous experience was mentioned fewer than half as many times as gaining experience on the job, although 'being a mum' was cited several times. Extrapolating from these data, it appears that previous experience of children, with opportunities to learn on the job, coupled with more formal training, are seen as leading to an effective LSA.

The other support mechanisms include building up networks and teams of people, good communication between schools and people and a whole-school approach to working with pupils with SEN, including consistency in that approach. A few LSAs mentioned the need for a career path for them with a better pay structure. One or two had some strong points to make about the inadequacy of their pay, although many others did not mention it at all.

This small extract from the Mencap research shows the importance assistants place on working together with other people. They value being part of a team and find that learning from working alongside and watching others is most effective. It may be that as few assistants have experienced further or higher education, they are less interested in college training. Interestingly, when the 24 teachers were asked the same question about what support LSAs needed to be effective, they cited formal training as being more important than learning 'on the job' (9 phrases relating to learning from others and 17 relating to training). Perhaps this reflects their greater knowledge and experience of more formal training.

Alongside opportunities for training, formal or informal, one of the difficulties facing assistants is the lack of career structure and possibilities for moving up a ladder of experience. There are no nationally agreed salary, training or career systems, which makes it difficult for individual schools to encourage assistants to become full members of classroom teams. Many assistants move in and out of classes, they are employed for a few hours a day, have little training and no prospects of improving their status.

## Conclusions

The partnerships between teachers and assistants that are effective, have to struggle in the face of many adversities. When they work, the partners are supportive of each other and of the children. They have sufficient time to plan and evaluate how best to work as well as efficient systems for communication. They use each other's experience and expertise well, responding to the needs of the pupils and enabling everyone in their care to learn to the best of their abilities.

In reality though, many assistants are undervalued and can even be seen as an 'intrusion' in the classroom (Thomas 1992). Teachers, who are already seriously stretched through excess paperwork, the pressures of standards and targets and relentless curriculum demands, can find the presence of other adults in the room just too much to manage. The current policy of attaching assistants to pupils through their statement of special educational needs can be compounding the difficulties felt by teachers. These 'other adults' are all too easily regarded as 'add-ons': yet another thing that demands scarce time. If funding was such that schools could employ assistants as a matter of course, rather in the way special schools work, then these people could become full members of the school team. It is tempting to think that it is a better deal to have six people for one hour each than one person for six hours, but in terms of effective support of pupils' learning needs and the satisfaction of the people themselves, it is not.

Much has been learned recently about teachers working with assistants. Good practice can be found in both special and mainstream schools and in both, what seems to be crucial is the quality of the partnership between these two groups of people. This partnership appears to be built upon mutual respect and trust, support of each other and a shared understanding of how to meet pupils' learning needs. It is underpinned by clear lines of communication, commitment to providing planning time and the security of a permanent job supported through a career structure and relevant training. Nothing less is sufficient.

# Chapter 10

# Working together in residential school settings

*(including material from Helen Parrott)*

The research that is drawn upon in this chapter comes from two distinct sources. The first is from the master's dissertation of Helen Parrott (2000) who conducted an action research case study in a residential school for pupils with learning difficulties and autism and the second is from observations and interviews on a visit to a residential school for pupils with emotional and behavioural difficulties (EBD) carried out to provide examples for this book.

These are some of the questions that underpin this chapter.

- *What models are being used to promote collaborative work across care and education in residential special schools?*
- *How important is a common approach across care and education?*
- *How is expertise transferred between care and education?*
- *What are the factors that promote effective collaborative work in residential settings?*

The two schools featured in this chapter have been given pseudonyms. The school for children with learning difficulties and autism will be called The Meadows and the school for children with EBD will be called St Michael's. They are both independent schools employing a wide range of staff to provide a 24 hour curriculum for the children. The two groups of staff who will be the focus of this chapter are education staff and residential staff. Both schools have spent some time trying to build a partnership between education and residential staff which will be interesting and illuminating to consider.

Traditionally education and residential staff have been almost completely separate from each other. Each had their own targets for pupils and their own ways of working which were largely unknown to the other. In recent years though, this has been seen as unsatisfactory. The argument has been that if children and young people are to benefit fully from attending residential school, it is important to provide a 24 hour curriculum with common aims across both education and care. The most difficult aspect of achieving this is in finding a model that enables education and residential staff to work together. The two schools used in this chapter have devised different models, although there are fundamental similarities between them.

## Transdisciplinary model

The Meadows has developed a transdisciplinary model of educare over a period of two years. The journey has been, and still is, difficult as it has involved fundamental changes to ways of working that have existed for many years. As with many examples of change of this scale, some people have been unable to adjust and have left the school. Others have thrived and have passed their enthusiasms on to new staff who have arrived willing to work within the new system. The general upheaval has been enormous and no one who has been involved would wish to minimise the sheer volume of work they have undertaken.

In brief, The Meadows provides 46 week residential schooling for approximately 12 pupils with profound autism, placed in three houses within a school of approximately 70 pupils. The school is built in a rural area and has extensive grounds which are used for small-scale agricultural activities. The staff involved in the autism special provision (ASP) consist of a care manager and a senior teacher who oversee the service, three team leaders, one for each house, managing teams of learning support workers. Other staff concerned are teachers, the consultant psychologist, psychology assistants and an occupational therapist. There are more people involved across the school site, but for the purposes of this case study, only those who are central to the case study will be mentioned.

## Learning support workers

The transdisciplinary model has been through several changes during its development, but its purpose is to encourage all staff who work within ASP to work together under common aims and systems, regardless of their discipline or status. The intention is to banish the 'us and them' culture so often found in residential schools and to put in its place a team structure within which pupils' education and care needs can be met in an integrated way. The linchpin in this model is the role of the learning support worker (LSW), so called to indicate the importance of learning across 24 hours of a pupil's day. No longer is there a clear division between the roles of classroom assistant and care assistant. Everyone is committed to supporting learning. After several working patterns were tried, it was decided that LSWs should be deployed in one of three ways:

- class-based LSWs
- house-based LSWs
- LSWs who work across both domains.

These roles should, as far as possible, be rotated so that everyone has experience of working in both care and education. However, it was found that several weeks in one role is necessary or it is hard to establish working relationships. Initially all LSWs worked across both education and care, but it quickly became evident that this created difficulties because the LSWs had no time away from the pupils within which to complete domestic tasks, carry out planning, write up paperwork or attend team meetings and training sessions.

A changing core of LSWs who work across both domains follow each student through their day ensuring quality programme delivery and consistency of approach to care and education because LSWs are skilled in both areas.

## A common approach

A crucial aspect of the transdisciplinary model is the common approach adopted by everyone. In the case of the ASP, the overriding framework is provided through TEACCH (Treatment and Education of Autistic and related Communication challenged Children). This is a programme aimed at providing a structure for people with autism. Briefly, TEACCH was developed in America by Schopler and Mesibov (1988) for people with autism spectrum disorders (ASD) and aims to build a structure and routine into their daily lives which will enable them to function more independently. It can be very effective in reducing anxiety in people with ASD which then enables them to become more receptive to learning and social interaction. One of the ways in which this approach is used at The Meadows is through a visual schedule. The activities in a pupil's day are each given a visual symbol which are then placed in the order in which they will occur. The pupils can then see their timetable sequentially and are thus better prepared for what is going to happen next. Some pupils will need to take the symbol to the next activity and then place it in an agreed 'finished' place afterwards as the act of moving the symbol seems to increase understanding.

Gradually everyone in the ASP is being trained in TEACCH so that it can be applied to all suitable areas of pupils' lives. For example, in the classroom, teachers and LSWs use the visual timetable to guide the order of matching and sorting tasks and in the house, LSWs use the timetable to guide the order of collecting and eating a meal. The expectations in each situation are similar as are the demands made by staff.

It could be said that it does not really matter (within reason) which common approach is adopted by education and care, what is important is the agreement between the two groups of staff. Of course, there is bound to be more commitment to an approach to which everyone subscribes and as this way of working is being seen to work over time, more staff are becoming committed. Training in techniques is cascaded through observation of work mates as well as delivered directly during formal courses. It was hard at first as so few people were trained in TEACCH and those who were struggled to get the approach underway. Two years later, staff have seen the structures working and are keen to increase their own skills.

## A common planning system

In most residential settings there are two planning and recording systems, one for care and one for education. At The Meadows this has been combined in a system of Individual Education and Care Planning (IECP). Pupils have one set of paperwork to which everyone contributes. Members of the transdisciplinary team, including parents, plan jointly and write programmes together which then may be carried out by a few key members of staff who have direct contact with each pupil. There is an identified service provider for each child and that person is responsible for drawing the plans together. The plan is implemented in full collaboration with all contributors and regular meetings are held to update and assess progress.

Discipline boundaries are broken down with the full cooperation of those involved; all agree to work together. Joint professional development is undertaken as part of the need to share expertise. The development of the IECP system has not been without its difficulties. Bringing together two ways of working that have been long established separately is not an easy option and it took great determination of the staff involved to devise ways in which to organise shifts to allow time for planning and reviewing. Meetings were rushed and disorganised at first, but have since developed into focused discussion and purposeful planning.

The establishment of key teams became the planning forum for the individual needs of each pupil. Membership of the key team is across the range of staffing expertise including care staff at different levels and a psychology assistant (that is an LSW with a degree in psychology). The key team is responsible for planning for two pupils in consultation with professionals from different disciplines. Identification of a need to introduce a new plan, or review one that requires changing, can originate from anyone whether they are members of the key team or the wider network of people involved with the individual pupil, but it is the key team members who are responsible for drawing up ideas with advice from others.

The process of developing IECPs is arguably more significant than the paperwork produced. It is a reflective approach based on evidence produced through, for example, behaviour charts and educational progression. The wealth of evidence collected is important in decision-making, providing a focus for discussion which has more weight than mere anecdote. Everyone in the transdisciplinary team can contribute carefully collected evidence whatever their status and this can then influence future plans for students.

## Crossing barriers

An important aspect of transdisciplinary teamwork at The Meadows is the way in which staff cross discipline barriers and transfer skills to each other. The occupational therapist (OT) began on a shift pattern like a LSW so that she could understand the demands of that role and the constraints under which LSWs work. Although she was initially excited at the idea of immersing herself in a different role, it soon became frustrating that she was spending so little time working as an OT. In retrospect, though, the OT feels that this early experience helped with building relationships with staff and with students and with working out realistic programmes.

There are a number of ways that the OT shares her knowledge and skills with others:

1. working individually with students while staff watch;
2. staff asking advice about games and equipment suitable for students;
3. discussing an issue informally;
4. filtering information from one member of staff to another;
5. working alongside a member of staff;
6. staff joining in with an activity;

7. staff leading an activity with support from the OT;
8. staff taking on an activity or programme but knowing they can ask for help;
9. OT planning a programme, the LSW working to the programme, the OT evaluating it periodically and replanning.

The OT describes these ways of working as 'filtering down' skills and expertise, which is more effective than expecting staff to implement a programme that she had written for them to follow. She also suggests that the model of LSWs working in both the school and the residential house meant that a programme could be tried out in one setting and then transferred, with the LSW, to the other. Her own knowledge of and skill with the TEACCH approach has been gleaned from watching and working alongside the teachers.

It has been suggested that professionals who share their skills as does the OT at The Meadows, feel undermined and threatened, and particularly that they will no longer be needed. In this case, the OT does not feel threatened at all and in fact, she suggests that the more she can pass on to others, the more she is freed to work in other areas. Sharing expertise can only increase the pool of knowledge and good practice, ensuring that students receive consistency of approach over the whole 24 hours.

## The role of psychology

Psychology assistants have been mentioned as one group of staff working at The Meadows. These are LSWs who have degrees in psychology and are thus trained in observation, assessment and data collection. Developing the role has been difficult as there is a conflict between the general nature of the LSW role in supporting students and the need for time to be given to the psychology assistants (PA) to observe, plan, discuss, recommend or analyse. Gradually work patterns have been altered so time can be given to activities which make best use of their expertise. Provision is made for them to work in the classroom and the house and for them to meet as a group and as part of the key teams. They are sharing their expertise almost imperceptibly through presenting a psychology perspective in meetings and through contributing to behaviour programmes for individual students.

There is also a consultant psychologist who is employed full-time by the school. Part of his time is spent in the ASP (autism special provision) and he sees his role and that of the psychology assistants as catalysts and intermediaries between education and care. As they are outside the two disciplines, they can provide the link between the two and facilitate communication. For example, psychology assistants call informal meetings between all members of the transdisciplinary team if there is a need to change part of the programme for a particular student.

There are also fortnightly staff support meetings which are chaired by the consultant psychologist. The purpose of these meetings is to discuss the needs of individual students, usually two each time. They are held on Monday afternoon, after school and everyone with direct interest in the student(s) is welcome to attend. From the discussion, an action plan is negotiated between the members of the transdisciplinary team. As the value of these meetings is being realised, says the consultant psychologist, so attendance is increasing and the level of discussion deepening.

Through the meetings of the transdisciplinary team, in different guises, and with the help and support of a psychological perspective, every team member is gradually realising that no one person has all the answers to working with students with such profound needs as those in the ASP. A problem solving approach which incorporates the discussion of collected evidence and suggestions from everyone, whatever their status, can lead to innovative ways forward.

## Collegial model

While developing the autism specialist provision (ASP), there have been several changes in the management structure at The Meadows. The current situation is that there is a care manager and a senior teacher for the provision and then three team leaders, one for each of the three residential houses. Students are allocated to houses according to age: post-16; secondary age; and primary age. To place this structure within the whole school, there is a Head of Care and a Head of Education who form the senior management team with the Principal, the Business Manager and the Director of Continuing Professional Development.

In the two years of development of the ASP there have been many changes in personnel, team structures, systems of working and approaches. Generally though the model that has underpinned the developments has been collegial, that is participative, for all staff. It was difficult at first for members of the transdisciplinary team to find time to meet together to discuss ways of working and the needs of students. Changing shift patterns and the role of the LSW has helped but more importantly, staff are realising the worth of meetings and that their voices matter: that team members can openly express opinions and these will be taken seriously. It takes time for staff, who traditionally had little say in what happened in the school, to build up trust, as well as the skills, to contribute.

The collegial model adopted by The Meadows contains the following features:

- authority of expertise, which is professional not positional (thus status is immaterial);
- a common set of values shared by members of the organisation;
- decisions reached by a process of discussion;
- issues resolved by discussion;
- participation in decision-making leading to a sense of ownership.

It is hard to achieve all of these in a large organisation such as The Meadows, either because democracy can seem very time-consuming and cumbersome, or the need to implement change quickly can mean that hierarchical structures need to be employed initially. Forcing through change can be alienating of staff and certainly The Meadows, in the introduction of a completely new model of working, has had a high turnover of staff. Not everyone employed before the changes felt they wanted to work in a different way and others, both newly employed and previous employees, tried working with youngsters with profound autism and found it did not suit them. Yet others have moved on through promotion after helping to implement the change at The Meadows.

As was indicated above, a collegial model of working needs time to develop. The consultant psychologist talks about 'a snowball effect', by which he means that staff need to see the model working before they can join in. Like a snowball, change should start small with a few committed people and grow gradually as others see how effective the change can be. Managers need to be persistent in employing the principles of participation and discussion, working out ways in which to facilitate them and build up staff confidence and trust. Until meetings are seen to be effective, sceptics will be not be persuaded to participate wholeheartedly.

## The role of the principal

The principal of The Meadows was the original architect of the model developed for students at the profound end of the autistic spectrum. He has a particular interest in a longer school year for those who need a constant structure and routine as well as in the bringing together of education and care. The role of the LSW was introduced to respond to a need for a 24 hour, 365 day curriculum: the need for students to be given every opportunity to learn, wherever they are.

Although the principal had a strong vision of the transdisciplinary and collegial models of working, the direct managers of the provision were given the freedom to develop them on the ground. In interview, the principal said that the model itself is essentially simple, but the implementation intensely complex, especially as it cut across such strong existing cultures in education and care. He saw the role of the senior management team as 'just advocating support for the programme but also being there to actually shape the philosophy' but added, 'it's not a rigid philosophical concept, it's one we're defining in the context of the school'. Other more practical ways in which the changes were supported was through meetings between the senior managers and the managers of the ASP. Reflection on what was occurring as a group was shaping the way the model developed.

The consultant psychologist was also asked about his perceptions of the role of the principal (and the senior management team) and his emphasis was on 'encouragement'. He felt that it was most important that the senior management team should be generally encouraging and supportive, enabling team members to work out for themselves the best ways of working together, rather than by providing specific solutions to problems. It is certainly helpful for those involved in major change to have a group of people with whom to reflect on successes and challenges. Merely articulating what has been occurring can assist in finding the way forward.

## Summary of the transdisciplinary approach

From the data gathered from a questionnaire to staff in the ASP and two interviews, the following are put forward as important features of transdisciplinary teamwork at The Meadows.

- LSWs are key players (but the working model must be flexible to meet the needs of individual students).
- There is a need to stress the educative role for all team members.
- Information-sharing and skill transfer are vital.
- TEACCH (a common approach) is a powerful tool.
- Communication systems need to be of high quality.
- Access to professional development must be a priority.
- Care and education staff need to familiarise themselves with each other's work.
- Team members should decide the goals of the provision (rather than managers).
- Working alongside each other to learn new skills is a good model of practice.
- A culture shift is necessary for the model to work.
- Senior managers should be supportive to developments, proactive to concerns and reactive to crises.

There have been enormous challenges to the development of completely new approaches to meeting the needs of students with the most profound autism at The Meadows, but after two years, the transdisciplinary and collegial models are well-established and staff are beginning to feel that they are really working together with common aims for the students. Some working examples demonstrate transdisciplinary work in practice.

---

**CASE STUDY**

A shopping programme has been prepared for JC. The purpose of this programme is to explore the possibility of introducing task demands to an established and familiar routine. The programme is graded and designed to develop J's ability to become more involved in planning and executing the task of shopping for his chosen items (usually videos and confectionery). Following discussion between the occupational therapists and the senior teacher, the possibility of introducing a coin recognition element into J's programme was explored. The OT accompanied J and an LSW on initial outings to establish the programme and this was then maintained by the LSWs who normally support J.

---

**CASE STUDY**

A graded and structured food handling programme was prepared for CF by the occupational therapist and a psychology assistant. The programme utilised the TEACCH structure to facilitate understanding and develop the ability to prepare a simple snack. After its establishment, the programme was maintained by the LSWs who support C both in the classroom and in the residential home.

---

**CASE STUDY**

A functional analysis of S's challenging behaviours was undertaken by a psychology assistant. This enabled the development of behaviour guidelines to counteract S's periods of sudden distress, incorporating such innovations as a choice board and 'first-then' cards. The guidelines were developed in a meeting with the rest of the key team who are now implementing them.

---

**CASE STUDY**

One of the latest transdisciplinary initiatives is the development of after-school clubs run by staff from different disciplines. Activities offered range across craft, sports and relaxation, making the most of the sensory and games rooms with some activities taking place in students' own houses. A part-time leisure coordinator has been appointed and this will enable the further development of the after-school clubs.

---

Major change such as that found at The Meadows is not comfortable for anyone involved. It involves shifts in values, beliefs and practices that have been in place for a long time. It is threatening to be expected to work in a completely different manner, however convinced you are of the efficacy of the new way. New practices need to develop gradually from the vision, in the control of those in the front-line, but supported by the visionaries.

## Partnership model

Although the bulk of this chapter has been spent on the transdisciplinary model of support for a 24 hour curriculum in a residential school, it is not the only possible model. St Michael's School has been as anxious as The Meadows to promote an integrated view of education and care to meet the needs of their pupils and they have implemented systems designed to promote this view.

St Michael's is an independent boarding school for approximately 60 boys between the ages of 10 and 16 who experience specific learning difficulties associated with behavioural problems. It is situated in and around a large country manor and has many opportunities for sporting and leisure activities beyond the classroom. Boys can study for GCSEs as well as advanced vocational awards. The residential areas are in the same building as the classrooms separated only by the main entrance hall. Offices for managers and administrators are all situated within the main house. Thus all staff and students live and work in close proximity.

### Roles

There are separate care staff and education staff, but the hours of work mean that there are many opportunities for these two sets of people to overlap and work together. A few residential care workers (RSWs) work in the classrooms, but generally the overlap with education staff occurs outside the classroom, during the many sporting and leisure activities both before and after school hours. Teachers take on residential duties, sometimes starting at 7.30 a.m. or alternatively starting at normal school time but continuing to 7.30 p.m. and/or by being available during weekends. Often they will be part of a team led by a member of the care staff, although they may also lead teams for leisure pursuits. People's abilities and skills are used whatever their status.

When roles of RSWs and teachers overlap as at St Michael's, there can be difficulties associated with differences in status, conditions of service, rates of pay and ways of working. Much effort needs to put into minimising these differences as far as possible. The actuality of working alongside each other can contribute considerably to breaking down barriers, as can social events and the supporting encouragement of senior managers. The status and responsibilities of RSWs have been increased recently and they may be running sport and leisure groups, leading teachers.

## A common system

Staff across care and education are divided into year groups so that relationships can be built up within a smaller group of people. Together they implement a grading system of the pupils' behaviour. This is mainly managed by the RSWs, but can be influenced and used by teachers. There are weekly year group meetings after school time where information is exchanged and individual pupils are discussed.

Underpinning the work across education and care are Individual Personal Plans (IPPs) which are managed by care staff, but to which education staff also contribute. They are reviewed termly by teachers and care staff together, but there are other opportunities for teachers to comment regularly on them and for there to be joint decisions made on priorities for and with individual pupils. Teachers' plans always include two objectives, in behaviour and participation, and these are regularly reviewed by both groups.

There are other supports for this common system in the form of daily logs, pupil behaviour checklists, incidents sheets and educational progress files. These are discussed in regular meetings where information is exchanged and individual pupils discussed. There are daily meetings at 8.55 a.m. for teachers, classroom assistants, Head of Care and the nurse and at 2.10 p.m. for the care staff, Head of Education and the other nurse. These are specifically to exchange information on what has occurred during the previous evening or in the morning. There are also weekly meetings for education and care staff separately as well as a joint year group meeting which is chaired by a member of the care staff.

There is a keyworker system and every member of the care staff works with a small number of boys. Keyworkers have responsibility for liaising with other members of the year group staff and with parents, enabling the integration of education, care and home life. They have an administrative role as well as a pastoral role.

## Close proximity

It was indicated at the beginning of this section on St Michael's School that all staff and pupils live and work in close proximity to each other. The care office is placed opposite to the classrooms and very close to the education staffroom which considerably helps the joint work of the two groups. Care staff are on call throughout the school day and can be in the classroom in seconds if necessary. Once called to a classroom this member of staff can remain supporting the pupils in lessons or she or he can take the pupil to a different space to calm down. Thus, although the teacher is ultimately responsible for the behaviour of the pupils in the classroom, there is always support on hand if the whole class is likely to be interrupted by the needs of one pupil.

The care office is large and open plan, making communication relatively easy between staff working there. The education staffroom is close by so messages can flow easily in both directions. There are constant cross-overs of staff at break times as care staff are responsible for pupils during breaks in the school day, so informal exchanges are occurring throughout the day. Recently the nurses' office has been moved closer to the hub of activity which has helped to include them more fully.

## Ethos of working together

There have been many mentions of the ways in which care and education staff work together routinely, but there are also examples of specific joint projects and activities. For example, daily assembly, called 'Thought for the Day', is attended by all staff who are on duty and can be led by any of them. There was also a joint group set up to produce the school handbook, written specifically for the pupils.

When new teaching staff are inducted, they are expected to spend some time working alongside colleagues in care and vice versa. At interview they are told that care and education work closely together and that they will be expected to work shifts whether they are teachers or RSWs. The head teacher feels that it is vital for teachers to work with pupils outside of the classroom if those pupils are to receive an integrated curriculum and approach.

Generally there is a strong ethos of working together, which has developed from a desire to 'bridge the gap' between education and care. Pupils who need 24 hour care are usually also in need of consistency and structure, alongside common aims and approaches. One of the reasons why pupils are transferred to residential care is that they lack consistency of approach across their lives. Home expectations may be very different from those at school which may be helping to exacerbate the emotional and/or behaviour difficulties. Bringing the two parts of pupils' lives together under one set of expectations may be the very thing that brings about change in behaviour.

## Conclusions

The partnership model provided by St Michael's School contains many of the features of the transdisciplinary model of The Meadows. There is more emphasis on a specific common approach at The Meadows with the adoption of TEACCH as a strategy to provide structure for students with profound autism, but there are the basics of a common approach in the behaviour grading system used across care and education at St Michael's. What seems to be important is the common thinking and the processes that have gone into acquiring this common thinking.

The IECP and the IPP systems at the schools are also seen as important. They provide the structure for communication across care and education and can promote the idea of common goals and targets. It is vital that any common system should be devised by everyone who uses it so that it will contain aspects of children's needs that are important across their lives. A common planning system should also support a common recording system so that everyone knows exactly what children are achieving.

Providing systems for communication does not necessarily mean that staff across education and care will use them effectively. There is more to partnership than systems. People are also important. Systems will not work unless people are committed to them. However, people cannot work together effectively unless they have the systems to support them. Both are needed. The Meadows and St Michael's recognise the importance of helping staff to build confidence for working together, while minimising the differences between them. Individual talents are recognised and encouraged and staff are equipped with new skills and expertise gained through formal staff development and through informally watching each other at work. People get to know each other by being together and by experiencing each other's worlds. And when they begin to know and understand each other, they can begin to work in partnership.

# Chapter 11

# Supporting LEAs through change

This chapter is based on work with four local education authorities (LEAs). Three are small urban LEAs reorganising aspects of their SEN provision and the fourth is the educational action zone (EAZ) of a large rural LEA wanting to develop the role of teaching assistants. For the purposes of this book, they will be called North, South, West and East LEAs. The aim of the chapter is to examine some of strategies that were used by both the outside consultant and those employed by the LEA to manage major changes in provision.

These are the questions that underpin this chapter.

- *What is the role of an outside consultant in the management of change?*
- *How can the change be managed effectively?*
- *How can staff development contribute to managing change?*

## The LEAs

Although the three urban LEAs have much in common in that they are relatively small authorities in metropolitan areas, they were trying to achieve different things in different ways and it would be helpful for the reader to hear about each LEA separately, including the rural LEA, before discussing the common themes that came out of the projects.

### North LEA

North LEA has three primary special schools catering for pupils with learning difficulties, all in poor state of repair. One is designated for pupils with severe learning difficulties (SLD), one for moderate learning difficulties (MLD) and the third for physical disabilities (PD). The LEA decided to combine the three schools into one and put up a completely new building for this so-called 'super-school' and sell the other two sites. It was intended that some pupils would be moved to mainstream provision when the three schools closed and the super-school would have about 180 pupils on roll.

Pupils, parents and staff faced major upheaval over several years as the school for pupils with PD moved out of their building to enable it to be torn down and rebuilt. They are being temporarily housed in an old secondary school. Generally parents are looking forward to the new school, although they are worried about the move and how it will affect their children, especially those who will have further to travel. Staff also have concerns about the changes, particularly those who feel they have built up expertise with a certain group of pupils and expect to have to work with another group in the super-school.

The consultant was bought in three years before the new super-school was expected to open to help support the LEA and the schools to manage the change as smoothly as possible. At the time of writing (February 2001), the new school is partly built and expected to be fully functional in the next academic year.

## West LEA

West LEA has eight special schools for pupils with learning difficulties, some of which have falling rolls. It is recognised that costly buildings can no longer be maintained and that fewer schools will be needed in the future. Thus the plan was accepted by the local council to reduce the number of special schools for pupils with learning difficulties to three and provide units attached to mainstream schools for some pupils. The designation of the three schools are primary complex and profound learning difficulties (CPLD), secondary CPLD and primary MLD plus. The latter designation refers to pupils who have moderate learning difficulties, but with additional needs such as autism or physical disabilities. A complex plan for redistributing pupils while rebuilding was carried out was drawn up with the promise to parents that pupils would not move more than twice during the period of change.

There were various complications for West LEA. Firstly, the plans for the changes took some time to be accepted by the Government and the local council which meant there was a very unsettling year when parents, pupils and staff were not sure what was going to happen to them. Secondly, the proposed changes were to be brought into effect extremely quickly following final approval: the decision was made in March for the first move in September. Thirdly, the LEA went through an unsuccessful inspection also in March, which meant that LEA officers were attempting to drive through major change while being severely criticised.

The consultant was bought in four months before the final decision on the changes was made to provide an outsider's view and to support both the schools and the LEA officers in the detail of future developments. At the time of writing, the heads of the new schools have been appointed, the first move for pupils has been accomplished and assistants are being interviewed and asked for their preference for workplace.

## East LEA

East LEA does not have the pressing need to change quickly like North and West LEAs. They have ten special schools and a long tradition of successful segregated special provision which is now out of tune with the current climate of inclusion. Some staff and LEA officers are committed to the idea of provision becoming more inclusive and they are attempting to encourage others to see the need for change. The only sector which is not fulfilling its current role and will need to change first is that of secondary provision for pupils with emotional and behavioural difficulties (EBD). The residential school has virtually no pupils in residence, there is no provision for girls with EBD in the authority and pupils with very severe difficulties are educated outside the LEA. Clearly there is a need for developments in this particular sector.

There are many successful projects joining special and mainstream schools together across the authority, especially for pupils with SLD and MLD and the intention is to build upon these successes in an organic way, rather than force sweeping changes overnight. In this way, East LEA is different from North and West LEAs: change can be gradual and planned over a period of years. The test here is to get the pace of change right: too slow and the innovators in the authority will move to other more dynamic LEAs; too fast and those who do not wish to change will become entrenched.

The consultant was bought in during the first consultation between the LEA and schools and parents. This consultation began with a questionnaire that was sent to all concerned to find out individual opinions of possible changes. Then more than 30 meetings were held to enable as many people as possible to comment on the proposals and also the consultation process. A second consultation was set up built on the results of the first, and at the time of writing this is still being carried out.

## South LEA

South LEA is a large rural authority with an EAZ that includes some of the authority's mainstream and special schools. The officers of the EAZ have many developments to steer through as part of the management of the funds given by the Government to boost areas of deprivation. The project to increase numbers and training of teaching assistants forms the basis of this particular case study.

The EAZ have provided funds for a large number of extra assistants primarily to help pupils with their literacy and numeracy. EAZ schools have employed assistants in different ways and with different conditions, but all are bound to the EAZ and funds will eventually be exhausted. The EAZ officers are anxious that the assistants should be as effective in raising pupil standards as possible and are thus anxious to plan, implement and evaluate the project thoroughly.

Like East LEA the change brought about by the EAZ in South LEA is not born from the need to save money or reorganise because of falling rolls. The change can be handled more slowly and in response to identified needs. There is, however, an imperative to succeed in raising standards, so, in a sense, there is an urgency that drives the innovation.

Generally there is great support for the extra assistants that have been allocated to schools, but this does not mean that every teacher and every school knows how to make best use of them. The consultant was bought in at the time when the EAZ officers were considering how to train both assistants and schools to make best use of the extra resources. At the time of writing, much consultation with schools and assistants has taken place and the first level of training has been piloted and is to be more widely disseminated.

## Advising and consultancy

Bringing in an outside adviser or consultant can be very helpful when organisations are faced with major change. The dispassionate view that the outsider can bring can be valuable, although it can be difficult to be seen to remain politically disinterested. West LEA's profile in both the press and the schools was not positive. Staff and parents were convinced of the incompetence of all involved in the proposed changes, signing petitions and protesting at the closure of schools. It would be very easy for a consultant bought in by the LEA to be seen in the same light and condemned by association.

Partly to counteract this possibility and partly to facilitate the proposed changes, the consultant set up various activities. Firstly, she suggested to the LEA officers that the head teachers of the schools involved should join them to form an implementation group for steering through the changes. Secondly, she organised and led three retraining sessions for staff wishing to move from working with pupils with MLD to working with pupils with SLD and PMLD. Thirdly, she deliberately spoke to her personal contacts in the schools, listening to their views and reassuring them that the LEA were not conspiring against them. Fourthly, she reported to the LEA her impressions of the feelings of staff in the schools.

In this way, the consultant attempted to:

(a) be seen to be listening to 'both sides'
(b) bring the two sides together (in the implementation group and as a go-between)
(c) give representatives of the schools power to influence the changes
(d) offer something positive (retraining) to those who will be forced to change.

It can be very difficult to balance the support given to everyone involved in major and sudden change, especially as a consultant is likely to be involved only intermittently. In the case of West LEA, the consultant met with the LEA officers twice and then with the implementation group four times over a period of six months so, of course, much was happening in between those meetings. Listening to school staff was achieved on an *ad hoc* basis when the occasion arose, which also meant the flow of information was not consistent. However, meeting intermittently also meant that the consultant was not expected to know all that had happened and could legitimately ask for a résumé.

The more leisurely pace of change in North LEA enabled the consultant to build up relationships with almost all the people involved in the creation of the new super-school. This began with meetings with the steering group which was made up of the three head teachers, the LEA SEN adviser and the deputy head of the secondary school for pupils with SLD. There were also meetings with the health and social services personnel involved in the new school. Alongside the planning and decision-making was a series of training days with all the staff of the three schools due to become one. These days had two main purposes, firstly to enable the three sets of staff to get to know each other and secondly to enable training in the areas of identified need. The consultant ran each of these days which contained activities such as a brainstorm of advice staff would like to give to the new head of the super-school (then not appointed). There were six training days planned to take place in the year before the new school opened.

The role of consultant can be difficult to achieve well. It demands the skills of:

- active listening and questioning;
- quick understanding and making connections between pieces of information;
- problem solving;

- knowing when to steer in a different direction;
- chairing discussions;
- managing conflict.

Consultants also need knowledge of:

- the effects of major change;
- ways of managing change;
- the likely situations in the LEAs and schools.

Of course, consultants also need to be thoroughly steeped in the topic of the proposed change, which in the case of the LEAs reported here was special educational needs. One of the reasons why the consultant was accepted by the people she was advising was her long history in special educational needs. When staff talked with her about pupils with the most profound disability or challenging behaviour, it was clear that she understood their perspective and could also encourage development in their thinking.

## Managing change

Those who are invited into a situation as an external adviser or consultant are usually agents of change. It is, however, an impossible job for an outsider to accomplish alone. Unless there are willing people within the situation, the consultant can advise but achieve little.

Most people are basically conservative by nature and do not wish to change, once they have established a situation that they can cope with. Even what looks to an outsider as an unsatisfactory situation, is preferable to many people than changing to something that might be better.

Staff in schools are no different from others in the population. They have established themselves in jobs in particular places, they have taken on responsibilities that now feel familiar, they have journeys to school that are predictable and return home at a time that is convenient for their own children and social lives. Closing schools, amalgamating them, altering their characters provides much scope for anxiety about the actual effects on people's lives. North, West and East LEAs are all intending to achieve major change and many staff will be expected to change the buildings they are working in, the children they are teaching and type of difficulties they will be expected to know about.

So one of the main issues that has been uppermost in the mind of the consultant has been how to anticipate the feelings of anxiety, how to allay the worst fears, how to offer a certain amount of compensation, how to find alternatives from which people can choose. What appears to be of great importance is treating the worries seriously. It is not helpful if the people who are steering the change (and who may not actually be expected to make the changes themselves) indicate that they cannot understand 'what all the fuss is about'. Simple things like getting bus timetables for people who will have to plan a new route to school can be useful.

North LEA is erecting a new school to replace three dilapidated buildings which is proving to be something of compensation to those involved in the changes. Both staff and parents are looking forward to having a purpose-built school that will provide a good working environment. Of course, there will be many compromises made as the new school becomes reality, but the general feeling is one of optimism for the future. Everyone is moving, although some staff will be returning to the site where they used to work, which means that there will be fewer territorial conflicts.

West LEA has experienced the first of the many moves that will be necessary to achieve three new schools instead of eight and already territorial conflicts are in evidence. Retiring head teachers have been unhelpful when new head teachers have been overseeing the furniture moves from one site to another. Staff who have remained in one building have been unwelcoming to staff who have moved in with them. It is certainly easy for an 'us and them' situation to arise when staff are brought together with little or no preparation and it can take many months for staff to begin to 'gel' and work together as a new unit. Often they need help through teambuilding activities and opportunities to get to know one another both formally and informally.

North LEA has spent some time arranging for staff from the three schools to get to know each other. Not only have there been the six training days together, but staff have been able to visit the other schools and become familiar with both staff and pupils who will be moving into the new super-school. It is intended that curriculum coordinators should exchange information and paperwork so that it will be easier to merge ways of working when the new school opens. The six training days discussed earlier are likely to help here.

South LEA has spent some time exploring ways in which to encourage teacher and assistant partnerships to become more effective following the appointment of large numbers of assistants in mainstream schools. Some teachers are resisting changing their practice to include working with another adult in the classroom, although there are others who are very willing to develop effective practice.

A small group of interested teachers and assistants who worked in partnership were called together to devise a package for schools that would help them and others to work together effectively. The outside consultant devised activities for the partners to try out, comment on and alter and eventually these were written down to form a pack to go into schools. The activities centred around:

- getting to know each other's roles and skills;
- creating common aims for the classroom;
- auditing how well time was being used in the partnership;
- developing face-to-face and paperwork communication;
- discussing the needs of one child;
- developing joint record-keeping.

The trial partners found the activities very helpful in developing the way they worked together and were confident that they could be used by others to change the way in which teachers and assistants were working together. At the time of writing, the pack is about to be trialled in schools.

During the discussions with teachers and assistants over developing the South EAZ pack, there was much talk about change and how people resist it. Some members of the group felt that there were some teachers, in particular, who were not used to working with another adult and who were not going to change what they did to make good use of the assistance offered. In those circumstances, generally, it is better to work with those people who are sympathetic to change, and at least for a while, not try to include those who show no interest. It can be very discouraging battling against people who say things like:

- 'I don't see why I should change, I'm happy as I am.'
- 'I've tried that before and it didn't work then so why should it now?'
- 'I'm fed up with having to change so often.'

Good advice from any consultant includes how to find sympathetic and empathetic colleagues with whom to start the change process. Development that can be slow and steady and constant is far easier to handle than sudden transformation, especially when it is made reluctantly. Behaving like a 'hero-innovator' is not advisable for anyone, but especially when colleagues are resistant or see no reason to change. Carrying out an audit of current practice is often a good place to begin to identify exactly what needs to change, especially when the change can be incremental.

East LEA is in the fortunate position of being able to change slowly over a number of years. The first step for them was to consult with everyone involved. The next step was to gather together all the examples of integration and inclusion currently occurring in the authority to locate good practice. Previous projects provided the LEA officers with examples of both good and not-so-good practice and examination of each one enabled lessons to be learned for the future. A consortium of three primary schools, one for pupils with SLD, one for pupils with MLD and one mainstream school, has been working together to meet a diverse range of needs and the management of this project can offer some helpful examples for others.

On the negative side, a primary school in East LEA was resourced to provide an inclusive assessment nursery, but unfortunately the staff in the main part of the school are reluctant to accept pupils with SEN and thus those pupils are placed in special schools instead of moving with their peers into the mainstream school. With hindsight, it could be said that the project was doomed to fail because of the attitude of the staff in the mainstream school to pupils with SEN. When that change was made originally, it was known that the head teacher was reluctant to be involved, but yet it still went ahead. This is a very clear example of a lack of attendance to the fundamentals of managing change. People will not change just because they are told to, not even if they are resourced to do so. They have to be convinced that the change is necessary and will improve the situation.

It is often feelings of helplessness which feed people's resistance to change. On the whole, people like to feel in control of what is happening to them. When change is imposed from outside, as in all of the LEAs used as case studies, people feel that control is slipping away from them. This creates anxiety which increases reluctance to change at all. Even when people can see that there is no option but to change, as for example in the case of replacing the crumbling buildings in North LEA, it is still uncomfortable for them if they feel they have no control over what is going to happen.

Employing some of the principles and processes of democracy can be helpful. Canvassing opinions and encouraging open debate can help people to feel genuinely involved even if expediency cannot allow all options to be seriously considered. East LEA have held 30 meetings in schools to listen to ideas and present possible scenarios for the future. They have also used a questionnaire offering possible alternatives. After further thought and discussion with the consultant, head teachers, parents and other agencies, the LEA officers are, at the time of writing, preparing a second questionnaire for which they have presented possible models of inclusive provision. This will go to all interested parties and will be accompanied by a further set of meetings in school. It is a long process, but if people are to feel in control of the change, then it cannot be hurried.

# Staff development

This final section expands further the notion of staff development as an element of managing change. Several references have already been made to training and retraining and these will be explored more fully.

People can feel deskilled when they are in the throes of major change. The special schools in West LEA are not only contracting in number from eight to three, but the pupils who will be left in segregated provision, following the changes, will all have complex needs. Two of the three schools will educate pupils with SLD and PMLD and the third has been designated 'MLD Plus' meaning that the pupils will have other needs as well as moderate learning difficulties. Those staff who have been teaching 'traditional' slow learning pupils with MLD are very uneasy at the choice that they face. They feel they are being asked to teach pupils about whom they know little.

A short course of three sessions on topics relating to teaching pupils with SLD and PMLD was offered to teachers and assistants. Eighteen members of staff from the MLD schools attended the course run by the consultant. The main aim of the course was to reassure staff that their expertise in teaching pupils with MLD could be transferred to working with pupils with SLD and PMLD. Much use was made of video alongside consideration of practical aspects of teaching pupils at an early stage of development. All participants said that they felt more confident about the future by the end of the third session. It cannot be claimed that all fears had been allayed by this short course, but it definitely made a contribution to the 18 people who attended.

North LEA has had a more extended training package which has been run over 14 months. Some participants were interested in gaining accreditation for their work and this was arranged through a university. Staff from all three schools joined together on six different occasions, using their five Teacher Education Days plus other voluntary sessions after school for those who wanted to gain the 20 credits for a portfolio of work. Four of the five days attended by everyone were devoted to sharing information about pupils' strengths and needs, teaching approaches and curriculum while the fifth was called a 'carousel day' which consisted of workshops on aspects of learning difficulties identified by staff (such as autism and challenging behaviour).

As was indicated earlier in this chapter, an important aim for these days was staff getting to know each other. There were many opportunities for discussion and staff were encouraged to move round and talk to different people. There is still six months (at the time of writing) before the final joining together in the new super-school and staff are definitely getting to know each other. They will be beginning working together from a base of having been in a learning situation together and having exchanged much information that has helped to reduce fears. This training will be followed up by other staff development activities, such as visiting each other's schools and exchanging videos of pupils at work. Two pupils on video have already been the subject of extended discussion on one of the training days.

Staff development and training appear to be essential aspects of managing change. Not only do they offer chances to develop new skills to suit the new situation, but they also foster new relationships between staff who are to work together.

Effective staff development and training to support change requires:

- initial negotiations between all participants to identify needs;
- an agreed programme between the school and training provider;
- taught elements that enable the change itself to be discussed sufficiently;
- opportunities to update or retrain in knowledge, skills and understanding;
- activities to encourage participants to work together towards the new situation;
- activities that include discussion of pupils to be taught in the new situation;
- possibilities for recognising the training through accreditation;
- ongoing evaluation of the success of the training in preparing people for the new situation;
- continuing professional development in the new situation that goes on relating to the changes until everyone feels sufficiently at ease.

## Conclusions

Supporting LEAs through major change can be both difficult and rewarding for an outside consultant. It demands many skills, but above all the ability to problem solve jointly. All support partnerships are, to a greater or lesser extent, reliant on the ability to problem solve together. Outside consultants need to be able to listen to different points of view from participants and come to conclusions swiftly before discussing ways of moving forward. They are not there to dictate what should happen, but to help insiders to be creative and innovative in their thinking. Sometimes insiders have an unrealistic expectation of what consultants can undertake or achieve, so it is important to establish the complementary roles of all people early in the relationship.

It can be helpful to refer to the model shown in Figure 11.1 of the passage of a consultant who enters an organisation to support change and who will exit once the job is complete.

It is important that each stage is given sufficient time. Diagnosing the situation in the organisation can be difficult for an outsider, but if the ethos within the

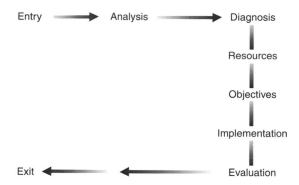

**Figure 11.1** Passage of a consultant supporting change

organisation is negative and even hostile to change it will be virtually impossible to achieve anything. These questions may be helpful to consultants for ascertaining the health of the organisation. They also provide guidance on the types of questions that it may be useful to ask while weighing up where to start with advice. If there are negative answers to all the questions, it would be fair to say that introducing major change would be enormously difficult.

- Is there general agreement on the aims and purposes of the organisation?
- Are people clear as to what their duties and responsibilities are in terms of delegated authority for decision-making?
- Does the communication system work with reasonable efficiency?
- Is the morale and social cohesiveness of the staff generally good?
- Are the staff either overloaded or underused?
- Is it generally accepted that power is fairly distributed?

Giving time to evaluating what has happened when the project is complete is often hard. The consultant has probably moved on to the next job and the insiders are often fully occupied with the consequences of the changed situation. However, throughout this book, there has been great encouragement to find the time to evaluate the way partners work together. Of course, this should be ongoing throughout the duration of the partnership, but a final evaluation can be helpful both for insiders and for consultants when planning for another innovation. Sometimes relationships drift apart instead of establishing a planned handover moment. The following questions can be helpful during that final evaluation before the consultant moves out of the organisation.

- What have we actually done?
- How did our partnership work?
- How might it have been improved?
- What do we think we have achieved/learned?
- What is there still to do?
- What do we intend to do next?

Answering these questions can bring the partnership to a positive close and help the organisation and its insiders to move forward in a planned way.

# Chapter 12

# Support partnerships between families and professionals

The material for this chapter has been collected from several different sources. Peter Limbrick (from the 'Springfield Project') has supplied the information for some of the cases studies used to illustrate ways of working in an effective support partnership between professionals and parents in the preschool stage. Other cases studies have been carried out specifically to provide data for this book and yet others have been collected over many years of personal experience of working with families of children with disabilities. The first part of the chapter is based mainly in the school years and the second part mainly in the preschool years.

These are the questions that underpin the chapter.

- *Why are partnerships between professionals and families so difficult to achieve?*
- *How can partnerships between professionals and families be developed?*
- *What strategies are helpful in establishing partnerships between professionals and families?*
- *What does the keyworker model offer to families of young children with multiple disabilities?*

## Partnership

Most people would agree that 'parent–professional partnership' is highly difficult to achieve in practice, but largely unproblematic in principle. Few would want to argue against encouraging professionals and families to work together, especially with children with disabilities and difficulties. Common sense suggests that if families and professionals have common aims, children are more likely to progress. However, constant practical difficulties with making partnership work and misunderstandings about the meaning of partnership between families and professionals has, in many cases, devalued its principle. Teachers and teaching assistants can often be heard to say that they would love to have a partnership with parents if only they (the parents) would come into school. Sometimes they continue by saying that parents seem not to care about their children, or cannot be bothered to do what the teachers have suggested, or are the direct cause of their children's difficulties. Judgements can fly around the staffroom or even, sometimes, the classroom where children can overhear.

It would, of course, be equally naive to suggest that all parents have the potential to be good partners with professionals, or have excellent parenting skills, or always have their children's educational, health or therapeutic needs in mind. What is needed by both 'sides' is more understanding of each other's needs and less rhetoric about partnership. As has been seen throughout this book, the first step towards any partnership is beginning to understand each other. Enabling both parents and professionals to experience or, at least, talk about the situation of the other would be very helpful. Unfortunately both 'sides' think they know about the other, parents because they went to school themselves and teachers because they are members of families.

---

**CASE STUDY**

A teacher of pupils with SLD devised a very successful behaviour programme to reduce the smacking by a child called Susie. Following the success of the programme at school, the family was contacted to ascertain whether it could be continued in the home environment. Susie's parents and three brothers were keen to try the programme and invited the teacher after school on Monday.

The teacher arrived and began to train the family in the techniques used at school. The family members were receptive and soon learned the procedure, but nevertheless, the teacher stayed all evening to support the transfer of the professional skills. On Tuesday when the teacher arrived after school, the family were pleased to see her and continued with implementing the programme with her support. On Wednesday, the family were a little less enthusiastic and on Thursday they asked the teacher not to return. They said that they preferred to continue with their own 'programme' to stop Susie smacking, which consisted of one family member sitting with Susie and holding her hands. They justified their rejection of the professional's programme on the grounds that there was no time to fit it into cooking the dinner, homework, the television and other aspects of family life.

---

So what went wrong? The teacher was careful to introduce the programme in the context where it was to be implemented and she was available to support the family physically until they felt secure, or until it was successful. She treated the family with respect and felt that she understood what was needed to ensure success of the programme.

What the teacher failed to do was to spend time getting to understand the family situation and the current approach to the 'problem' and then working jointly with the family to develop a strategy that was 'in tune' with their lives. It is very easy for an outsider to a situation to make suggestions, or provide programmes that seem to meet the need identified, but fail to realise the implications of adding that programme to an already busy situation.

There are many other examples of one partner overloading another by developing programmes in isolation which are often 'the last straw'. The home teacher can easily do this with families. The teacher works with the family (usually the child and mother) and leaves an activity to be completed and reported on. Families often feel under enormous pressure to complete the activity even if it is really burdensome to find the time. They may even complete the activity at the expense of other activities that may be just as good if not better than that proposed.

Visiting professionals to schools can create the same problem for classroom staff by developing a programme, for example, for speech and language therapy based only on the needs of the child and not the context within which she or he is being taught. This can put strain on the already very busy staff who resent having to 'fit in' yet another thing. It can make the difference between classroom staff including children with special needs or rejecting them on the grounds that they do not have time to provide something different from the rest of the class. Developing programmes and approaches together in both home and school situations can avoid this feeling of 'adding on' to current pressures.

## A blame culture

Returning to the story about Susie and her family, working jointly with the family may or may not have been successful in reducing Susie's smacking. If it had been unsuccessful it may have been attributable to other circumstances that were not immediately solvable. For example, Susie's parents, at the time, were experiencing enormous difficulty in supporting each other. The stress of caring for a severely disabled youngster was forcing them apart and eventually they did divorce. Even if the teacher had been scrupulous with her joint problem solving, the situation may not have been conducive to working in partnership in the way envisaged by the teacher. What might have been needed was more general support in terms of a listening ear, baby-sitting, respite care, home help. Perhaps the family was not ready for a specific programme. Maybe they never would be. What is important is that the professional negotiates with the family what support they want and learns about the situation in a non-judgemental way. It is impossible fully to understand what it is like to care for a child with severe disabilities in any given situation and equally impossible to attach blame to anyone within the situation.

---

**CASE STUDY**

Liam has autism. He has various rituals and needs that interfere with family life, for example he likes everyone to sit down in a darkened room with the television on, but not tuned to a channel (to watch the 'snow'). He will only eat chips or crisps and will not have anything else on the table. If his demands are not granted he will scream and get very distressed. Sometimes he will be violent towards property, but not to people. Not surprisingly members of the family usually acquiesce and thus spend much time in the dark and either eat Liam's diet or hide to eat other things.

---

It is very easy for a professional to look at this situation and blame the parents for allowing Liam to be so dominant. They might perceive Liam as being 'spoilt' and his parents as being weak, but both may be completely inappropriate. Blame can be placed in the other direction as well. Parents can feel that schools (or playgroups or colleges) are uncaring of their children or are unrealistic in their learning targets or withhold information. Wherever the blame is placed, it does not help professionals and parents to work together in any kind of partnership.

## Developing partnership

The following is an account of how one school set about developing partnership with parents.

---

**CASE STUDY**

Tudor School spent some time developing partnership with parents in the early years department. They appointed a part-time home–school liaison worker who was also the school nurse. She spent three days a week on nursing matters (funded by the health authority) and two days on working with parents (funded by the school). There was a room in the school designated 'The Parents' Room' and this also contained a toy library as well as coffee making facilities and a small library of books about disabilities and ideas for working with young children with disabilities. Parents, usually mothers, came to school on the transport provided with their children on Tuesday mornings and many were taken home in the school minibus at the end of the morning. Some used public transport to return home and a few remained in school to help with afternoon activities and returned home with their children. A crèche was provided during the morning for siblings.

The morning meeting was used for a variety activities, some related to learning about disabilities or benefits or services such as respite care and others devoted to making home-made books or games for their children. Sometimes there was an invited speaker, who could be a member of staff or someone from outside the school, but on other occasions the sessions would be organised by the nurse or by the parents themselves. The emphasis was on informality and there was time set aside for the nurse to talk individually with parents.

Apart from the Tuesday morning meetings, parents could use the parents' room at any time they wished, which someone did on most days. Mothers would arrange to meet there for informal chats with each other, perhaps after helping in the classroom for an hour or two or before a clinic appointment.

Although many families did make use of the room and activities provided in the school, not all wanted to nor could come into school. The nurse allocated some of her time (during the day or in the evenings) to visiting these families at home, or in a place named by the families as a suitable place to meet. Her training in counselling skills and her experience in home visiting meant that she could help families make the best use of these visits, providing links with school and other agencies. In school the nurse would spend time talking with classroom staff, providing them with links to the families.

The health service used the school for regular doctors' and therapists' clinics and the nurse arranged appointments to suit the needs of the families

---

> as far as she could. The school was seen as a local resource and health funds were available to support this. Parents regarded the school as the central provider of services and perceived the nurse as an ally when strategic decisions were being made.

The work undertaken at Tudor School demonstrates the commitment felt by staff to developing a partnership with families. Funds had been set aside to provide a home–school liaison worker and different ways of meeting family needs had been provided. Of course, not every family was able to take advantage of the services because of other factors that were out of the hands of the school and the liaison worker, but the majority of families were reached and felt that they had both support for their needs and a voice to express their opinions.

## Difficulties in developing partnership

As was mentioned earlier, many school staff say that they cannot get parents to come into school and some will perhaps explain this by saying that the difficulties experienced by the children are related to poverty, unemployment, parental inadequacies and general social exclusion. Often these parents will have experienced difficulties during their own schooling and have memories of rejection from teachers and other professionals and of their own parents not being welcome in school. Encouraging people such as these to overcome their negative feelings is very hard and each school will need to experiment with different approaches before they find the right formula. Staff from a school in the deprived area of a new town said that the prospect of a bonfire seemed to draw parents into school. Annual reviews and meetings could not attract nearly as many parents as a bonfire. Perhaps in this particular neighbourhood, starting with building up confidence outside the school is necessary before people will venture in. Perhaps the school is the very place *not* to meet to talk where the local pub or social club might be.

Some schools may need to be more imaginative with their approaches to families and not expect either a conventional relationship or nothing. There are myriad reasons why the conventional relationship (where parents attend parents' evenings, annual reviews and generally give and receive information) is unsuitable, especially for the families who have a member with a disability or difficulty. In some cases it has to be accepted that partnership between professionals and particular families is too difficult to achieve, but with the majority of families, it can be said that if partnership is not established then the professionals have not yet found the right approach.

## Equality or equity?

Once a positive relationship between families and professionals has been developed, how does that grow into a partnership? What does partnership mean when it relates to these two groups? Can one talk about 'equality' when power does not seem to be equal between the partners? It is not always clear who has the power in the relationship as sometimes professionals hold power in terms of knowledge and access to services, but sometimes parents hold power through their role as consumers and evaluators of services, or through their greater knowledge of their own children.

It may be better to conceive of the relationship to be based on power sharing and on equity rather than equality. In other chapters in this book, it has been suggested that partnership and collaboration do not rely on sameness and equality, but on utilising differences. It is about valuing contributions from different sources and respecting those who hold information and expertise that together with other people's will be even more valuable. Parents and professionals are engaged in a joint enterprise which requires one to support the other in order to succeed.

## Strategies to support partnership

If schools and families are to be successful in their joint enterprise what strategies can help them to succeed, other than the home–school liaison worker and a parents' room cited in the Tudor School example?

---

**CASE STUDY**

Park Special School uses home–school diaries to encourage children to provide the liaison between families and classroom staff. The children 'write' their own diaries telling families about school and staff about home. Some children can actually write or draw, some use symbols on the computer, others choose photographs or pictures and yet others are 'involved' while someone records a taped message or draws a cartoon. Both at home and at school, these messages are used to encourage children to engage with family members and classroom staff in recalling their activities.

At Park School this kind of home–school diary is completed at least once a week, sometimes more if there are activities to be reported. The diary is also used more conventionally with information on social, health and educational issues flowing in both directions. If either side does not use the diary then the other assumes that there was insufficient time. Anything urgent and confidential is usually conveyed on the telephone or in a sealed envelope.

---

Home–school diaries have been used, particularly in special schools, for many years and it is useful for school staff to agree with families on the form that they will take. One mother of a child with multiple disabilities wanted all seizures recorded alongside the amount the child ate and drank during the day so that she would know how much food and drink to give the child at home. In return the mother reported on how the child had been in the night and whether she had had any breakfast. Both sets of correspondents added humorous comments to relieve the boredom.

It is helpful to review the use of home–school diaries regularly as it is easy to keep on in the same way when needs, on either side, have actually changed.

Reviews of any kind are useful in all partnerships as it gives a chance for partners to stand back and evaluate what is good and not so good about their relationship and then decide how to develop in the future. It is quite rare for schools and families to spend time reviewing how they work together, although often they are very good at reviewing the progress of the children.

In the Tudor School example, two other strategies were used that will be helpful to explore briefly: parents working in classrooms and parent workshops. In other examples of support partnerships in this book, working alongside each other has been identified as a helpful strategy for developing collaboration. Parents working alongside teachers, teaching assistants and therapists in school can pass over their skills and knowledge as well as learn new skills. Apart from exchanging expertise, everyone can get to know and understand each other better. As children get older it may be more beneficial for some parent helpers to work in classes that do not contain their own children, but that is not universally so. The longer parents and professionals can work together the more the child will benefit from a unified approach.

Of course, not every parent is able or willing to volunteer to work in schools, although it seems important to offer the facility of working alongside professionals somewhere for at least a short while so that each can learn from the other. It may be necessary to arrange home visits to achieve this.

Running workshops is another way of passing on information to parents, although it is perhaps less good for receiving information from parents unless the sessions are deliberately interactive. Where it is appropriate it is very helpful for parents and professionals to attend workshops together so that they hear the information at the same time and work out how they are going to use it afterwards. Joint courses can be very powerful in promoting collaboration as they provide a focus for doing and for discussing topics together.

## Preschool partnership

When a child's disabilities are diagnosed, families can be completely overwhelmed, not only by the news, but by the range of assistance available to them. They may receive visits from several agencies and be expected to attend many hospital appointments, usually completely unconnected with each other. Children with extreme medical difficulties may have spent a considerable amount of time in hospital and/or may have complicated routines and equipment for families to manage at home. Parents may find themselves repeating information over and over again as each service or professional tries to help. The confusion that can surround families in the first few years of the life of a child with disabilities is not deliberately created by agencies, but the result can be benevolent chaos. On the whole, professionals really desire to help, although the outcome is often to make families feel as if they must beg for services which may be granted to them out of the goodness of the hearts of agencies. What seems to be lacking are the systems to organise services that should be available by right to families whose needs are greater than those of the majority of the population.

One system that has been developed, evaluated and refined is the keyworker model used by the 'Springfield Project'. The Springfield Project was a registered charity working during the 1990s in a northern county with families who had a baby or young child with multiple disabilities and complex health needs. The charity provided a keyworker whose job it was to help parents to promote their child's development, play and learning. There was also a need for the keyworker to respond to the emotional needs of the families and help them to benefit from the services available. As the charity developed it became clear that the focus should shift from the child to the family, particularly as the diagnosis of multiple disability can result in tremendous pain and distress for all family members.

The keyworker became 'an assistant parent', generally helping and supporting during the first months and years of living with and bringing up a child with multiple disabilities. Keyworkers were people who are good at listening, who also possessed counselling skills as well as being knowledgeable about child development and the services available for families to access. They developed close relationships with families, maintaining a positive but realistic stance and avoided becoming yet another professional 'expert'.

Part of the role of the keyworker is to help families coordinate the professionals and agencies so that:

- appointments are rationalised;
- professionals know what each other is doing;
- duplication and contradictory advice is avoided;
- services provide collectively for the whole child and family.

Keyworkers also help parents to integrate all interventions so that:

- they have an holistic picture of the child's abilities and needs;
- there is a whole approach which embraces all developmental activities, learning programmes and goals.

There are four main stages in the relationship between keyworkers and families:

1. *Introductory phase* – getting to know the child and family and working to establish mutual friendship and trust.
2. *Regular visits phase* – over an agreed period of time.
3. *Winding down phase* – which is negotiated with the family.
4. *Keeping in touch phase* – which is also negotiated.

Various records are kept so that the relationship is properly conducted and documented. There is a family file which is kept by the keyworker and consists of official notes, letters and reports. The family have access to the file as does the supervisor of the keyworker. A log of each visit is kept by the keyworker and this also includes any action promised. The family keep their own records of their child's progress perhaps through a whole-picture book or video recordings.

Parents of 'Mark' describe their experience of a Springfield Project keyworker.

> **CASE STUDY**
>
> Our son Mark was eight months old when he was seriously ill with pneumococal meningitis. The illness left Mark with severe learning difficulties, autism and epilepsy. We will be forever indebted to the marvellous doctors and nurses who looked after Mark while he was in hospital.
>
> However, in the months after Mark's return home, and as the side-effects of his illness began to emerge, we began to feel increasingly isolated. We were 'hitting a brick wall' with our concerns over his lack of development; being cast as paranoid parents when trying to deal with his fitting, sometimes numerous times a day; and being offered little or no guidance over where to seek help.
>
> Enter the Springfield Project, purely by chance, and Sally, who was to be Mark's keyworker. It immediately became clear when we first met Sally that here was someone who was taking the time to listen and genuinely understood our concerns for Mark.
>
> Sally then began to discuss with us how best to tackle the problems we faced, developing plans on who we needed to see, the questions we needed to ask, helping to ensure that the numerous people who were helping Mark were coordinated in their approach. Right from the beginning, Sally showed her ability to work effectively alongside us so that we adopted the best strategies for getting Mark help. At the same time, she provided invaluable support to us, whether it be attending appointments with us, or just being there to listen during our many low points.
>
> Thanks to the Springfield Project, and Sally in particular, we began to feel that Mark was at last getting the help he needed. Sally's work culminated in assisting with Mark's Special Needs Statement. Mark is now six, making good progress with his development, attending a school he loves and his epilepsy is much more controlled.

Mark's parents are clearly certain that the presence of a keyworker who was able to listen to and support the whole family helped them to lay the foundation for nurturing their multiply disabled son. Other examples provided by Peter Limbrick can illustrate the way in which a keyworker model can work.

> **CASE STUDY**
>
> When the special care baby unit (SCBU) were preparing to discharge Jack at ten weeks of age, his mother was extremely anxious that she would not manage. Her fear was that Jack would have some sort of crisis and she would not deal with it properly without doctors and nurses at hand. She imagined him dying during the first weeks at home. The family approached the voluntary agency, who provided a keyworker to help. The keyworker was not a medical person and it was agreed with the family that her role was to visit the mother at home and offer emotional support.
>
> Jack's discharge waited until his parents and the keyworker had got to know each other and the keyworker attended the discharge planning meeting to introduce herself to the SCBU medical team and the specialist home

> visitor. For the first few months the keyworker visited two or three times a week and then on a reducing scale until Jack was admitted to a nursery. Some years later Jack's mother commented that the whole service she received in the first years could not have been better.

As can be seen from both the stories, families require the support of someone who has the time to listen and physically support them when they feel unable to care for a child with complex medical needs. The next story shows the importance of bringing together the advice of therapists into a set of activities that the family can manage.

---

**CASE STUDY**

John was six months old and had many problems from birth. His mother, a single parent since the disabilities were confirmed, was anxious for her child to have every opportunity to learn and develop, but felt unequal to the task. A physiotherapist and occupational therapist had got to know John, but his mother did not feel able to carry out their suggestions at home. The Springfield Project provided a keyworker who agreed a dual role with John's mother. He would become someone she could talk to when she needed and he would help her to learn to play with John in activities that would include the therapists' goals. Some of these play sessions were recorded on videotape so that John's mother could show them to her parents to help them when they had John for weekends.

---

The Springfield Project has provided several examples of the way in which a keyworker system can work. The important aspect in that project was the independence of the keyworkers. They are not employed by an official agency or service, but can look at the whole situation in an unbiased manner, supporting and advising in a way that is relevant for each family.

## Conclusions

Although the independent keyworker system can work very well, it is not the only way in which an effective partnership with parents can be established. The last story used in this chapter comes from parents of a child with multiple disabilities and complex needs, who write about partnership with a professional which sounds very similar to the keyworker model. It neatly sums up so many of the aspects of a support partnership between families and professionals.

---

**CASE STUDY**

A successful professional and parent partnership is hard to find, but when you find it and it works well you can conquer almost everything! We found this with Jean, Anna's speech therapist.

Jean was involved with Anna from six weeks old, when she could not feed properly. From the first time we met Jean, she did not give us any false hopes.

She told us everything as she saw it. Total honesty, that's all we want, and that's what we got!

We tried a number of different ways to feed Anna, and when they did not work, Jean never sounded disappointed or pushed us to keep trying. She was just positive, asking us our thoughts on the situation and moving on to another way of feeding. If I found I could not cope myself with a particular way of feeding, we would get together and discuss another way. Jean encouraged us all the way and praised and respected everything we did and said. She understood all the problems we had with Anna and always listened to what we had to say.

Jean suggested a gastrostomy for Anna, but the paediatrician thought she would learn to feed in her own time eventually. Jean worked very hard to encourage Anna to cooperate with various tests to convince the paediatrician she needed the operation, not only for her, but for us as a family to take the pressure off feeding times, which could take up to 16 hours through the day and night. She did it and it changed our lives. At least we could go out now and do more 'normal' day-to-day activities with a feeding pump.

Next was communication. Makaton was introduced to us when Anna was about 12 months old. Jean was straight with us and told us that she would have speech problems and almost certainly have behavioural problems if she could not communicate. It was amazing. Anna really picked it up quickly and for the first time she could ask for a drink or a biscuit. Jean was really enthusiastic and encouraging.

When Anna started specialist and mainstream playgroups, Jean would arrange meetings with everyone involved with Anna to go to playgroup and meet the teachers and invite us along to discuss Anna's progress and make plans and goals for the next three months or so and regularly review and meet again. Each time we were involved. The playgroups were grateful for input as it helped them to teach Anna correctly.

Anna is now four years old and she has started mainstream nursery with a nursery nurse who uses Makaton signs. We could never have expected Anna to go to mainstream school, but Jean has always had faith in Anna's ability to learn and has wanted to prove other professionals wrong. Jean has worked so hard and encouraged Anna to make verbal sounds and now she has convinced a plastic surgeon to operate on Anna's throat to improve the quality of speech and eating, which has taken nearly three years of hard work.

This partnership has been successful because Jean has come into our home, has got to know us as a family and our family needs, has encouraged us to fight for Anna when she has been 'written off' so many times, has believed in Anna and has discussed her progress and what lies ahead. She is friendly and approachable, honest, a fantastic listener and most all, Anna loves going to see her, which I think says it all.

Partnership between families and professionals takes time to build and not every agency or professional is prepared to devote the time necessary. Partnership can make all the difference though between a family with a child who is thriving and developing well and one that is virtually dysfunctional. Early intervention within a supportive partnership can be the key.

# Chapter 13

# Joint professional development

One of the aspects of support partnership that has been mentioned several times, but not yet explored in any depth, is that of professional development. It has been suggested repeatedly that professionals require opportunities to learn how to work together effectively if they are to meet the needs of learners who have special needs and this chapter contains the results of a three year research project set up to implement and evaluate an example of joint professional development. It is hoped that it may provide the basis for others wishing to develop a course suitable to support and develop the teamwork of people working in the human services.

This course was part of an action research project designed to answer the questions:

- *How can I run a day workshop for teams of people in organisations which has an impact on their collaborative practice?*
- *How can I develop a teaching approach which enables participants to reflect on and develop their own practice?*

The day workshop was developed, progressively trialled and altered until a framework suitable for a variety of settings was settled upon. The action researcher recounts the project.


## Training for collaboration workshops

The workshops designed to help organisations such as schools, colleges and services to develop their collaborative teamwork were carried out and evaluated 19 times. Each had broadly the same framework, although the detail was altered in the light of evaluations and according to the needs of the organisation in which it was being run. In total almost 400 people have been involved with the workshops that were part of the action research project.

As expressed to organisations who wish to develop their collaborative teamwork, the general aims of the workshop are:

- to exchange information concerning present multidisciplinary collaboration in your organisation;
- to consider the problems and possibilities for collaborative work between staff;
- to discuss the components of effective collaboration;
- to move practice forward in your organisation.

The teaching medium is mainly discussion: a mixture of dialogue between participants and me (the workshop leader), large group discussion, small group discussion and directed activities. This aspect of the workshops will be considered separately later in this chapter, when I briefly consider my teaching style and how that developed during the project. It will be sufficient to say at this point that my aim throughout the day is to engage in dialogue with participants: firstly, to listen to what they perceive as their successful and less successful aspects of teamwork; and secondly, to offer possibilities for developments gleaned from my research and experience, relating directly to their concerns.

The first exercise is a SWOT, which summarises the strengths, weaknesses, opportunities and threats relating to teamwork in the organisation. My motive for using this exercise is the need for me to understand the way in which teams work in the setting so that I can be of help in developing collaborative practice. This first discussion includes the whole group in order that everyone can hear what is being said about their organisation. During this session, which usually lasts until coffee time, I can interject with questions and ideas. My intention is to include definitions of terms such as the differences between liaison, cooperation, coordination and collaboration, but I fit these into the discussion as the need arises.

After a coffee break, I encourage the discussion to move away from the organisation for a while and we brainstorm problems and possibilities for teamwork generally. This is the time when I pick up on any particular topic suggested by those who engaged me and on any other which seems to be prominent. In one organisation, for instance, I deduced quickly that meetings were posing a particular problem and we spent some time considering how these could be improved. We made a list of things people like about effective meetings and then discussed how some of these could be introduced into their own.

After lunch, I divide participants into groups of approximately six to play the 'Effective Collaboration Game'. This time of day is often characterised by difficulties in concentration and a small group task is helpful for keeping the momentum going. I explain that the game is an excuse for discussion and that the rules are simple with no obligation to keep to them. There are 15 statements which follow the stem, 'Effective collaboration means:'

1.  team members have well-defined roles which have been agreed between members.
2.  team members' expertise and interests are known to all.
3.  specialisms are used so that pupils/clients get the best from each team member.
4.  certain central tasks can be carried out by any team member.
5.  pupils'/clients' work is jointly planned by team members.
6.  there is one set of records open to all team members.
7.  all team members' views are heard and debated whatever their status.
8.  there is strong leadership in terms of providing direction for the team, but this leadership can vary depending on the needs of the pupil/client.
9.  there is an atmosphere of support so that team members feel comfortable giving their views.

10. team members trust each other when they are working independently from each other.

11. team members watch each other at work and learn from each other.

12. team members feel confident of their own abilities and can pass on relevant skills to other team members.

13. team meetings are well run and decisions are made.

14. joint training is available for all team members.

15. there are regular reviews of the work of the team.

The group must discuss every statement and either say how they achieve each one in their organisation, or talk about how they might achieve them. I tell them that all statements are important and that they have a hour in which to complete the game. If they wish they can group the statements or place them in some kind of a hierarchy. At the end, we briefly share any important aspects from each group.

Following this task, the final activity of the day begins. For this, participants are usually divided into their day-to-day teams, though with one group, they opted to remain as one large group because their interest was in developing ways in which three separate under-eight's services could work together. The purpose of the task is to review teamwork at grassroots level and encourage the writing of an action plan to move it forward in the light of the day's discussions. This begins with a 'bragging and moaning' session where team members are asked to list the good and not-so-good points about their teamwork. Then they select one of the not-so-good which can be improved in the near future and write an action plan. To this they add names and dates by which the plans will be carried out and finally set a date for evaluation of the success of the plan. I have experimented with ways of ensuring this evaluation, sometimes pairing off teams and sometimes handing over that element to managers.

In summary, the workshop is an attempt to affect the teamwork practice in organisations through open discussion and action planning. I deliberately do not have a fixed agenda, although I have a very full bank of possible avenues down which we can go. I want to respond as far as possible to the needs of individuals and their work together. Previous research reported in the literature suggests that short courses which have the greatest impact are those which directly relate to immediate needs and which engage participants actively in reflecting on their own practice (see Chapter 5). My approach has taken both these into account. I turn now to consider the evaluations I have received and from those attempt to gauge the impact of the workshops.

## Impact of the workshops

The main tool for judging the impact of the day course was an end-of-day questionnaire used nine times and, in the case of one school, a follow-up questionnaire several months later. I also made notes of my reactions to what occurred on three of the days which will be used in support of the written responses. In addition, I administered an opening questionnaire to three of the organisations so that I would have a record of respondents' perceptions of the teamwork in their organisation, especially as each organisation was at a different

**Table 13.1** Numbers of respondents to the end-of-session questionnaire

| Organisation | Number of respondents |
| --- | --- |
| School | 7 |
| School | 22 |
| School | 26 |
| Intensive support service | 7 |
| Autistic community | 13 |
| Autistic community | 10 |
| Community health team | 13 |
| Adult training centre | 13 |
| Under eights service | 32 |
| Total | 177 |

stage in their development of teamwork and wanted to discuss different aspects during the day.

Table 13.1 gives a breakdown of the workplaces and numbers of respondents to the end-of-session questionnaire, although not every question was answered by all participants. I refined the questionnaire over the three years so that it gave me better feedback for future planning, therefore not every question appeared in exactly the same way all nine times.

As the questionnaires were open-ended in nature, I will present the results in terms of the themes which arose from comments. A tabular form will help to make these themes clear. I will indicate the total number of respondents to a particular question (sometimes not everyone offered a comment) and the total number of responses (this may be greater than the total number of respondents as some comments contained more than one theme).

One question concerned what participants felt they might have learned as a result of the day course (Table 13.2):

*What do you feel you learned about collaborative teamwork during the day?*

**Table 13.2** What respondents felt they had learned about collaboration

| Comments | Number of responses |
| --- | --- |
| the importance of communication and support between members | 80 |
| an understanding of what collaboration means and what is possible | 46 |
| the importance of teamwork | 28 |
| that we already do it | 13 |
| how difficult it is | 13 |
| Total number of responses | 180 |
| Total number of respondents | 149 |

One of my central messages is that 'you cannot be a team unless you talk together'. This appears to have been appreciated by at least half of my listeners, although they highlighted different aspects of this, for example: meetings; sharing information; planning. It is also interesting that understanding the meaning of collaboration is seen as important. On several occasions people have spoken to me following one of these days, saying that they thought they were collaborating well or their teamwork was good, until they analysed it with me. However, none have indicated that this was a negative experience, which could have been the case.

As my interest is in the impact of the day course on practice, I asked the question:

> *What aspects of the day do you anticipate will be most helpful in your future teamwork practice?*

The answers were varied (see Table 13.3) but three were mentioned most often: the action planning at the end of the day, a general increased awareness of team colleagues and the opportunity afforded by such a day for talking and working together.

Two of the activities in which they were involved were mentioned by 23 people (the Effective Collaboration game and the SWOT analysis), although the reference to talking and working together must include these as they played a major part in the groupwork. No one made any negative comments in this section: everyone could find something they thought would be useful in their practice. Table 13.4 contains a few examples of the comments from individuals. They were selected to indicate the range of comments and to give some idea of how I reduced these to the seven categories used in Table 13.3.

I did specifically ask for ideas for improvements to the day and from 170 responses, 120 had no comment to make or said it should remain the same. 15 people wanted more small group activities and 11 had comments to make on my

**Table 13.3** What respondents anticipated would be most helpful elements of the day in future teamwork practice

| Comments | Number of responses |
| --- | --- |
| action planning | 52 |
| gaining awareness and understanding of other people's roles, needs | 53 |
| the opportunity to talk and work together | 41 |
| gaining an understanding of teamwork | 14 |
| the Effective Collaboration Game | 14 |
| the SWOT analysis | 9 |
| mention of something specific to be done following the day | 8 |
| Total number of responses | 191 |
| Total number of respondents | 177 |

**Table 13.4** Examples of comments concerning the most helpful elements of the day

'planning action'

'have had time for discussion'

'talking to each other and sharing ideas'

'awareness of others' strengths and weaknesses'

'making sure I give myself (and other members of our team) time to evaluate present practice and to *implement* change where necessary – not let it go on and on'

'the acknowledgement from care staff and heads of houses of the "isolation" of education and the need to communicate with them on this aspect of life at SC'

'bragging and moaning'

'deciding upon things to improve in the future. Develop a better team, knowing what others consider to be important'

'opportunity to air views and grievances regarding multidisciplinary working'

style, such as wanting five minute warnings before discussion time was up and encouraging more people to speak in large groups. I will discuss this in more detail in the final section of this chapter which is concerned with my teaching approaches.

From the questionnaire, I wanted details regarding the action planned in the final session of the day to see what developments were intended for the near future. Although it is unwise to take this as concrete proof that practice was to be affected, it is certainly an indicator of the intention of participants to develop their practice. Table 13.5 shows which aspects of teamwork were identified as ready for improvements.

**Table 13.5** The aspects of collaboration included in action plans

| Comments | Number of responses |
| --- | --- |
| communication | 85 |
| time management | 30 |
| relationships and support of one another | 49 |
| specific projects planned | 30 |
| planning, organisation and review | 18 |
| individual's personal aspects | 14 |
| vague improvements | 6 |
| Total number of responses | 232 |
| Total number of respondents | 148 |

**Table 13.6** Examples of action plans in one school

---

'to meet each morning at 8.30. Finishing earlier to leave time for toileting and record keeping'

'time to discuss ideas. Utilise skills to extend ideas – > practical activity'

'joint planning of topics in order to gather suitable resources. Time to discuss ideas and decide which to adopt'

'buy a clock; daily morning meetings; planning activities; leaving time for changing; allowing time for record keeping'

'meeting to be planned to discuss individual children's goals with teacher, assistant and therapist'

'time management: making time for staff communication; enough time for changing and self-help skills; improve activity planning so children aren't rushed'

'to implement planning meeting for individual children involving all disciplines'

'to organise regular meetings, possibly a two hour session per class, per term'

'five mins meeting a.m. and p.m. and meeting with OT once a week'

'try to set up integrated nursery'

---

In the case of one school, I was able to send a follow-up questionnaire which is a better gauge of impact on practice. Twenty-six people filled in the end-of-session form and 15 the follow-up. Table 13.6 contains examples of the action plans recorded on the first form. Of the 15 people who filled in the follow-up questionnaire 14 said that they had carried out their plan. The fifteenth put a question mark and added the remark, 'We still do not interact with other classes very much, but practically it would be difficult to do otherwise.' When asked what they actually did, ten said they had meetings and discussions, two referred to time management and one to better teamwork. Three mentioned a specific outcome such as adopting the programme MOVE (Movement Opportunities via Education) which they felt was attributable to the plan devised on the day course.

I also asked if they carried out the evaluation session that was set up as part of the action plan. Only two said they had. I was disappointed that this part had not worked, but as almost everyone had carried out their plan, perhaps this did not matter unduly. I would still suggest, though, that regular evaluation is important, but recognise that it is not seen as a priority in many teams. I went on to find out (a) if any more developments had come about as a direct result of the day course and (b) if they anticipated any more in the future. These results are shown in Tables 13.7 and 13.8 respectively.

Although fewer people felt that there would be future developments attributable to the course, a good proportion felt that there had already been specific effects which is encouraging when seeking evidence of impact.

I was also interested in whether individuals felt that their own teamwork had improved since the course. Seven were positive and five were not, although one comment read, 'not really – still working closely with therapists' and other negative responses were given by people who felt their teamwork was good before the workshop began. Table 13.9 includes a summary of the ways in which people felt they had improved. Some people cited more than one aspect.

**Table 13.7** Other developments attributable to the workshop

| Comment | Number of responses |
|---|---|
| Yes | 9 |
| No | 5 |
| Don't know | 1 |

**Table 13.8** Anticipated future developments

| Comment | Number of responses |
|---|---|
| Yes | 5 |
| No | 7 |
| Don't know | 2 |
| No answer | 1 |

**Table 13.9** Ways in which respondents felt their teamwork had improved

| Comments | Number of responses |
|---|---|
| more discussion, passing on of information | 4 |
| more awareness of others and their skills | 3 |
| more confidence | 1 |
| felt more included | 1 |

## Conclusion concerning the day course

From the evidence offered above, I would claim that the day course was successful both in terms of the approaches to the day and in terms of its impact on practice. My understanding of the literature (see Chapter 5) led me to believe that what I had planned would be useful for development in both individuals and their organisations and this has been borne out in terms of self-reported effects. I am aware, though, that this evaluation falls into the category of research carried out by course providers which is criticised in the literature as less satisfactory than outsider research. However, I am excited by the fact that the course appears to have been a catalyst for many people. I am sure that there was a halo effect evident in some cases and that it faded quickly, but the follow-up questionnaires showed that, in the case of one school, effects of the action plans had been definite and were still having impact. For others, it had been a confirming experience and they found comfort in realising that their teamwork was sound. No one who filled in the end-of-session questionnaire suggested that she or he had learned nothing, which demonstrates that there are approximately 300 people with open minds ready to reflect and learn. There have been examples of individuals who have appeared less responsive at the time, for example a classroom assistant at one school felt that the discussion concerning annual reviews was not relevant to her. I think that she was convinced that it had some relevance after arguments from me and then from other staff in the school, especially when involvement of assistants in the process was debated and adopted.

## My teaching approach

*How can I develop a teaching approach which enables participants to reflect on and develop their own practice?*

The final part of this chapter reporting on the action research project relates to the approaches to teaching and learning which underlie the workshops I ran. I was anxious to encourage the reflective practice suggested from the literature (see Chapter 5) and developed a style which I called 'teaching through comment' to facilitate this.

The course questionnaire contained three open-ended questions that referred to the way in which the day was run: 'What aspects of the day do you anticipate will be most helpful to your teamwork practice?', 'Please comment on the way the day was run. What did you particularly like?' and 'What do you feel should be changed when I run this day another time?' Although, these did not always draw out comments that referred to my style of teaching, many participants used these questions as an opportunity to express their feelings concerning my approach.

Before I present the results of the evaluation, it will be helpful to recap on the framework for the day, but this time characterising my teaching style. Essentially the day is concerned with teambuilding which takes reflecting on current practice as a basis for change in the future. I encourage and facilitate evaluation of the participants' own work through the medium of action plans, getting commitment to develop new ideas. Although I have an agenda for the day, I start from their own practice and, through using question and answer and brainstorming techniques, I comment on what they tell me.

My approach has been to encourage the participants to talk about their organisation, its strengths and weaknesses and its vision. By asking pertinent questions I can direct them towards the aspects of teamwork which I consider are crucial to success and failure and by engaging in discussion I can make suggestions for improvements. If the group is under 20 then it is possible to conduct this exercise as a whole group discussion, even though there may be some members who will not contribute in this kind of forum. If numbers are in excess of this, or if the large group is dominated by a few vociferous members, then small group discussion precedes the full group feedback to enable everyone's views to be heard.

If small group discussion, followed by feedback, is used then I ensure that the feedback is more than merely a repeat of that discussion. It is easy to become bored if the session is not continually moving forwards. For instance, if small groups are asked to share their experiences of teamwork, they are asked to find instances of successful and unsuccessful teamwork. I will take this information a stage further in the feedback by dividing it into four sections: strengths, weaknesses, opportunities and threats (SWOT). From this they will have a detailed analysis of their organisation upon which to base the rest of the day. Informal evaluations have revealed that it is usual for several people to learn something new about their workplace after this exercise. On many occasions this new knowledge has led to greater understanding of the way in which colleagues work, their beliefs and the constraints under which they work.

The morning is spent in a variety of different discussions and question and answer sessions, some very specifically related to the organisation under scrutiny, such as, 'What kind of records do you keep?' leading to the importance of joint records, and others more general, such as, 'Why collaborate?' leading to team planning of individual programmes. The afternoon is rather different and begins with 'The Effective Collaboration Game'. This is merely another stimulus for discussion and I make that very clear to participants, who are often resistant to playing 'silly games' and engaging in role play.

For this game, participants are divided into random groups but for the final exercise, it is imperative that they work in their day-to-day teams. This is the zenith of the day. In their working teams, they have a 'bragging session' in which they record on paper all the good things about their teamwork. Then they have a 'moaning session' where they record the problems they have. After that they select one problem which they feel is solvable in the next few weeks and write themselves an action plan to improve the situation. The day is not finished until they have shared the outline of the action plan with the whole group and agreed on who is going to do what by when. The final act is to decide on an evaluation date and who is going to be involved.

## What am I trying to do?

So, how would I characterise 'teaching through comment'? What am I trying to do? My intention is to lead participants to reflect on the strengths and weaknesses of their present practice and from that to plan ways in which they can develop more effective ways of working. I tell them about what I have found in my research in other organisations and make suggestions about what I consider to be good practice, but I only offer this when I judge that they are ready to consider it. I could produce transparencies and handouts and work my way through the aspects of teamwork I think they are going to need, but my belief is that this would not be as effective as commenting on what they tell me about their work. I have gathered information on theories of groups and teams and can provide explanations and arguments which could lead to greater understanding and perhaps to more effective practice. I am not, however, convinced that it is helpful for me to pass on all this information unless it is solicited.

As I was developing my practice along these lines, during the four years of the project, I was becoming aware of the principles upon which I was building my beliefs. These related to the way I viewed educational knowledge and the understanding I had of the way in which experienced professionals learn. Why didn't I simply want to tell them what I'd found out about how to work in teams? What did I believe that made that approach so alien to me? In my analysis I tried to answer the question, 'Why don't I want just to tell them?' and my answers seem to come from many different sources.

My first belief is that learners are essentially active constructors of their own personal knowledge and understanding and that they strive to make sense of their environment. Piaget's work on young children (see Wood 1998) seems to me to be also relevant to adult learners and it relates to what Borger and Tillema (1993) are writing on the active ways in which teachers can be encouraged to transfer knowledge into classroom teaching. So learners of all ages have to make their own connections between what they already know and understand and what is new to them. They will not make those connections if they are not 'ready' to do so, but I know I must be careful not to fall into the trap so many infant teachers did in the 1960s and 1970s as they waited for young children to become 'ready to read'. It is my responsibility as a teacher to lead learners to readiness. I cannot wait, but must offer opportunities for development. Although I indicated that I did not want to deliver lectures on group theory unless they were requested, I have an obligation to make sure that I am asked, through posing the sorts of questions which cause participants to come to the point of wanting to know themselves.

Question and answer techniques are basic to teaching in schools, but are perhaps less used in INSET sessions. Combining this with use of brainstorming appears to offer me a powerful tool for encouraging people to reflect on their present practice. I comment on what I am hearing, trying to encourage expansion of understanding and enabling participants' tacit knowledge to become more explicit. I know that I must work close to what I discern as present understanding, taking into account the work of Vygotsky on young children (see Wood 1998) concerning the importance of placing teaching in the child's 'zone of proximal development'. Too close or too far from current understanding will not be effective. Mindful of this, I spend a considerable amount of time asking questions so that I can find the group's zone. I try to make this clear, telling them that I can be much more effective in my teaching if I understand where their practice and their thinking are now. Then I am able to negotiate with them where they might want to be next.

Studies of teacher and in-service education have suggested that teachers find it difficult to put theory into practice (see Chapter 5). They possess the theoretical knowledge but need help in applying this to practical situations. My approach appears to provide a framework for at least some crossover from theory to practice. I make this explicit, giving time for action planning before the session is ended, so that groups of people who normally work together can discuss the implications for them of the wider discussions. I would argue that I am attempting to use some of the principles of action research which writers such as McNiff (1993) claim combines research and development, thus avoiding the difficulties teachers have with relating professional research to classroom practice. This is much truncated as, in the case of the one-day workshops, time is limited, but my framework encourages: sharing data concerning present practice; imagining solutions; and forming the first plan for action. I set up an evaluation session but this is left in the hands of the organisation. I cannot of course be sure that it is carried out and in fact the follow-up evaluations in one particular school, six months later (see above), revealed that formal evaluation sessions did not take place, though participants could pinpoint changes attributable to action plans made on the INSET day.

## Evaluation of my teaching style

Analysis of the 177 questionnaires given at the end of the day, gives some insight into the perceived effectiveness of my attempts to teach through comment, although it is wise to treat such evaluations with caution when assessing the

**Table 13.10** What participants enjoyed most about my teaching style

| Comments | Number of responses |
|---|---|
| listening to each other and engaging in discussions | 103 |
| action planning | 58 |
| SWOT analysis | 10 |
| encouraging reflection | 12 |
| an informal, relaxed and flexible style | 39 |
| Total number of responses | 222 |
| Total number of respondents | 177 |

effects on future practice. As they contained open-ended questions, the remarks have been categorised to reveal trends (Table 13.10). Most respondents commented on more than one aspect so the total responses add up to more than 177. There were 235 mentions of my teaching style and all but 13 were positive. The negative comments all referred to the need for even more small group work.

My main intention, when deciding to use end-of-the-day evaluation forms, was to generate an aid for planning the next teamwork day, rather than to provide a valid research tool, but analysis of the total number of questionnaires has provided data to support the teaching style that I have adopted. This can be further supported through a dialogue I had with two colleagues. I asked them to observe my teaching and give me feedback so that I could move my practice forward. The general tenor of the discussion was very positively in favour of using an interactive approach. When I asked whether they felt I had got enough information across to participants or 'Would it be better to deliver a lecture?' they both vehemently answered together, 'No, no absolutely not'. They also agreed that the question and answer style was effective and that participants had been encouraged to reflect on what they already did and understood as the basis for future developments. We discussed handling an argumentative participant and the possibility for being diverted by 'red herrings'. This can be a danger when the teacher is trying to follow the lead of the learners and I have tried to develop the skill, over time, of leading discussants back to a central point. There was, however, one occasion when participants were so concerned with the results of a recent management decision that I felt I had to enable them to leave the main topic and discuss what had happened as they were unlikely to be receptive to my arguments until they had talked through their current concern. Working in an interactive style demands a very subtle sharing of control between teacher and learners. I must allow them to run but must 'reel them in' when they stray too far.

## Summary and conclusions

This chapter has contained a single example of a workshop designed to enable participants to reflect on and improve their collaborative teamwork. There is no suggestion that this kind of workshop is the only way to achieve effective teamwork. There are many different kinds of professional development which would be capable of achieving the same end. What is most important is that time is given to teambuilding and development. Teams and partnerships cannot flourish when people are merely thrown together and expected to work in a collaborative manner. It takes time and training to become fully effective.

The case presented in this chapter described a one-day workshop and organisations are likely to benefit from such short courses for all their staff. They also require at least some staff to have been engaged for much longer in the process of developing teamwork. They can then become the source of expertise on that topic, as others might be on communication, leisure activities or a National Curriculum subject. Organisations such as schools, colleges and services such as speech therapy or visiting teachers would benefit from appointing (at least) one person who is responsible for the effectiveness of the teamwork or partnerships between staff or between staff and families. It would be his or her job to facilitate the smooth running of the teamwork, but also to ensure that there is adequate time set aside for professional development issues. As with other specialists, these people may be able to carry out some of the development themselves but they should also be responsible for organising outside speakers, visits and study days to enable teamwork to be given sufficient encouragement.

# Chapter 14

# Support partnerships: Where are we and where should we go next?

This final chapter contains both a summary of the strategies that promote partnership between professional groups that have appeared in the thirteen previous chapters, and also a summary of the current position of research into support partnership and possible ways forward both in terms of research and in terms of practice. In addition it includes an audit for partners who would like to review the way in which they work together. This is based on the audit that appears in Lacey and Lomas (1993).

These are the questions that underpin this chapter.

- *What are the lessons that have been learned about how to achieve effective support partnerships?*
- *What are the strategies that promote partnership?*
- *What are the questions that organisations and services should ask themselves when wishing to improve their partnerships and collaboration?*
- *What are the current concerns of research into partnership and collaboration?*
- *What should be the future concerns of this research?*

## Lessons from support partnerships

The case studies presented in the second part this book represent a tiny sample of support partnerships across a small range of situations. However, they could be seen to represent the main aspects of partnership and teamwork across the human services and by drawing them together many of the messages about working collaboratively can be heard. The advantage of in-depth case studies, such as those presented in Chapters 6–13, is the detail that it is possible to present. Professionals who wish to learn from other people's practice require considerable detail to understand what is happening and how far they can transfer what they are reading about to their own situations.

In order to distil the essence of effective support partnerships, the outcomes from a Mencap conference entitled 'What's Good Support?' will be used. A video and a booklet were produced from the conference and through the voices of people with learning disabilities and their supporters, professionals can learn about what constitutes good support (Mencap undated). In this context, supporters are volunteers who help people with learning disabilities to speak out and give their opinions. They do not speak for people with learning disabilities, but help them to get their views across. Their role is to enable others; to pass on their expertise; to find out what their partners need and provide that in the best possible way.

## Lessons from the conference

People with learning disabilities and their supporters have a very clear view of what makes good support and their words sum up some of the most important aspects of support partnerships very well.

*'People with learning difficulties were part of the project from the start.'* (Partners should plan jointly the activities they are going to undertake together.)

*'Everyone who came to the weekend had something to give, we wanted everyone to feel equal.'* (Partners should value each other's contributions in an atmosphere of equality or equity.)

*'All the papers and meetings had to be made accessible, people needed information early so they could prepare.'* (Partners should make sure that they do not use unnecessary or unexplained jargon and they need to give each other time to prepare for meetings and joint activities.)

*'Some things went wrong so we had to act fast to fix them.'* (Partners should be ready to sort out difficulties which arise from working together.)

*'I think support is about power. A supporter can either empower or disempower people very easily with a word, a look, with an intervention or a block.'* (Partners should be aware of power relationships and ensure that power is distributed between them.)

*'I think the supporting role is still a new thing to some people in the professional world. They sometimes forget the expertise people need to support somebody, the time and effort and the money that's there to support people.'* (Developing a support partnership takes time, money and effort.)

*'Because I had good support I was able to do more things, work to a higher standard and be a National Councillor for Mencap.'* (Partners can help each other to develop new skills and understanding through passing on expertise.)

*'Good supporters put their partner first, but know that it's OK to say no, OK to get angry sometimes. Good supporters have a real belief in their partner, a real commitment to equal opportunities.'* (Partners encourage each other to give their opinions and are not afraid of positive conflict.)

*'You've both got to have a clear vision and clear aims, unless you share the same belief you can't provide quality support.'* (It is important for partners to agree on common aims and work together towards them.)

*'We found that the most important thing is to have a relationship where there is: good communication; and a lot of flexibility.'* (Good communication between partners is vital.)

*'If you have a bad supporter they want to do everything for you and you don't need that.'* (Partners do not take over from each other, but support each other to increase expertise between them.)

## Strategies to promote partnership

In order to encourage the most effective support partnerships to develop, certain systems and strategies (as has been seen in the case studies in this book) have been found to be helpful.

### Management systems

At all levels of teamwork, there seems to be a need for management systems that support individuals who strive to work together. At strategic level representatives of the different agencies need a forum for writing policies and making plans for developing practice across disciplines. At operational level it is advisable to bring together different members of the team under a single management system. It is much easier, for example in schools, for teachers and therapists to be supported to work together if they have the same line manager, vision and approaches. At fieldwork level, practitioners require common systems that enable them to share and carry out work jointly.

### Management support

Not only do members of teams need common systems, but they are also likely to flourish if they have encouragement from managers. Expectations from managers that team members will work together is important as is the facilitation of ideas for helping the partnership to develop. Active management support can also be vital, for example by providing non-contact time for meetings, or an office in which to meet. Sometimes the seemingly smallest support is the most important.

### Flexible time management

Time needs to be seen as the servant, not the master, of teamwork. If time is regarded as flexible and its use changeable, negotiations between partners seem to be possible. Partners need to agree on the priorities for their time and have the ability to change how it is used if it will help the team to be more effective.

### Leadership

Although partners and team members should have equity of voice, the work of the team is likely to be more effective if someone takes a leadership role. This person is not 'the boss' but 'the facilitator' for the team. She or he helps the teamwork to flourish, injects motivation when necessary, coordinates the work and generally takes responsibility for what happens. Leaders do not always emerge and in many cases it is helpful to agree who will take on the role (and for how long).

## Communication

Even when the team has only two members it seems to be important to decide upon lines of communication both for face-to-face meetings and for written reports. The process of talking about what is required seems to be as important as the actual methods used.

## Common focus

The partners who appear to work together well generally have a common focus to their work, for example motor education (see Chapters 6 and 7) or TEACCH (see Chapter 10). They have a common understanding, vocabulary, outlook and ways of working.

## Shared learning

Partners who learn together tend to work together effectively. It can be an advantage for team members to attend courses together so that they can hear the same message at the same time. They can also explore each other's perspectives and learn how to make the best use of the different viewpoints.

## Teambuilding

An important part of shared learning seems to be time set aside for building up the team. It is almost impossible for, even two, people to meet once and then immediately work together effectively. People need time to get to know one another, understand each other's roles, agree on the common aims, work out how they will work together and how they will work apart.

Partnership and teamwork can be seen as impossible dreams, especially if they are grafted on to the traditional way of working. Working together in a collaborative manner demands different structures and systems and is unlikely to work if these remain the same. Learning support assistants (see Chapter 9) will continue to have no time to plan with teachers if they are not employed at times when teachers are free to plan with them. If collaboration is to be possible, terms of employment and ways of working will have to change.

# Conducting an audit

This section is based on Lacey and Lomas (1993) *Support Services and the Curriculum: A practical guide to collaboration* and is designed to help practitioners to consider the different aspects of provision within the human services in a systematic and reflective manner. Questions to ask will be suggested which arise from the discussions which have formed the heart of this book. Areas for consideration within an audit will be highlighted in order that an action plan can be devised which relates to specific teams and partnerships or 'would-be teams and partnerships'.

It has become fashionable to exhort professionals to carry out audits of their work and it is easy to feel overwhelmed by such procedures. Schools have been obliged for some time to write school development plans (or school improvement plans) and the procedure that is being advocated can relate directly to this. If priorities for collaborative work can be developed alongside other aspects of the work of organisations and services, a set of realistic possibilities can be suggested.

If staff are going to feel in control of the audit process, it is expedient for them to develop their own agendas and sets of questions to ask. This ensures that the process is relevant to individual situations. Thus it is advisable to see the following set of audit questions as starting points only and to spend time devising an audit which directly relates to each situation. Not all the questions posed will be applicable for all the situations in which support teams can be found.

## Strategic level

In the absence of a single service for meeting special needs, collaboration or at least cooperation between services must begin at a strategic level or fieldworkers will continue to be hampered by rules and conditions out of their control. An audit should indicate such questions as:

- What is being done to address the differences in structures, funding mechanisms and priorities within health, education and social services?
- What are the structures in place for LEAs, social services departments and health trusts to ensure effective implementation of new policies about common client groups?
- Who is responsible for interservice cooperation?
- What joint planning and consultation is there between education, health and social services?
- How is financial responsibility for provision decided?
- How does each service know the extent of its role and how is role confusion and overlap avoided?
- How is information about individual pupils with SEN (clients) collected and collated? Does the structure encourage or actively facilitate collaboration?
- How are families involved?
- How effective are the lines of communication between education, health and social services?
- Is there a policy statement or handbook setting out procedure for cooperation, available to all services?
- Does staff development include the chance for members of the different services to meet and discuss common strategies?
- When senior staff move on, what mechanisms are there to ensure that interservice cooperation is continued?
- Is collaboration (or at least cooperation) in the job descriptions of key people?
- Is there an agreement about confidentiality and its extension across services?

- How often is interservice cooperation reviewed and evaluated? Who and what is included in this review?

The *ad hoc* links that exist between education, health and social services will continue to frustrate real collaboration until such time as there is some form of regional or local initiative to support interagency work. In the absence of a single state department for services for people with special needs, the bulk of the work must be done at local and fieldwork level. One of the single most important factors is the appointment of professionals whose jobs include a significant amount of time for liaison between services. Initiatives will begin to happen if there are senior appointments made with this in mind. If those changes are to be made, directors of services must see it as a priority and must allocate resources.

## Operational level

This is the level at which heads of schools (colleges and centres), health services and district officers decide how to manage priorities within their own section. An audit should include such questions as:

- What structure exists at head of service/school level to ensure effective collaboration?
- Whose job is it to liaise with other services?
- What is contained in contracts between services, and in contracts between services and schools (colleges and centres)?
- How are managers' responsibilities defined where there is interservice work?
- How are joint decisions made at managerial level?
- What joint training is available for service managers and for fieldworkers?
- What training is available for collaborative work/running meetings/interpersonal skills/teambuilding?
- How are services organised to enable time for team members to meet for discussion?
- What has been done to enable team members to share physical proximity while they work in the field (e.g. sharing premises)?
- How are such potential problems as: status differentials/professional jealousies/service jargon/power games/conflicting loyalties handled as people work together?
- How are team members encouraged to work across the boundaries of their professional role ('role release')?
- How are team members chosen for each child's (client's) team? Is there any thought given to unnecessary overlap because of shared skills?
- How does the organisation of caseloads aid the timetables of fieldworkers?
- How is the keyworker or coordinator for each child's (client's) team decided?
- When do team members who service the same school (colleges, centres) get together to share information/skills/experience/knowledge?
- How are fieldworkers kept informed about decisions that affect them from any of the relevant services?

- What are the lines of communication between team members?
- In what way are families involved in their son's or daughter's team?
- What do job descriptions contain about collaboration?
- How are jargon-free reports encouraged?
- How often is interservice collaboration reviewed? Who and what is included in this review?

As at strategic level, one of the most important factors in enabling collaborative work at operational level is the recognition of the need to allocate time for liaison. Contracts can help considerably here, by building in time for planning and evaluation. Support departments in mainstream schools would find it useful to draw up their own forms of contract with individual departments and teachers. This would be an excellent forum for the discussion of the vexed problem of where to find time to meet and plan.

## Fieldwork level

The audit at this level centres round the way in which a support partnership or team achieves the overall aim of meeting the needs of children (or adults) with disabilities and difficulties. It focuses on the team itself and the way in which individual members contribute to making it effective. The questions are based in a school setting, but could easily be converted into a health or social service setting, a preschool or an adult situation The questions are deliberately formed to encourage forward thinking as far as possible. There are a lot of questions, but there does not have to be a response to them all. *They are suggestions.*

- Who is included in the support partnership/team?
- From which services do they originate? How does this affect their time/ commitment/resources?
- What is contained in the school or service contract on collaborative teamwork?
- How often are full team meetings held? What influences this?
- What arrangements are there for joint planning and regular exchange of information/assessment/records?
- How is it decided what kind support is being used: advising/direct support/ in class support/withdrawal?
- In what way are parents part of the child's team? How are they encouraged to be effective members?
- How are individual programmes for children written? How do team members agree priorities? What evidence is collected to inform those decisions? How is the procedure evaluated?
- What is the procedure for ensuring that children's priorities/general information etc. are communicated to all relevant staff?
- How does staff development include *all* staff? Is there joint training/ exchange of skills and knowledge/joint problem solving/training for effective teamwork?
- What is the procedure for passing on information and inducting a new person when a team member moves on?

- How is professional jargon avoided?
- How are roles defined to avoid the potential conflict caused by two adults working in the same room?
- How do team members know what tasks they are to perform? Is everyone clear about team and classroom tasks?
- What steps are taken to avoid unnecessary overlap, particularly in assessment and record-keeping?
- How does each team member work with pupils? Is there a blurring of roles when appropriate so that pupils receive similar input?
- How far is this input integrated into the curriculum and natural settings?
- What steps have been taken to reduce potential difficulties caused by professionals working together who have different backgrounds/funding arrangements/conditions of service?
- In what ways do team members support each other?
- What procedure enables team goals and priorities to be set?
- How is each child's core team decided? How many people does this generally include? Is the size conducive to effective teamwork?
- What procedures are there for calling upon a wider network of support when necessary?
- Of how many different teams is each support staff a member? Is this the most efficient division?
- Where are support staff placed physically? Can the proximity of the core team be improved?
- How is it ensured that 'everyone pulls their weight' in the team and that no one person is left to do all the work?
- Who is the coordinator of each child's team? Does this vary according to need? Is this person the child's keyworker?
- How effective are team meetings? What procedures are there for evaluating agendas/chairpersonship/decisions made/action taken etc.?
- What is the review procedure – for (a) the children's progress, (b) the work of the team?

At fieldwork level, staff must be committed to working together. They must genuinely believe that joint efforts offer a better service to the children (adults) with whom they work, or teamwork will continue to be half-hearted. It is very difficult to persuade doubters that after the initial struggle to find time, joint work becomes a way of life rather than a burden.

## Moving forward

Conducting an audit is the first stage in the process of moving practice forward. The data collected as part of the procedure should be rich in information about present practice and the constraints under which everyone works. Some of the questions have been weighted towards suggesting an ideal and developing towards all of these at once is not possible. It is necessary now to decide upon priorities. These will be different according to whether the team under scrutiny is at a strategic, operational or fieldworker level. Each team, at whichever level, will be at different stages of development, so the result of this section will be unique to each situation.

The three lists which follow contain suggestions for the areas in which schools and services may wish to decide upon priorities.

**Strategic level**
1. Funding and resources across services (including cross service funding)
2. Interservice cooperation (including communication and joint decision-making)
3. Structures and roles (including appointments and job descriptions)
4. Staff development across services (including opportunities for training in collaboration)
5. Policy documents (including handbooks of information)
6. Review and evaluation procedures

**Operational level**
1. Funding and resources within the service/school
2. Collaboration at service/school level (including communication and joint decision-making)
3. Structures and roles (including appointments and job descriptions)
4. Staff development (including joint training opportunities)
5. Contracts and policy documents
6. Review and evaluation procedures

**Fieldwork level**
1. Resources at organisational level (including problems with overlap)
2. Collaboration within support teams for each child (including organisational procedures and joint decision-making)
3. Roles and tasks of team members (including an agreement on which areas are shared)
4. Staff development (including opportunities for exchange of skills and knowledge as well as teamwork training)
5. Assessment and record keeping (including procedures for collaboration)
6. Curriculum delivery (including planning and working together in the classroom)
7. Review and evaluation (of both pupil progress and the teamwork process)

## Writing the action plan

After the process of audit and deciding upon the priorities for immediate development, it is important to commit this to paper in a manner which enables evaluation to be carried out easily. Action needs to be decided upon and a time-scale needs to be set against which progress can be measured. Special educationalists are skilled at writing objectives for individual pupils. That skill can easily be translated to objectives for themselves and their schools or services.

**EXAMPLE**

The audit may have revealed two people working together in the same classroom who have very different ideas about how support staff should be used. Although it may be impossible for them to agree on every point, one of the priorities for the next term must be that they are given time to exchange views and find an effective way of working together. Often misunderstandings occur because individuals are not given time to discuss their own points of view with each other.

Alongside this discussion should be more general staff development which increases the understanding those two individuals have of the nature of support teaching and the benefits of working together in an agreed manner.

Objectives might be written thus:

(a) Staff development sessions for this term will address:
   • innovative support teaching techniques
   • ways of working together.
(b) A and B will be timetabled for liaison sessions once a week.
(c) Class teachers and their specific support staff will produce a brief joint report on their work together for discussion at the end-of-term team meeting (contents to be agreed during a staff development session).

Although none of this guarantees that A and B will work together more effectively, positive steps towards this goal have been taken and the discussion at the end of term will reveal whether the situation has improved. If it has not then further steps can be taken, involving further training or even moving staff so more compatible individuals are working together.

This book has offered practical examples of working collaboratively in schools/services and family homes with children and young people who have a variety of special needs. This final chapter has included a basic structure of conducting an audit and developing an action plan for moving practice forward. Organisations and services will no doubt be able to create their own lists of suitable questions, but those which have been identified can act as an initial prompt. Specifics can be added or taken away according to need.

## Research and support partnerships

The concluding section of this final chapter is devoted to the consideration of research into collaboration. As was indicated in the literature chapters of Part One of this book, there has been very little research evidence to direct the practice of people wishing to work in partnership or teams. Common sense has guided most people's drive to collaborate. It seems sensible to try to reduce overlap, share ideas, report back to each other, pass over skills and problem solve together. It is almost impossible to set up a situation where it could be proved that collaboration is better than non-collaboration. Who could say which factors were most important? You cannot measure something so complicated in the same way as you can chemicals in the laboratory or sales figures in the business world.

It is, however, possible to carry out some research into collaboration as was seen from the review of the literature. For example, over the last two years (1998–2000), there have been several useful, mainly small-scale, studies that have provided evidence that collaboration is not only desirable but possible. Many of the studies have utilised the case study approach and the body of evidence is gradually growing. Four examples of recent research are described below and will form the basis for summing up current research interest and for preceding suggestions for future research.

## Effective Communication between Schools, LEAs and Health and Social Services in the Field of Special Educational Needs (Dyson *et al.* 1998)

In this study the researchers aim to identify obstacles to effective interagency cooperation in the context of the Code of Practice; to establish models of inter-agency cooperation and recommend ways in which cooperation and decision-making can be improved. Interviews and case studies were conducted in ten LEAs and suggested models were validated in regional and national workshops.

As part of their report the researchers identified some principles which seem likely to underpin effective interagency cooperation.

- Effective interagency work appears to depend on efficient information-management within and between agencies.
- Interagency cooperation needs specific location and opportunities within which it can develop (e.g. close proximity of offices, common caseloads).
- The development of effective cooperation appears to require a clearly-defined focus which is of significance to each participating professional (e.g. Code of Practice, drug abuse, children from a 'deprived' housing estate).
- The shared aims of the agencies must be powerful enough to counter the agencies, very different core purposes.
- In some cases, cooperation requires the intervention of one or more individuals with a vision to provide an initial stimulus.

The researchers warn that their small-scale study is limited but their recommendations support what has been found in the case studies presented in this book.

## Unlocking Key Working: An analysis and evaluation of key worker services for families with disabled children (Mukherjee *et al.* 1999)

In this study, the researchers planned, developed and implemented multi-agency key worker services for families with disabled children in two local authorities. Managers and practitioners in these authorities worked in partnership with the research team in order to observe, monitor and evaluate the process. Everyone involved in the projects, including parents, were interviewed about their experiences of the key worker service.

The key workers gave emotional support, advice and information to families, they identified and addressed family needs, acted as an advocate for the family and coordinated the different agencies and services. Families valued different aspects of the service, but all thought it important to identify and meet the family needs, not just those of the child. Key workers felt it was important to start the service at the point of diagnosis and that the key workers' role should be raised in profile in their services. Managers suggested that clarity of role was vital.

There were many recommendations from the case studies. At the point of starting a key worker service, it is recommended that there should be strong commitment from agencies and from people backed by a steering group of representatives of all interested parties. Planning should be given sufficient time so that aims, principles, roles and approaches can be agreed. During the implementation phase, communication is vital as are ongoing training, systems of support and time for further planning. The most important priorities are identified as:

- having time for planning;
- making sure the service is the outcome of agreed ownership between agencies;
- having an external facilitator to support the change process;
- involving families in evaluation.

The researchers point out several times in their report that all did not run smoothly during the project. They felt they learned as much from the difficulties as from the successes and could make recommendations based on both.

## 'Multi-disciplinary team working in practice: managing the transition' (Lowe and O'Hara 2000)

Questionnaires were used to evaluate the effect of setting up multidisciplinary teams in one authority that had a tradition of uni-disciplinary, profession-based practice. The new teams were focused on particular groups of clients, for example there was a children's team of occupational therapy, physiotherapy, speech and language therapy and the child development centre. Structures were put into place to support the new configuration which consisted of coordination and communication; monthly joint meetings for collaborative decision-making; annual appraisal and objective setting for team members; frequent team meetings and shared goal planning.

The development of the teams was encouraged through giving the members autonomy to decide their own priorities and ways of achieving goals. They were enabled to set their own standards and given time for reflection. Joint training was also available.

Feedback from service users and staff unanimously agreed that the services had improved in effectiveness, efficiency and quality. They cited improvements in goal setting, less repetition and more efficient use of time. Staff also reported feeling more supported and less threatened by other professionals who were now working in the same team. In terms of even more improvement, everyone called for more time for planning and liaison.

The researchers are very positive about the changes to the service since the introduction of multidisciplinary teams, though they warn readers about the fundamental changes necessary, not only in structures and systems, but also in professionals as they reappraise their own roles. Managers had to abandon their traditional models of managing and everyone has had to develop new skills and attitudes to fit the new way of working.

## 'Preparing students for interprofessional teamwork in health care' (Gilbert *et al.* 2000)

This is a report of a two-day interprofessional teambuilding workshop for health care students in British Columbia, Canada. Interestingly it was much easier to recruit students who were keen to learn about teamwork than university staff, who repeatedly cited other commitments as precluding such volunteer work.

The workshops utilised shared learning principles within interactive activities such as teamwork simulation using Lego bricks and patient case study problem solving. During the simulation exercise, each group was given different instructions and a different management model to adhere to, despite all being expected to produce the same Lego model. Discussing the models following the task seemed to be very helpful for the students developing their ideas about working in teams. The case studies provided participants with an opportunity to apply team theory and to demonstrate the effectiveness of interprofessional teamwork.

The workshops were evaluated as they progressed using periodic debriefing sessions and then written evaluations on completion. A follow-up evaluation was carried out six months after. The initial evaluations were very good, indicating that the experiences of teambuilding and case study problem solving were very good ways of enabling students to learn about interprofessional work. The participants were all appreciative of the learning opportunity. However, from the follow-up questionnaires, respondents had difficulties in implementing what they had learned. This seemed to be due to the lack of training of others in teamwork and in the lack of knowledge of university staff who did not know what had been taught.

The researchers recommend that interprofessional learning requires considerable rethinking of the learning environment, particularly in the understanding of the professional roles of others and in the collaboration between university departments. They also call for more examples of interprofessional learning to provide illustrations of successful teaching and learning.

## Conclusions and future research

The four small-scale studies selected for brief discussion above encompass several of the aspects of support partnership that have been the subject of this book. Multi-agency work within schools, with families and in services have all featured, as has shared learning. None of the studies appear to take the thinking about collaborative teamwork on any further than has been seen in the case studies used in the book, but they have provided helpful summaries of what has been achieved in recent years. It is actually quite dispiriting that four studies carried out in the last two years have very little more to offer than was being said about collaboration 30 years ago. It has been said that, in the field, the difference between the most innovative practice and the least is about 25 years, so perhaps the current round of studies indicate the tail catching up? This seems rather an optimistic view of the state of collaborative teamwork in a multidisciplinary context. Unfortunately there are many services that perhaps recognise the good features of teamwork, but seem unable to develop them in practice. They are, perhaps, unwilling or unable to make the fundamental changes necessary to work in a different manner.

This book has been filled with examples of changing structures, systems, people and approaches. Developing collaborative teamwork in support partnerships is not easy and the case studies have provided many illustrations of the hard roads trodden by those wishing to change. More exemplars are needed and the following list of possible questions represents a few ideas for future research to help build up the body of evidence, firstly, that collaborative teamwork is effective in providing services that meet client needs and, secondly, to provide models from which others can learn.

- What is the most effective way of changing service structures to facilitate collaboration?
- What models are there other than collaborative teamwork that are effective in meeting clients' needs?
- How tolerant can multidisciplinary teams be of a member(s) who is resistant to collaborative teamwork?
- What difference does it make to multidisciplinary teams to have a properly designated leader?
- How important is it for team members to experience each other's jobs?
- What is the effect upon the effectiveness of the teamwork of an outside facilitator or an intermediary?
- What effect does a multi-agency strategy (such as a forum for service managers or joint departments) have on the day-to-day work of practitioners working in collaborative teams?
- How important is legislation to the development of local multidisciplinary teams?

There are so many possible questions still to be answered or answered sufficiently to be convincing. Very few people need to be persuaded of the importance of working together and providing 'joined up services', but what still seems to be missing is the willingness of large organisations like schools, hospitals and services to change. Collaboration cannot be tacked on to traditional ways of working. It demands fundamental change.

# Glossary of terms

This is a list of the terms used in this book which refer to multidisciplinary teamwork or people working together. It does not cover all the terms used but is concentrated upon those used most frequently or likely to be confused.

| | |
|---|---|
| Collaboration | The most advanced working together, implying sharing and joint purpose, mutual trust and support. |
| Consultancy | The process of giving advice and of handing over skills and knowledge from one person to another. |
| Cooperation | People in a network ensure that they respond to requests for information from each other and do not cut across each other's work. |
| Coordination | People in a network ensure that their work is streamlined and timetabled so that children receive a balanced package of education and care. |
| Interagency | More than one agency or service work together in a coordinated manner. |
| Interdisciplinary | Members of more than one discipline work together in a coordinated way. Usually they will meet to discuss children's needs but will work with them individually. |
| Keyworker | One team member who undertakes to coordinate the work of the team for one particular child and be the point of contact for all network members. In special schools, this is often the teacher. |
| Liaison | Making contact with individuals and organisations in the network and maintaining that contact. |
| Motor group | A group of children with motor disabilities working towards functional motor control, through an integration of education and therapy. |
| Multi-agency | More than one agency working together. |
| Multidisciplinary | Members of more than one discipline working together (from liaison to collaboration). It can also mean that each discipline works completely separately from each other. |
| Multidisciplinary teamwork | A generic term meaning a group of people who represent different disciplines and who work together (from liaison to collaboration). It can also mean a group who work separately from each other (see above). |
| Network | A pool of people who offer services to individual children and their families. They usually have infrequent contact with the child. |
| Support partnership | Two (or more) people working together using the expertise of each to problem solve jointly. |
| Team | A group of people who work together (daily or at least weekly) to meet the needs of individual children. |
| Team leader | An individual in the team who takes responsibility for coordinating, directing and evaluating the work of the team, motivating team members and ensuring good communication between them. It is not a hierarchical position. |
| Transdisciplinary | Members of more than one discipline working together in a collaborative manner. |

# References

Adair, J. (1973) *Training for Communication.* Farnborough: Gower Press.

Adair, J. (1983) *Effective Leadership.* London: Pan Books.

Adair, J. (1984) *The Skills of Leadership.* Aldershot: Gower Press.

Adair, J. (1986) *Effective Teambuilding.* London: Pan Books.

Ainscow, M. (1991) *Effective Schools for All.* London: David Fulton Publishers.

Ainscow, M. (1997) 'Towards inclusive schooling', *British Journal of Special Education* **24**(1), 3–6.

Ainscow, M. *et al.* (1994) *Creating the Conditions for School Improvement: A handbook of staff development activities.* London: David Fulton Publishers.

Anderson, J. *et al.* (1993) 'Issues in providing training to achieve comprehensive behavioural support', in Reichlie, J. and Wacker, D. (eds) *Communication Alternatives to Challenging Behaviour.* Baltimore: Paul Brookes.

Ash, E. (1992) 'The personal–professional interface in learning towards reflective education', *Journal of Interprofessional Care* **6**(3), 261–71.

Audit Commission (1986) *The Reality of Community Care.* London: HMSO.

Audit Commission/HMI (1992a) *Getting in on the Act: Provision.* London: HMSO.

Audit Commission/HMI (1992b) *Getting the Act Together: Provision for pupils with special educational needs.* London: HMSO.

Babington Smith, B. and Farrell, B. (1979) *Training in Small Groups.* Oxford: Pergamon Press.

Bailey, T. (1991) 'Classroom observation: A powerful tool for teachers?' *Support for Learning* **6**(1), 32–6.

Bairstow, P. *et al.* (1993) *Evaluation of Conductive Education for Children with Cerebral Palsy. Final Report (Part II).* London: HMSO.

Ball, S. (1987) *The Micro-Politics of the School: Towards a theory of school organisation.* London: Methuen.

Balshaw, M. (1991) 'Classroom assistants: Staff development issues', in Upton, G. (ed.) *Staff Training and Special Educational Needs.* London: David Fulton Publishers.

Barker, D. (1980) *TA and Training.* Aldershot: Gower Press.

Barr, H. (1994) 'NVQs and their implications for interprofessional collaboration', in Leathard, A. (ed.) *Going Interprofessional – Working Together for Health and Welfare.* London: Routledge.

Bayley, M. (1973) *Mental Handicap and Community Care: A study of mentally handicapped people in Sheffield.* London: Routledge and Kegan Paul.

Beattie, A. (1999) *Service Co-ordination: Professionals' views on the role of a multi-agency service co-ordinator for children with disabilities.* Birmingham: Handsel Trust.

Belbin, R. M. (1981) *Management Teams: Why they succeed or fail.* Oxford: Butterworth Heinemann.

Bennett, R. (1984) 'Management education for real', in Kakabadse, A. and Mukhi, S. (eds) *The Future of Management Education.* Aldershot: Gower Press.

Berne, E. (1964) *Games People Play.* New York: Grove Press.

Blau, P. (1964) *Exchange and Power in Social Life.* New York: John Wiley.

Booth, T. *et al.* (1992) *Policies for Diversity in Education.* Milton Keynes: Open University Press.

Borger, H. and Tillema, H. (1993) 'Transferring knowledge to classroom teaching: putting knowledge into action', in Day, C. *et al.* (eds) *Research on Teacher Thinking: Understanding professional development.* London: Falmer Press.

Bowers, T. (1991a) *LMS and SEN Support Services Resources and Activity Pack.* Cambridge: Perspective Press.

Bowers, T. (1991b) *Schools, Services and Special Educational Needs. Management Issues in the Wake of LMS.* Cambridge: Perspective Press.

Bradley, H. *et al.* (1994) 'Developing teachers, developing schools', in Bradley, H. *et al.* (eds) *Developing Teachers, Developing Schools.* London: David Fulton Publishers.

Bridge, G. (1993) 'A personal reflection on parental participation: how some mothers of babies with disabilities experience interprofessional care', *Journal of Interprofessional Care* **7**(3), 263–7.

Brighouse, T. (2000) 'Beyond wildest dreams', *Times Educational Supplement,* 20 October.

Bronfenbrenner, U. (1979) *The Ecology of Human Development.* Cambridge: Harvard University Press.

Brookfield, S. (1986) *Understanding and Facilitating Adult Learning.* Buckingham: Open University Press.

Brown, J. (1994) 'The caring professions', in Malin, N. (ed.) *Implementing Community Care.* Buckingham: Open University Press.

Brown, J. (1995) 'Foundation course', *Nursing Times* **91**(49), 56–7.

Brown, M. (1994) 'Voluntary agencies, young children and their families: preschool playgroups', in

David, T. (ed.) *Working Together for Young Children: Multiprofessionalism in action.* London: Routledge.

Bush, T. (1986) *Theories of Educational Management.* London: Paul Chapman.

Butt, N. (1989) 'In-service training in the new era', *Support for Learning* **4**, 67–74.

Cade, L. and Caffyn, R. (1994) 'The King Edward VI family: An example of clustering in Nottinghamshire', *Support for Learning* **9**(2), 83–8.

Cade, L. and Caffyn, R. (1995) 'Family planning for special needs: The role of a Nottinghamshire family special needs co-ordinator', *Support for Learning* **10**(2), 70–4.

Carpenter, B. (1997) 'Early intervention and identification: finding the family', *Children and Society* **11**(3), 173–82.

Carpenter, J. and Hewstone, M. (1996) 'Shared learning for doctors and social workers: evaluation of a programme', *The British Journal of Social Work* **26**(2), 239–57.

Casto, M. (1994) 'Education for interprofessional practice', in Casto, M. and Julia, M. (eds) *Interprofessional Care and Collaborative Practice.* Pacific Grove: Brooks/Cole Publishing.

Challis, D. *et al.* (1998) *Care Management Study: Report on national data.* London: Social Services Directorate.

Clough, P. and Lindsay, G. (1991) *Integration and the Support Services: Changing Roles in Special Education.* Windsor: NFER Nelson.

Cocker, C. (1995) 'Special needs in the infant school', in *Support for Learning* **10**(2), 75–8.

Cohen, L. and Manion, L. (1989) *Research Methods in Education,* 3rd edn. London: Routledge.

Conner, C. (1994) 'Higher degrees that serve the school or institution: is there still a justifiable place for study at master's degree level in the current in-service climate?' in Bradley, H. *et al.* (eds) *Developing Teachers, Developing Schools.* London: David Fulton Publishers.

Connolly, B. and Anderson, R. (1988) 'Severely handicapped children in the public schools: A new frontier for the physical therapist', in Jansma, P. (ed.) *The Psychomotor Domain and the Seriously Handicapped,* 3rd edn. New York: Universal Press of America.

Cooley, E. (1994) 'Training an interdisciplinary team in communication and decision making skills', *Small Group Research* **25**(1), 5–25.

Cottam, P. (1986) 'An approach for the mentally handicapped', in Cottam, P. and Sutton, A. (eds) *Conductive Education: A system for overcoming motor disorder.* Beckenham: Croom Helm.

Cottam, P. and Sutton, A. (1986) *Conductive Education: A system for overcoming motor disorder.* Beckenham: Croom Helm.

Coulshed, V. (1993) 'Adult learning: implications for teaching in social work education', *British Journal of Social Work* **23**(1), 1–13.

Critchley, B. and Casey, D. (1986) 'Team building' in Mumford, A. (ed.) *Handbook of Management Development,* 2nd edn. Aldershot: Gower Press.

Crom, S. and France, H. (1996) 'Teamwork brings breakthrough improvements in quality and climate', *Quality Progress* **29**(3), 39–42.

Dale, N. (1995) *Working with Parents of Children with Special Educational Needs.* London: Routledge.

David, R. and Smith, B. (1991) 'Collaboration in initial training', in Upton, G. (ed.) *Staff Training and Special Educational Needs.* London: David Fulton Publishers.

Davie, R. (1993) 'Implementing Warnock's multi-professional approach', in Visser, J. and Upton, G. (eds) *Special Education in Britain After Warnock.* London: David Fulton Publishers.

Day, C. (1989) 'INSET: the marginalising of higher education', *British Journal of In-service Education* **15**(3), 195–6.

Delamont, S. (1992) *Fieldwork in Education Methods: Pitfalls and perspectives.* London: Falmer Press.

Dempster, N. (1991) 'University agencies for in-service education: survival in an educational market economy', *British Journal of In-service Education* **17**(3), 181–8.

Department for Education (DfE) (1994) *The Code of Practice on the Identification and Assessment of Special Educational Needs.* London: HMSO.

Department of Education and Science (DES) (1978) *Special Educational Needs* (The Warnock Report). London: HMSO.

DES (1989) *A Survey of Support Services for SEN, Report by HMI.* London: HMSO.

DES (1991) *Interdisciplinary Support for Young Children with Special Educational Needs.* London: DES.

DES (1993) *The Education Act.* London: HMSO.

Department of Health (1986) *Disabled Person's Act.* London: HMSO.

Department of Health (1989a) *The Children Act.* London: HMSO.

Department of Health (1989b) *Caring for People: Community care in the next decade and beyond.* London: HMSO.

Department of Health (1990) *NHS and Community Care Act.* London: HMSO.

Department of Health (1998) Circular 1998/201. London: HMSO.

Dey, I. (1993) *Qualitative Data Analysis.* London: Routledge.

Drucker, P. (1974) *Management: Tasks, responsibilities, practice.* Oxford: Butterworth-Heinemann.

Dyer, W. (1977) *Team Building: Issues and alternatives.* London: Addison Wesley.

Dyson, A. (1994) 'Towards a collaborative learning model for responding to student diversity', *Support for Learning* **9**(2), 53–60.

Dyson, A. and Gains, C. (1993) (eds) *Rethinking Special Needs in Mainstream Schools: Towards the Year 2000.* London: David Fulton Publishers.

Dyson, A. *et al.* (1998) *Effective Communication between Schools, LEAs and Health and Social Services in the Field of Special Educational Needs.* London: DfEE.

Elliott, J. (1991) *Action Research for Educational Change.* Buckingham: Open University Press.

Engel, C. (1994) 'A functional anatomy of teamwork', in Leathard, A. (ed.) *Going Inter-professional: Working together for health and welfare.* London: Routledge.

English, R. (1995) 'INSET: initiating change or merely supporting it?' *British Journal of In-Service Education* **21**(3), 295–309.

Eraut, M. (1988) 'Management knowledge: its nature and its development', in Calderhead, J. (ed.) *Teachers' Professional Learning.* London: Falmer Press.

Evans, J. *et al.* (1989) *Decision Making for Special Educational Needs.* Loughborough: Tecmedia Ltd.

Farrell, P. *et al.* (1999) *The Role, Management and Training of Learning Support Assistants.* London: DfEE.

Ferlie, E. (1994) 'The creation and evolution of quasi-markets in the public sector: Early evidence from the National Health Service', in *Policy and Politics* **22**(2), 105–12.

Fish, J. (1985) *Special Education: The way ahead.* Milton Keynes: Open University Press.

Forman, D. *et al.* (1994) 'Shared management learning at the University of Derby', *Journal of Interprofessional Care* **8**(3), 275–8.

Fox, N. (1994) 'Self-directed approaches to multidisciplinary health studies', *Journal of Interprofessional Care* **8**(3), 247–54.

Freeling, P. (1993) 'Interdisciplinary master's degree in health sciences' (letter to editor), *Journal of Interprofessional Care* **7**(1), 77.

Fullan, M. (1991) *The New Meaning of Educational Change.* London: Cassell.

Funnell, P. (1995) 'Exploring the value of interprofessional shared learning', in Soothill, K. *et al.* (eds) *Interprofessional Relations in Health Care.* London: Edward Arnold.

Gains, C. and Smith, C. (1994) 'Cluster model', *Support for Learning* **9**(2), 94–8.

Georgiades, N. and Phillimore, L. (1975) 'The myth of the hero-innovator and alternative strategies for organisational change', in Kiernan, C. and Woodford, P. (eds) *Behaviour Modification with the Severely Retarded.* London: Association of Scientific Publishers.

Gilbert, J. *et al.* (2000) 'Preparing students for interprofessional teamwork in health care', *Journal of Interprofessional Care* **14**(3), 223–35.

Gilbert, N. (1993) *Researching Social Life.* London: Sage.

Gill, J. and Ling, J. (1995) 'Interprofessional shared learning: A curriculum for collaboration' in Soothill, K. *et al.* (eds) *Interprofessional Relations in Health Care.* London: Edward Arnold.

Glaser, B. and Strauss, A. (1967) *The Discovery of Grounded Theory.* London: Weidenfeld and Nicolson.

Glatter, R. (1982) 'The micropolitics of education: Issues for training', *Educational Management and Administration* **10**(2), 160–5.

Goble, R. (1994) 'Multiprofessional education: European network for development of multiprofessional education in Health Sciences (EMPE)', *Journal of Interprofessional Care* **8**(1), 85–92.

Gould, N. and Harris, A. (1996) 'Student imagery of practice in social work and teacher education: a comparative research approach', *The British Journal of Social Work* **26**(2), 223–37.

Gregory, E. (1989) 'Issues of multiprofessional co-operation', in Evans, R. (ed.) *Special Educational Needs: Policy and practice.* Oxford: Blackwell/NARE.

Guirdham, M. (1990) *Interpersonal Skills at Work.* Hemel Hempstead: Prentice Hall.

Halpin, D. *et al.* (1990) 'Teachers' perceptions of the effects of in-service education', *British Educational Research Journal* **16**, 163–77.

Hamel, J. *et al.* (1991) *Case Study Methods.* Newbury Park: Sage.

Hammersley, M. (1992) *What's Wrong with Ethnography?.* London: Routledge.

Hammersley, M. and Atkinson, P. (1995) *Ethnography: Principles and practice*, 2nd edn. London: Tavistock.

Handy, C. (1985) *Understanding Organisations.* Harmondsworth: Penguin.

Hanko, H. (1990) *Special Needs in Ordinary Classrooms: Supporting teachers*, 2nd edn. Oxford: Blackwell.

Harris, T. (1973) *I'm OK – You're OK.* London: Pan Books.

Hart, S. (1991) 'The collaborative dimension: Risks and rewards of collaboration', in McLaughlin, C. and Rouse, M. (eds) *Supporting Schools.* London: David Fulton Publishers.

Hastings, C. *et al.* (1986) *Superteams: A blueprint for success.* London: Fontana.

Hattersley, J. (1995) 'The survival of collaboration and co-operation', in Malin, N. (ed.) *Services for People with Learning Disabilities.* London: Routledge.

Hersey, P. and Blanchard, K. (1982) *Management of Organisational Behaviour: Utilising human resources*, 3rd edn. Englewood: Prentice-Hall International.

Hevey, D. (1992) 'The potential of NVQs to make multidisciplinary training a reality', *Journal of Interprofessional Care* **6**(4), 215–22.

HMI (1991) *Interdisciplinary Support for Young Children with SEN*. London: DES.

Homans, G. (1974) *Social Behaviour: Its elementary forms*. New York: Harcourt Brace Jovanovich.

Home Office, Department of Health, Department of Education and Science, Welsh Office (1991) *Working Together under the Children Act 1989*. London: HMSO.

Horder, J. (1995) 'Interprofessional education for primary health and community care', in Soothill, K. *et al.* (eds) *Interprofessional Relations in Health Care*. London: Edward Arnold.

Hornby, S. (1993) *Collaborative Care: Interprofessional, interagency and interpersonal*. Oxford: Blackwell Scientific.

Horst, M. *et al.* (1995) 'St. Joseph's Community Health Centre model of community – based on interdisciplinary health care team education', *Health and Social Care in the Community* **3**, 33–42.

Howard, S. *et al.* (1995) 'The changing face of child language assessment: 1985–1995', *Child Language Teaching and Therapy* **11**(1), 7–22.

Hudson, B. (1995) 'Is a co-ordinated service attainable?' in Malin, N. (ed.) *Services for People with Learning Disabilities*. London: Routledge.

Hunter, D. and Wistow, G. (1987) *Community Care in Britain*. London: King's Fund.

Iles, P. and Auluck, R. (1990) 'Team building, interagency team development and social work practice', in *British Journal of Social Work* **20**, 157–64.

Janis, I. (1972) *Victims of Groupthink*. Boston: Houghton-Mifflin.

Johnson, J. (1990) *Selecting Ethnographic Informants*. London: Sage.

Jolleff, N. *et al.* (1994) *An Approach to Combined Therapy Assessment*. Unpublished conference paper for 'Practical Teamwork for Children with Multiple Disabilities'.

Jones, K. (1989) 'Community care: old problems and new answers', in Carter, C. *et al.* (eds) *Social Work and Social Welfare*. Milton Keynes: Open University Press.

Jones, K. *et al.* (1989) *Staff Development in Primary School*. Oxford: Blackwell.

Jordan, A. (1994) *Skills in Collaborative Classroom Consultation*. London: Routledge.

Joyce, B. and Showers, B. (1982) 'The coaching of teaching', *Educational Leadership Now*, November, 4–7.

Katzenbach, J. and Smith, D. (1993) *The Wisdom of Teams*. New York: Harper Business.

Kersell, J. (1990) 'Team management and development', in Montserrat and Anguilla, *Public Administration and Development* 10, Jan/Mar, 81–91.

Kinder, K. *et al.* (1991) *The Impact of School-focused INSET on Classroom Practice*. Slough: NFER.

Klein, J. (1956) *The Study of Groups*. London: Routledge and Kegan Paul.

Knapp, M. *et al.* (1992) 'Smart moves', *Health Service Journal*, 29 October, 28–30.

Lacey, P. (1995) 'In the front line: special educational needs co-ordinators and liaison', *Support for Learning* **10**(2), 57–62.

Lacey, P. (1996a) 'Classroom teamwork: teachers and support staff working together', *Primary Practice* **6**, 25–8.

Lacey, P. (1996b) 'Supporting pupils with special educational needs', in Mills, J. (ed.) *Partnership in the Primary School: Working in collaboration*. London: Routledge.

Lacey, P. (1997) *Multidisciplinary Teamwork in Special Education: Practice and training*. PhD Thesis, The University of Birmingham.

Lacey, P. (1998) 'Multidisciplinary teamwork', in Tilstone, C. *et al.* (eds) *Promoting Inclusive Practice*. London: Routledge.

Lacey, P. (2000) 'Multidisciplinary teamwork: problems and possibilities', in Daniels, H. (ed.) *Special Education Reformed: Shaping the future*. London: Falmer Press.

Lacey, P. and Lomas, J. (1993) *Support Services and the Curriculum: A practical guide to collaboration*. London: David Fulton Publishers.

Lacey, P. and Ranson, S. (1994) 'Partnership for learning', *Support for Learning* **9**(2), 79–82.

Lally, V. *et al.* (1992) 'A collaborative teacher-centred model of in-service education', *Educational Review* **44**(2), 111–26.

Larson, C. and LaFasto, F. (1989) *Teamwork: What must go right, what can go wrong*. Beverley Hills: Sage.

Law, S. and Glover, D. (1995) 'The professional development business: School evaluations of LEA and higher education INSET provision', *British Journal of In-service Education* **21**(2), 181–92.

Lawn, M. and Woods, R. (1988) *Team Building with Industry in Initial Teacher Education*. Aldershot: Indtel.

Leathard, A. (1992) 'Interprofessional developments at South Bank Polytechnic', *Journal of Interprofessional Care* **6**(1), 17–23.

Leathard, A. (ed.) (1994) *Going Interprofessional: Working together for health and welfare*. London: Routledge.

Limbrick-Spencer, G. (2000) *Parent Support Needs: The views of parents of children with complex needs*. Birmingham: Handsel Trust.

Linder, T. (1990) *Transdisciplinary Play-based Assessment*. Baltimore: Paul Brookes.

Ling, J. *et al.* (1990) 'Shared learning', *Nursing Times* **86**(3), 65–6.

Liswood, I. (1990) *Serving Them Right: Innovation and powerful customer retention strategies.* New York: Harper and Row.

Lomax, P. (1994) 'Action research for professional practice: a position paper on educational action research'. Paper presented at the Annual Conference of BERA September 1994.

Lomax, P. (1995) 'Action research for professional practice', *British Journal of In-service Education* **21**(1), 49–57.

Losen, S. and Losen, J. (1985) *The Special Education Team.* Boston: Allyn and Bacon.

Lowe, J. (1991) 'Teambuilding via outdoor training: experiences from a UK automotive plant', *Human Resource Management Journal* **2**(1), 42–59.

Lowe, F. and O'Hara, S. (2000) 'Multi-disciplinary team working in practice: managing the transition', *Journal of Interprofessional Care* **4**(3), 269–80.

Lunt, I. *et al.* (1994a) *Working Together: Inter-school Collaboration for Special Needs.* London: David Fulton Publishers.

Lunt, I. *et al.* (1994b) 'Collaborating to meet special education needs: effective clusters?' *Support for Learning* **9**(2), 73–8.

Lyons, G. and Stenning, R. (1986) *Managing Staff in Schools.* London: Hutchinson.

Macleod, R. and Nash, A. (1994) 'Multi-disciplinary education in palliative care', *Journal of Interprofessional Care* **8**(3), 283–8.

Malcolm, L. *et al.* (1996) 'Powerless children: powerful systems', *Children and Society* **10**, 210–16.

Malin, N. (1994) *Implementing Community Care.* Buckingham: Open University Press.

Manford, P. (1991) 'Why collaborate?' *Special Children* **45**, 7–9.

Marshall, M. *et al.* (eds) (1979) *Teamwork: For and against.* Birmingham: BASW (Report of workshops).

Mathias, P. and Thompson, T. (1992) 'Interprofessional training: learning disability as a case study', *Journal of Interprofessional Care* **6**(3), 231–41.

Maxwell, J. (1996) *Qualitative Research Design: An interactive approach.* London: Sage.

Maychell, K. and Bradley, J. (1991) *Preparing for Partnership: Multi-agency support for special needs.* Slough: NFER.

McCormick, L. and Goldman, R. (1988) 'The trans-disciplinary model: implications for service delivery and personnel preparation for the severely and profoundly handicapped', in Jansma, P. (ed.) *The Psychomotor Domain and the Seriously Handicapped,* 3rd edn. New York: University Press of America.

McGrath, M. (1991) *Multidisciplinary Teamwork – Community Mental Handicap Teams.* Aldershot: Avebury.

McLaughlin, C. (1989) 'Working face to face: aspects of interpersonal work', *Support for Learning* **4**(2), 96–101.

McNiff, J. (1988) *Action Research: Principles and practice.* London: Routledge.

McNiff, J. (1993) *Teaching as Learning: An action research approach.* London: Routledge.

McNiff, J. *et al.* (1996) *You and Your Action Research Project.* London: Routledge.

Mencap (1999) *On a Wing and a Prayer: Inclusion and children with severe learning difficulties.* London: Mencap.

Mencap (undated) *What's Good Support.* Video and booklet. London: Mencap.

Merriam, S. (1988) *Case Study Research in Education.* San Francisco: Jossey-Bass.

Merry, U. and Allerhand, M. (1977) *Developing Teams and Organisations: A practical handbook for managers and consultants.* London: Addison-Wesley.

Middleton, L. (1998) 'Consumer satisfaction with services for disabled children', *Journal of Interprofessional Care* **12**(2), 223–31.

Miles, M. and Huberman, M. (1994) *Qualitative Data Analysis,* 2nd edn. Thousand Oaks: Sage.

Miller, C. (1996) 'Relationships between teachers and speech and language therapists', *Child Language Teaching and Therapy* **12**(1), 29–38.

Morgan, C. and Murgatroyd, S. (1994) *Total Management Quality in the Public Sector.* Buckingham: Open University Press.

Morton-Williams, J. (1985) 'Making qualitative research work: aspects of administration', in Walker, R. (ed.) *Applied Qualitative Research.* Aldershot: Gower Press.

Mukherjee, S. *et al.* (1999) *Unlocking Key Working: An analysis and evaluation of key worker services for families with disabled children.* Bristol: The Policy Press.

Murray, P. (2000) 'Disabled children, parents and professionals: partnership on whose terms?', *Disability and Society* **15**(4), 683–98.

Nash, K. (1994) 'Teaming at work in Australia: a progress report', *Work and People* **15**(1), 16–17.

Newton, D. and Newton, L. (1994) 'A survey of the use made of non-contact days: the infamous five', *British Journal of In-service Education* **20**(3), 387–96.

Nunkoosing. K. and Phillips. D. (1999) 'Supporting families in the early education of children with special needs: the perspectives of Portage home visitors', *European Journal of Special Needs Education* **14**(3), 198–211.

O'Hanlon, C. (1991) 'The facilitator's role in action research for teachers of pupils with SEN', in Upton, G. (ed.) *Staff Training and Special Educational Needs.* London: David Fulton Publishers.

Orelove, F. and Sobsey, D. (1991) *Educating Children with Multiple Disabilities: A transdisciplinary approach*. Baltimore: Paul Brookes.

Ovretveit, J. (1994) *Co-ordinating Community Care: Multidisciplinary teams and care management*. Buckingham: Open University Press.

Parrott, H. (2000) *An Investigation into the Effectiveness of the Transdisciplinary Team Approach to the Education and Care of Students at the Profound End of the Autistic Spectrum in a Residential School*. MSc dissertation, University College, Worcester.

Payne, M. (1982) *Working in Teams*. London: Macmillan.

Payne, M. (1993) *Linkages: Effective networking in social care*. London: Whiting and Birch.

Penson, P. (1996) 'What teambuilding won't cure', *Training* 33(3), 90.

Pietroni, P. (1994) 'Interprofessional teamwork: its history and development in hospitals, general practice and community care (UK)', in Leathard, A. (ed.) *Going Interprofessional: Working together for health and welfare*. London: Routledge.

Potts, P. *et al*. (1992) *Learning for All Unit 5: Right from the start*. Milton Keynes: Open University Press.

Poulin, J. *et al*. (1994) 'Interdisciplinary team membership: a survey of gerontological social workers', *Journal of Gerontological Social Work* 22(1/2), 93–107.

Powney, J. and Watts, M. (1987) *Interviewing in Educational Research*. London: Routledge.

Pugh, G. (1992) 'A policy for early childhood services?' in Pugh, G. (ed.) *Contemporary Issues in the Early Years: Working collaboratively for children*. London: Paul Chapman.

Qualifications and Curriculum Authority (2001) *Curriculum Guidelines for Pupils with Learning Difficulties*. London: QCA/DfEE.

Rainbird, H. (1994) 'The changing role of the training function: A test for the integration of human resources and business strategies', *Human Resource Management Journal* 5(1), 72–90.

Rainforth, B. *et al*. (1992) *Collaborative Teams for Students with Severe Disabilities*. Baltimore: Paul Brookes.

Renshaw, J. *et al*. (1990) 'Climate for communication', *Social Work Today* 21(25), 18–19.

Robinson, K. (1988) *A Handbook of Training Management*. London: Kogan Page.

Robson, C. (1993) *Real World Research*. Oxford: Blackwell.

Robson, C. and Sebba, J. (1991) 'Staff training and development', in Segal, S. and Varma, V. (eds) *Prospects for People with Learning Difficulties*. London: David Fulton Publishers.

Rose, S. (1993) 'Social policy: a perspective on service development and interagency working', in Brigden, P. and Todd, M. (eds) *Concepts in Community Care for People with a Learning Difficulty*. London: Macmillan.

Rouse, M. (1987) 'Bringing the special needs department out of the cupboard', in Bowers, T. (ed.) *Special Educational Needs and Human Resource Management*. Beckenham: Croom Helm.

Rouse, M. (1994) 'Linking individual and institutional development for special educational needs', in Bradley, H. *et al*. (eds) *Developing Teachers, Developing Schools*. London: David Fulton Publishers.

Royal National Institute for the Blind (RNIB) (1992) *Curriculum Materials used with Multihandicapped Visually Impaired Children and Young People: Report from the working party*. London: RNIB.

Schon, D. (1992) 'The crisis of professional knowledge and the pursuit of an epistemology of practice', *Journal of Interprofessional Care* 6(1), 49–63.

Schopler, E. and Mesibov, G. (eds) (1988) *Diagnosis and Assessment in Autism*. New York: Plenum Press.

Sebba, J. (1994) 'Developing reflective practitioners in special schools', in Bradley, H. *et al*. (eds) *Developing Teachers, Developing Schools*. London: David Fulton Publishers.

Sergiovanni, T. (1984) 'Cultural and competing perspectives in administrative theory and practice', in Sergiovanni T. and Corbally, J. (eds) *Leadership and Organisational Culture*. Chicago: University of Illinois Press.

Sharp, A. (1994) 'Co-ordinating provision: the story so far in one local authority', in David, T. (ed.) *Working Together for Young Children: Multi-professionalism in action*. London: Routledge.

Shaw, I. (1993) 'Learning together: social work and nursing', *Health and Social Care in the Community* 1(5), 255–62.

Shaw, I. (1994) *Evaluating Interprofessional Training*. Aldershot: Avebury.

Sheal, P. (1992) *The Staff Development Handbook*. London: Kogan Page.

Shonk, J. (1992) *Team-based Organisations: Developing a successful team environment*. Homewood: Business One Irwin.

Sims, A. and Sims, D. (1993) 'Top teams', *Health Service Journal*, 24 June.

Sinclair, R. and Grimshaw, R. (1997) 'Partnership with parents in planning the care of their children', *Children and Society* 11(4), 231–41.

Smith, J. (1986) 'The development of Portage in the United Kingdom', in Cameron, R. (ed.) *Portage: Pre-schoolers, parents and professionals, ten years of achievement in the UK*. Windsor: NFER-Nelson.

Solity, J. and Bickler, G. (eds) (1994) *Support Services: Issues for education, health and social service professionals*. London: Cassell.

Stainback, W. and Stainback, S. (1990) *Support Networks for Inclusive Schooling*. Baltimore: Paul Brookes.

Starr, A. and Lacey, P. (1996) 'Multidisciplinary assessment: a case study', *British Journal of Special Education* **23**(2), 57–61.

Steel, F. (1991) 'Working collaboratively within a multidisciplinary framework', in Tilstone, C. (ed.) *Teaching Pupils with Severe Learning Difficulties.* London: David Fulton Publishers.

Stein, J. and Brown, H. (1995) 'All in this together: an evaluation of joint training on the abuse of adults with learning disabilities', *Health and Social Care in the Community* **3**(4), 205–14.

Storrie, J. (1992) 'Mastering interprofessionalism: an enquiry into the development of masters programmes with an interprofessional focus', *Journal of Interprofessional Care* **6**(3), 253–9.

Sturmey, P. (1987) 'The implications of research for the future development of Portage', in Hedderby, R. and Jennings, K. (eds) *Extending and Developing Portage.* Slough: NFER-Nelson.

Sutton, A. (1986) 'The practice', in Cottam, P. and Sutton, A. (eds) *Conductive Education: A system for overcoming motor disorder.* Beckenham: Croom Helm.

Swan, W. and Morgan, J. (1993) *Collaborating for Comprehensive Services for Young Children and their Families.* Baltimore: Paul Brookes.

Teire, J. (1986) 'Using the outdoors', in Mumford, A. (ed.) *Handbook of Management Development,* 2nd edn. Aldershot: Gower Press.

Thomas, G. (1992) *Effective Classroom Teamwork: Support or intrusion?* London: Routledge.

Titchener, J. (1986) 'An approach for the physically handicapped?' in Cottam, P. and Sutton, A. (eds) *Conductive Education: A system for overcoming motor disorder.* Beckenham: Croom Helm.

Tjosvold, D. (1991) *Team Organisation: An enduring competitive advantage.* Chichester: John Wiley.

Tozer, R. (1999) *At the Double: Supporting families with two or more severely disabled children.* London: National Children's Bureau.

Trethowan, D. (1985) *Teamwork in School.* London: Education for Industrial Society.

Tuckman, B. (1965) 'Developmental sequences in small groups', *Psychological Bulletin* **63**, 384–99.

Walker, R. (1985) 'An introduction to applied qualitative research', in Walker, R. (ed.) *Applied Qualitative Research.* Aldershot: Gower Press.

Wallace, M. and Hall, V. (1994) 'Go collaborative! Subvert reform for the sake of the children', in *Support for Learning* **9**(2), 68–72.

Webb, R. (1989) 'Changing practice through consultancy based INSET', *School Organisation* **9**(1), 39–52.

West-Burnham, J. (1987) 'Effective learning and the design of staff development activities', in *Educational Change and Development* **8**(2), 17–23.

Westland, P. (1988) 'Progress in partnership: a case study', in Wistow, G. and Brooks, T. (eds) *Joint Planning and Joint Management.* London: Royal Institute of Public Administration.

Whalley, M. (1992) 'Working as a team', in Pugh, G. (ed.) *Contemporary Issues in the Early Years: Working collaboratively for children.* London: Paul Chapman.

Whitehead, J. (1993) *The Growth of Educational Knowledge: Creating your own living educational theories.* Bournemouth: Hyde Publications.

Whittier, K. and Hewitt, J. (1993) 'Collaborative teacher education: the elementary education/special education connection', *Intervention in School and Clinic* **29**(2), 84–8.

Wideen, M. (1992) 'School-based teacher development', in Fillan, M. and Hargreaves, A. (eds) *Teacher Development and Educational Change.* London: Falmer Press.

Williams, A. (1992) 'Building a highly motivated team', *Senior Nurse* **12**, Mar/Apr, 22–3.

Wistow, G. (1988) 'Beyond joint planning: Managing community care', in Wistow, G. and Books, T. (eds) *Joint Planning and Joint Management.* London: RIPA.

Wistow, G. and Hardy, B. (1991) 'Joint management in community care', in *Journal of Management in Medicine* **5**(4), 40–8.

Wood, D. (1998) *How Children Think and Learn.* Oxford: Blackwell.

Wood, J. (1994) 'Shared or joint training?' in Harris, J. and Corbett, J. (eds) *Training and Professional Development: An interdisciplinary perspective for those working with people with severe learning disabilities.* Kidderminster: BILD.

Woods, P. (1986) *Inside Schools.* London: Routledge and Kegan Paul.

Working Group on Joint Planning (1985) *Progress in Partnership.* London: DHSS.

Wright, J. (1992) 'Collaboration between speech therapists and teachers', in Fletcher, P. and Hall, D. (eds) *Specific Speech and Language Disorders in Children.* London: Whurr.

# Index